The Battleground

SYRIA AND PALESTINE

The Battleground

SYRIA AND PALESTINE

The Seedplot of Religion

———————

HILAIRE BELLOC

IGNATIUS PRESS   SAN FRANCISCO

Original edition:
© 1936 by Hilaire Belloc
Published in 1936 by J. B. Lippincott Company
Philadelphia and London

© by the estate of Hilaire Belloc
Reprinted by permission

Cover photograph: Jerusalem © iStockPhoto.com

Cover design by John Herreid

Foreword © 2008 by Ignatius Press, San Francisco
All rights reserved
ISBN 978-1-58617-235-0
Library of Congress Control Number 2007938143
Printed in the United States of America ∞

TO

EDMOND L. WARRE

CONTENTS

LIST OF MAPS

PREFACE

This book needs a brief apology. The writer has not only taken for granted that there is a God, but also design in the Universe and in the story of Mankind.

He has affirmed a special design in the story of Syria and particularly of Israel, reaching a climax at the Crucifixion. He even seems to imply the Divinity of his Saviour.

All this must sound so unusual today that it may be thought an affectation, deliberately assumed to startle and offend. Such a feeling will be enhanced by the discovery that he takes the Gospel of St. John to have been written by St. John and even allows some historical value to the Old Testament.

The sole excuse he offers for his extravagance is that the present generation is tolerant of novel ideas, and that therefore he may hope for indulgence.

KINGS LAND

HILAIRE BELLOC

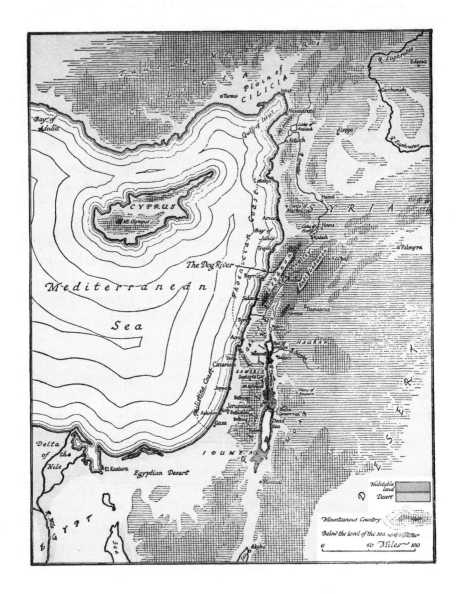

THE BATTLEGROUND

I

The Structure of the Land

IN THE BEGINNING of our Europe, when the work of its creation was accomplished and its shores had taken the shape we know, some Atlantean boat sailed eastward from through the Mediterranean beyond Crete to find what might be found. They of the boat, moving by sails and oars, set out upon discovery to know new lands and see whether bounds had been set to that inland sea, or whether they should be led onwards and out again into the strength of ocean which surrounds the world.

It was the early springtime of the year, when the long rain storms of winter are past and men can trust an open heaven. The northerly breezes of that season befriended them as they left the mountain of Rhodes behind them and still made easting more and more, anchoring by night in the shelter of Lycian combes until, from the shores, rose those splendid heights of snow which now, since the curse came out of Asia, bear uncouth Mongolian names, but then were the unknown habitations of the gods. For this was before the evils fell upon us, and all was young.

So they went on along that coast of Asia Minor till the hills receded northward. They might be tempted to turn and follow the friendly nearness of the strand, but a new sight called them. Very far away indeed, but beckoning them to a direct course, was a grey line with more brilliant edges that might be cloud, but proved fixed. At last, as they risked the passage across the broad bay, these appeared as the shining snows of summits where the light ended.

For these mountains they would make, daring a night journey, and steering by the stars. With the second morning they had plainly before them more splendours of high snows, the summits of the Cilician Taurus. They had crossed the wide Adalian bay and could continue their course, still eastward; and soon on the seaward side they caught, a long way off against the sun, the line of some great island. It was Cyprus they saw and the faint peak of its Olympus. They were in the Channel between it and the mainland. The hills of that mainland to the north once more receded but this time enclosed no bay; where water might have been was a broad plain on which Tarsus was to rise. They passed the mouths of its rivers. The shore line still led them on until at last these men who thus first explored the vast Mediterranean Sea entered a profound gulf: a sheet of water, broad and still, leading far into the land, with solemn hills encircling it on every side.

Those hills were of a vivid green, steep grass cut here and there by ribs of naked rock; and on the highest of the slopes, mist gathered, hiding the summits and making as it were a roof above them. No wind blew, and there was no sound save the plash of their oars. They had reached, at the far end of this loch, the end also of their eastward searching. There was no issue beyond. They could no longer explore onwards.

They turned back to where, at the seaward end of this wide and sheltered gulf, a long day's rowing back westward, a mountain higher than the rest had guarded their entrance into the deep recess. Perhaps, that Cape once rounded, they could still make onward for the east again. But when they had rounded it they found it was not so. They were bound to a new course altogether. The shore henceforward ran southward at right angles to the way they had come and was so to run day after day uninterruptedly. They were not following the coast of a peninsula, turning the end of which they might come upon further worlds; they were following a barrier line. There were no further waters. They had found the boundary of the inland sea.

With their new course they were passing a new land. The air grew warmer, and there was something more violent in the light. More than once, as they lay anchored in the silence and the dark, the night would be filled with a stifling air, as from an oven, which reached even to the sea line. It would pass; but they had felt, without knowing its source, the breath of the desert. But what marked especially this novel country was its *wall*. This continuous shore down which they were to sail and row, for near four hundred miles, under the northerly light airs or often becalmed, was backed everywhere, unceasingly, by a continuous *wall* of high land. The mountain ran monotonous, without peaks, in a line now rising, now falling, here and there so low as to make a saddle, but always close to the eastward of the shore with but a few miles of enclosed flats between. Spurs from the hills would often thrust out high capes into the sea itself; and the valleys descending from the hilly country ended in short stretches of level rich land through which the last of a mountain torrent ran.

So it was at the beginning of their new southerly sailing into the unknown, but later on longer stretches of plain intervened. The headlands still reached the water, indeed, from time to time, but more rarely; and for a whole day's run there might be a stretch of plain between the water and the heights. But everywhere that horizon of lifted land followed them, and it was over its crest that the sun rose on their port beam morning after morning.

They opened a few small harbours. Now and then, at long intervals, a group of small islands near the strand gave a roadstead: some sort of shelter between them and the beach. (One of them, a flat large rock, was to bear, centuries hence, the wealth of Tyre.) Here and there a hammer-headed projection of land gave shelter on its lee for anchorage (one such was to bear, centuries hence, the wealth of Sidon). Here and there a crook of slightly advanced cape protected a little bay, its arm half bending. But still this was the character of all that even shore: few harbours and these small and too open.

In the midst of their journey, half-way down the coast, the inland ridge lifted so high that, even so far south, snows appeared upon it, above dark forest belts. Further to the south again it was to sink into what were no more than stony hills; but still everywhere it barred the eastern sky and looked down upon the sea. This last shore of the sea was enclosed, banked in.

They, the first sailors, or perhaps later the people of the land itself, gave that stretched length of heights some name which clung to the place from the beginning of time, some name meaning "the high land". That name had for its root sounds "R" and "M", and it was in the form *"Aram"* or *"Arim"* that it came to be known; whence came all its titles, to strangers as well as to the people of the shore. It was Arim for the oldest of the Greek poets; it was "Aram" for those who, a thousand years before him, called its inland part "Aramean". In the Hebrew traditions, today four thousand years old, it was also "Aram". It would be more fitting if those hills and the sea-plain which they watch between them and the waters and the inland country beyond, had kept this most ancient name; but the growth of a great Empire changed it; Assyria overflowed it, and, from that name Aram came to be known (officially at least) some two thousand years ago as *Syria** to the world's central Government at Rome. Syria it is still called.

In the central part of their southward sailing, where the inland ridge reached its greatest height, standing thousands of feet up into the air and shining in a broad unbroken band of snow, the desire to possess the secret of what lay beyond had grown upon the mariners. It was determined to land a party which should push eastward beyond the mountain wall and return in some days to the ship with the story of their journey.

Since such wind as had blown had been continuously from the northward, down the shore, they looked for a projecting hook of land in the lee of which they could anchor together. They found one such providing a sheltered roadstead—it is known today as the Bay of Junie—and there, with good holding ground in five fathom of water close inshore, they dropped anchor and landed their detachment under its captain, provisioned for ten days.

No men had been seen, nor cities; but there would be wild

---

* But there is a guess that the name had a different source. Tyre was the main port later best known to the Greeks. Now the early and native name for Tyre was *"Tsur"*—"the rock"—and it is suggested that of this sound the Greek merchants made "Syria".

beasts in the scrub of the sea-plain and in the forests which covered the slopes of the long mountains up to the snow line, so they went well armed and bearing with them a brazier of fire, slung from a pole which two men carried and constantly fed with fuel lest it should fail.

Next, once on land, they must look for some way of approach towards and over the very high barrier which towered above them. Such an approach would be given by some large stream among those which, at this season of melting snows, ran full over stony beds to the sea. They found such a one a short day's march down the shore, so full and wide as promised a good supply of water as well as an open valley upward into the hills, and by the mouth of this (it is called today the Nahr-el-Kelb, that is, "The Dog River") they lit their fire and camped for the night.

With the dawn they went up stream in a band along the northern bank and all day long rose further and further into the hills. By evening they had toiled so far and so high that they had reached the spring whence the torrent was fed, gushing as do a hundred others of this land, out of a limestone cleft. The trees were growing rare. A little higher on they ceased, and at their limit the second bivouac was made, with its protecting fire. With the first light their leader made for a notch in the ridge, where the snow lay light and thin between a tangle of rocks. He, going before, first reached the summit, and suddenly there broke upon him a view astonishing, abrupt and very grand.

At his feet lay a profound valley floor some thousands of feet below him and only a few miles wide. Its intense green contrasted violently with the bare rock and snow of the wall he and his men had surmounted. Beyond that valley, some six to ten miles away, another towering, unbroken mountain wall, parallel to that he had crossed, shut out whatever lay beyond: northwards to his left, southwards to his right that level green floor stretched away. It rose slightly, far off to the northward, where, as it seemed, should be a water parting. But that low lift hardly broke the general level of the swampy meads and its enclosed fertility, guarded on either side by such huge ramparts. This straight depression continued till it was lost at the very limits of his vision.

They descended to the valley floor and made their way still eastward through deep grasses, till they came to the narrow waters of a stream which ran southward through the centre of that deep marshy vale. Here, by the waterside, they made their third bivouac, and on the fourth day they advanced across the further part of the valley floor to the high, second ridge beyond. A stream and its rising cleft once more led them up into the heart of this opposing wall. They camped for a fourth time on its higher course and, after the night, they climbed this second, opposing wall as they had climbed the first. Like the first it was a long monotonous high ridge afforested, until they reached once more the treeless summit where snows and rocks intermingled: and from this second summit a contrast, more violent than the first, met their leader. To the eastward below, under the fierce sun, he saw, stretching away forever to a far horizon, the Desert. He had not traversed forty miles from his leaving of the coast, and already the narrow belt of habitable land, so strongly marked by the two parallel ranges, was exhausted.

Down that eastern slope to the bare sands fell torrents here and there, as on the seaward side of the first ridge. As they met the stony level their last waters nourished oases of verdure on the very edge of the parched waste, but the diminishing streams were swallowed up very soon and disappeared.

So they stood after an arduous morning's climb on the bare pass under a terrible sun, and looked down on to a landscape such as they had not thought could belong to this world—for beyond the oases far off and below was that other sea, not the human sea of their legends and voyages, the sea by which they lived, but a sea of desolation, of burning drought under a sky of fire.

There was peril of death if they should adventure further and attempt what was never meant for men. They had known all that could be known of this strange land. They had measured its breadth in so short an advance between the waves and the desert.

Their leader led them back to the last camp. Thence by the trail they had first made they returned again across the valley floor, across its small central river, and up again to the summit of the last high range. There they saw once more the very broad band of the sea rising up, up, to the skyline; and thought they could distinguish, a speck under its protecting cape, their vessel where their companions awaited them. Down the river they went to its mouth, camped for the last time, and before noon of the ninth day they were hailing their ship from the shore.

They weighed anchor and sailed on before the northerly breeze. Perhaps a cape would be turned and show a passage eastward? None such appeared. They saw the mountains diminish, the heights of Lebanon fell to lower heights; they saw between them and the inland hills a plain broken by the thrust of Carmel but still broadening. It grew more parched: the desert had come through and reached the sea. Just as they thus came to the end of living things the shore began to turn westward. They must run with the north wind first on the starboard quarter, then abeam. They knew that they had sailed down the last shores of their waters and that no way by sea would open eastward now. This long sea-land which they had coasted was the boundary of that inland sea-world.

In that short exploration inland through the empty hills the travellers had tested Syria. They had taken a sounding and a sample. They had grasped the soul of that land; for what Syria had shown itself to be in that one march and counter-march from the sea to the desert and back again to the sea—up the high wall of Lebanon, down into profound depression below, up the opposing second wall whence the dead, burnt plains stretched eastward forever—that Syria remained from one extreme to the other: from the Gulf of Alexandretta in the north down to the Egyptian wilderness on the south, four hundred miles away.

All along that constricted ribbon runs the same plan: the sea-coast, the narrow fertile patches along it, then the first great lift of highlands close by, everywhere looking down upon the sea, the deep cleft beyond, the second highlands eastward; then at their foot the Desert.

How shall the structure of that country, the ribs and form of it, be made clear?

Looking down from the air upon the whole scheme, from the Gulf of Alexandretta in the north to the Gulf of Akaba in the Red Sea, the one impression you would receive would be that of a long narrow piece of habitable land, running exceptionally between the empty desert and the empty sea.

In that belt of human conditions between the desert and the sea, you would not, as along the Nile, see a violent contrast of green marking the well-watered land, and of tawny rock and dust, marking the land where water was not. Rather was the bulk of that corridor bare stone and rock, but also a place to be suited later for cities and for men. You would know this by the marking of it throughout with lines of vegetation, which were the winter watercourses, by patches of brown earth within the folds of limestone hills, by the young growth on the plains along the coast.

But what would strike you most in that survey from above would be an unbroken thread of vivid verdure running straight through the heart of the land between the mountains parallel with the coast. It broadens here and there by some few miles, it is marked here and there, from north to south, with sheets of water, large and small. This green central line is the central cleft on either side of which all Syria is built.

Seeing it thus clearly from the air, the unbroken ribbon of fertility could only be the gift of living water (at any rate as far south as the Dead Sea) and one might suppose it to be the course of some great river, such as has elsewhere given life to the sands of Egypt and of Mesopotamia. But there is no such stream in Syria; the line of green, though, so strict and continuous, is built up along the banks of more than one stream, each of which, as you go southward, carries on the direction inherited from its forerunner to the north.

The northernmost of these is the Orontes, flowing from a low saddle in the depression, and running northward till it slips through a gap into the Mediterranean on the extreme ends of Syria. From that low saddle whence the Orontes springs, flow-

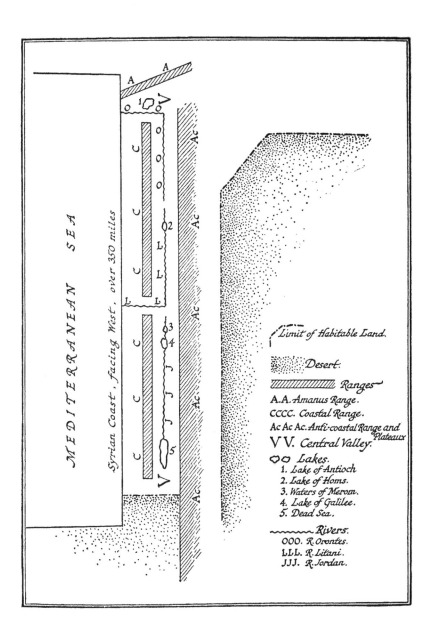

MEDITERRANEAN SEA

Syrian Coast, facing West, over 350 miles

Limit of Habitable Land.

Desert.

Ranges
A.A. *Amanus Range.*
CCCC. *Coastal Range.*
Ac Ac Ac. *Anti-coastal Range and Plateaux*
VV. *Central Valley.*

⌒⌒ Lakes.
1. *Lake of Antioch*
2. *Lake of Homs.*
3. *Waters of Merom.*
4. *Lake of Galilee.*
5. *Dead Sea.*

~~~~~ *Rivers.*
OOO. *R. Orontes.*
LLL. *R. Litani.*
JJJ. *R. Jordan.*

THE STRUCTURE OF THE COUNTRY

9

ing northward, springs another river, the Litani, flowing south: and just where the Litani makes an elbow sharply westward to find the Mediterranean in its turn, through a profound chasm in the hills, yet another river rises, to run southward again, still carrying on the north-south line of the Orontes and Litani axis. This third river is the Jordan; the eye may follow its deep, too luxuriant, half-tropical valley, to the expanse of the Dead Sea lying in its awful hollow to the south.

Beyond that, no stream prolongs the line of the ravine. Its further extension is watered only by imperfect brooks from the slight rainfall of the eastern hills. That moisture soon disappears in the drought of desert land.

This, then, is what a man might see from the air at a great height, overlooking the Syrian earth below, whose great inequalities and mountain ranges are flattened and reduced to a level for such an observer.

He would see the tracks of the torrent watercourses marked all along the few miles next to the coast. He would see, parallel to this coast and but a few miles inland, a long bare strip which is the coastal highland, and in its central part white ridges of snow. Next, eastward, another very few miles, would run another parallel; the bright green line of the successive rivers, and strung along that line the big marshy lake of Antioch to the north, the lesser mere of Homs, the little water of Merom, the larger oval of Genesareth (which is the Sea of Galilee), and lastly, far to the south, the enclosed waters of the Dead Sea. To the east, again, of this green cord another parallel bare strip which is the run of eastern highlands. Then the immense stretch of the desert, boundless, confused at last a hundred miles away with the hot haze of its horizon sky. And all these successive parallels would build up among them between the desert and the sea a border not more than a long day's ride across from side to side: forty miles at its narrowest, sixty at its most.

But even such a view, in its apparent flatness, does not teach a man the strange, the unique, structure of Syria.

To grasp that, it would be necessary to fly low above the coastal plain, rising but little higher than the passes over the coastal hills, nowhere over four thousand feet, save in the central knot, where Lebanon and Anti-Lebanon lift their monotonous great opposing walls. In such a flight, a man looking inland would find how truly Syria was built round that central valley of the Orontes, Litani and Jordan. It is the simplest of schemes, a central valley deeper in some sections than in others, but everywhere profound and clearly marked, like a trench dug by design and on a plan. It is a rift like nothing else on earth, running in its unchanging, direct line, undeviating from the north to the south, bounded as by levees to east and west, and these opposing barriers never far apart.

In the north, the highlands near the sea, to the west of the central chasm, are confused, though they form, along the watershed, a connected range; and gradually become one sharp ridge, the ridge of Lebanon, twice nearly reaching ten thousand feet. Beyond the narrow floor of the cleft, to the east thereof, the highlands bounding the Orontes valley also remain confused in structure to a point somewhat farther south than the rise of Lebanon on the western wall; but at last, after the lake of Homs, these eastern highlands also rise to a definite ridge, comparable to Lebanon, which stands over against them a few miles away. That eastern ridge is Anti-Lebanon. A man flying not much higher than the mountain passes would here see the central cleft in its most striking form, where it is deepest, and where its guardian mountain barriers on either side are at their steepest and most sharply defined; the secluded trench, where both the Orontes and the Litani rise.

As he still flew south, he would find the Anti-Lebanon ending abruptly in the sharp terminal lift of Hermon, the high mountain in which Anti-Lebanon ends.

Yet farther to the southwards, the hills to the east and west of the cleft become confused again, and no longer so high; rounded, indefinite; the highlands of Galilee to the west of the trench, of the Hauran to the east of it. Nor do the hills, as one still goes southward, rise so high whether on the western or on the eastern parallel run of highlands.

This being so, it might be thought that the peculiar central

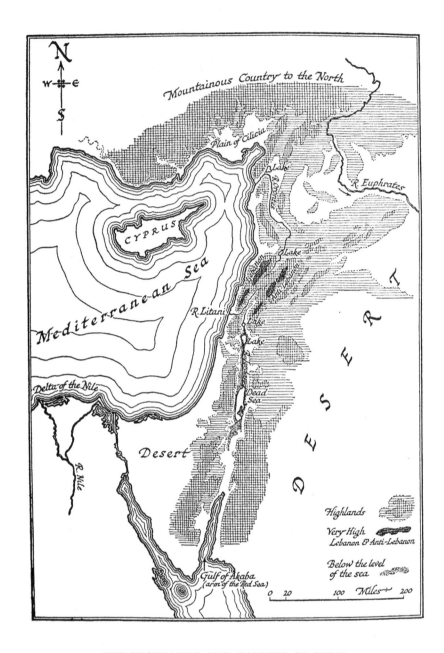

THE HIGHLANDS AND VALLEYS OF SYRIA

cleft would become less distinct and remarkable; by a singular exception, the like of which we have not elsewhere, this central valley becomes, on the contrary, more pronounced and individual than ever as it proceeds southward.

This is because the bed of it sinks steadily till, at last, in the depths of the Dead Sea, it is 2,600 feet below the Mediterranean. Throughout its whole course, the Jordan (save in its uppermost, brook, portion, under the slopes of Hermon) runs below sea level. The Sacred River follows a chasm which plunges deeper and deeper into the earth, until at last, where it falls into the enclosed waters of the Dead Sea, whence there is no issue, it is sunk lower than any river of the world. Even at its beginnings in the Sea of Galilee it was 680 feet below the lowest of the general earth on which men live, the shelf of the seashore; by the time it has run its further course, and loses itself in the salt waters beyond Jericho, a hundred miles away, it is more than 1,200 feet below, and the profoundest sounding of the Dead Sea itself, the lowest point of the cleft is half a mile deep, burrowing into the foundations of our world.

Thence forward, southwards on to the Red Sea at Akaba, over another hundred miles, the cleft continues, but in a different form, though it is still clearly marked, with the eastern hills forming a wall and boundary for it, the floor of it rising to a more normal level, reaches a summit and then sinks again gradually towards the sea at Akaba.

Thus then is Syria built, in five layers, each very narrow for its length, and laid along side by side; the string of sea plains in the north, at first no more than river mouths; later, farther south, increasing in size, but nowhere more than a few miles broad; the western highlands; the strange central ravine; the eastern highlands; the edge of the Desert.

So formed, so standing on the edges of Asia and of Africa, so providing a passage squeezed between sea and sand, so facing the commerce of all the great Mediterranean—looking down its length from the east—Syria has been of the highest moment to our race: above all in this, that it has been our Battleground.

It has been the place of meeting and of shock between

opposing cultures and men, of conflict between those forces which sweep and mould the world beyond all others, which are supreme above all others, those sources from which all cultures flow—religions.

Here the gods of Egypt appeared, not without majesty, but disdaining to plant their worship; here in the Syrian belt the very evil gods of Lust and Torture were to await the proclamation of Israel and to be locked in battle with the God of Israel—the One Jehovah—and to succumb; Moloch and Ashtaroth and Baal. Here the Spirits of loveliness were to waft in from the West in the wake of the Greek armies, and here Aphrodite mourned for Adonis dead. Here in the fulness of time came the flower of our Revelation, the kindling of the Gospel, the founding of the Church, the violent, obscure, creative tragedy whence our Western civilisation arose. Herein arose the Main Challenge: whether the Christ had come indeed or not.

From that day onwards, that battleground became a battle-ground indeed. The Faith was established to the confusion of its foes; the True Cross was present and worshipped in Jerusalem; it was the centre and the symbol of the Christian thing. But still there was to be no peace. Asia swept in again, under the Persian name, ravaged and destroyed; and immediately afterwards the most powerful of the heresies arose, under the followers of Mohammed, and all that high culture rooted in Rome and Athens was flooded and overwhelmed.

The lowest degradation followed; the Mongol Turk out of the northern steppes came in as conqueror; the Christian West awoke, and there followed for two centuries the triumphant charge, the dogged reluctant retreat, of the Crusades. Mighty castles arose, and the French Principalities were formed to hold Asia off for a hundred years—then, at the Horns of Hattin, we Christians lost the East.

For two lifetimes more the pertinacious but doomed effort to retain what could be retained held on, losing ground step by step, and at last the Holy Land was altogether abandoned and what remained therein of clarity and order was ruined. Islam had conquered.

But even so peace was not to come securely in the destruction of the better by the worse. The battleground remained a battleground, awaiting its time; it saw during a few brief weeks the bayonets and heard the guns of Napoleon.

Today[1] there has risen before us in that same land a new menace, a triple riddle to be answered under pain of death. In Syria, artificially divided, Islam is at issue with French power in the north; in the south, in Palestine, England has taken it for a task to re-establish in the teeth of Islam what will shortly be an imperilled Jewish State—and all around either Western power are the watchful millions of Islam, of the desert, and of Asia beyond.

---

[1] Hilaire Belloc is writing in the mid–1930s.—ED.

II

The Desert and the Rain

THE BATTLE BETWEEN THE DESERT AND THE RAIN—
THAT IS, THE BATTLE OF LIFE AND DEATH

SYRIA, the battleground of great empires and of much more important religions, was, at its beginnings, and remains to this day, a battleground of nature: the battleground between the desert and the rain.

Syria is a fringe of life established precariously and artificially, as it were, on the edge of death's empire. It is a frontier occupation by an invading power—the power of moisture and fertility which has attacked the dominion of sterile sand and stone. That invading power has never been able to reach more than a few miles from the sea-coast. Over those few miles it has entrenched itself and it holds them permanently. That is Syria. That, at least, is habitable Syria, for the name is extended over the whole vast desert land behind the fields and the harvests of the coastal hills.

By rights all Syria, coastal or inland, ought to be under the dominance of drought and death. It ought to be one of those wide districts united by sterility everywhere. The desert ought to come down, by rights, to the sea-coast, from a little below the northern mountains on the edges of Asia Minor right down to the corner where the shore bends westward and the approach to Egypt begins. But the scheme has been interrupted by sea moisture, and that interruption has created the habitable Syria we know.

There is in our northern hemisphere a zone, beginning to the south of our temperate latitudes, in which zone rain does not fall, or if it falls falls neither frequently enough nor densely enough to support the full life of mankind. The lands lying under those rainless skies are the deserts. You can see them stretching on the map from our own extreme west in Africa into and across Asia, to the extreme east: from the Atlantic to the Pacific. It is not an uninterrupted silence and desolation. It is a chain of deserts, isolated each from the other by exceptional lands (and coastal Syria is one) where water is present and men can live. But taken in the mass this zone is a desert zone in which the habitable interruptions are exceptions.

There is no definition of the desert, for, like every other obstacle and physical enemy which man has to challenge, the strength and severity of the inhuman aridity varies. Many a district which seems desert to the traveller born and bred in a happier world of fields and forests and many streams, is not such to the traveller coming thither from lands to the south even more stricken. What at first sight seems desert to us Northern and Western men, has carried a high civilisation and nourished great cities. The south of Tunis, the bare hills of Atlas farther west, look desert enough to an Englishman who sees them for the first time. They seemed a paradise to the Mohammedan conquerors coming in from over the Libyan sands. The ultimate frontier of the desert is the line between that which will bear crops and that which it is futile to cultivate.

Sparse, rare crops can be grown on the edges of the desert. Between what may be called absolute desert (such as, for instance, the great billows of mere sand stretching for hundreds of miles south of the Atlas) and fully habitable land such as the Phœnician coast or the Algerian Tell, there are many degrees of drought. Moreover there is hardly any district in Asia or Africa so cursed that chance nomads may not wander in it, feeding their animals on the sparse scrub or, where even this is lacking, making long marches from one oasis to another. But if it be difficult to define the desert we Western men know well enough what it is: the dominion of death. A wind of death blows from it and it bears an aspect, majestic but terrible, which is also the aspect of death when we look down upon it from the last ridges of the boundary hills.

Two conditions present the desert with water—and when that gift is afforded men and vegetation can live.

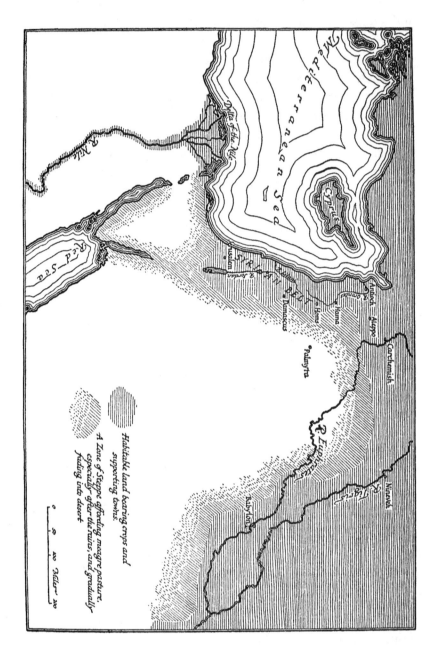

RAINY AND DESERT AREAS IN PALESTINE AND EGYPT

Habitable land bearing crops and
supporting towns.

A Zone of Steppe affording meagre pasture,
especially after the rains, and gradually
fading into desert.

These two conditions are (1) high land, sufficiently near the sea to bring down rain, and (2) the presence of some great river, sufficient in volume when it issues from its sources in a well-watered land, to carry on through the sterile wilderness and reach the sea without absorption by the porous earth or the heat of the skies above.

Now the first of those conditions is present in Syria itself, the second sufficiently near Syria to mould its history. Syria itself is a strip of coastal highland; attainable from Syria to the east and the south-west are the great desert rivers, Nile and Euphrates.

There runs down from the northern mountains of Asia Minor to the Egyptian desert, close to the sea all the way, that continuous system of highlands already described. Such highlands provoke rain. No one knows why this should be, but so it is. A group of hills or mountains will often—not always—cause such moisture as comes upon them from any neighbouring sea to condense and fall as rain. It is in part perhaps explained by the fact that (for some reason also unknown) the air gets colder as one rises through the first few thousand feet above the earth. In this as in every other department of physical science modern research and experiment push explanation further and further off as knowledge accumulates.

The connection of rainfall with highland is capricious. You get far greater condensation in some hilly regions than in others and the cooling of the air with height cannot be reduced to rule. The snow line on the Pyrenees, for instance, right up against the Atlantic and facing a cool climate to the north, is far higher than it is in the Alps, though these are much farther from the ocean and face on their southern side the warm climate of the Italian plains.

Anyhow, in general, hills will provoke rain and there will be rainfall on the heights and in their neighbourhood where there would be none if the land were flat. So it is with the narrow belt of Syrian highlands which runs all the way from the Amanus range in the north above the Gulf of Alexandretta to the beginnings of the wilderness beyond Hebron on the south. There is a fair rainfall even towards the end of that strip, although it tends to lessen as one proceeds southwards.

The rainfall is naturally heavier on the seaward side of the Syrian ranges than it is on the landward side to the east. There it becomes so slight, after a very short advance, that it is insufficient for vegetable growth and the desert begins. In the north you can go from the sea right to the upper Euphrates over land which has been well cultivated in the past, is still somewhat cultivated, and might under good government be fully cultivated again. All that district, of which Aleppo is the modern chief town, lies under those fairly favourable conditions. When you get down sixty miles south of that, the rainfall to the east of the heights is less. The desert begins within a short distance of Homs, within a shorter distance still of Hama and comes within a very few miles of Damascus. One might almost say that it lies at the gates of that city; for though the torrents, coming from the Anti-Lebanon, and which nourish Damascus, continue some way beyond till they are lost in marsh, the land beyond that marsh, and indeed to the north of it, is hardly habitable. A caravan comes into Damascus from the uninhabitable desert as a sailor comes into a haven from the uninhabitable sea.

Farther south the rule continues. The rainfall, though somewhat lessened, is still considerable on the heights west of the Jordan ravine. It is appreciable on the hills beyond, so that the Hauran and the hills of Moab can be cultivated. There is a fairly wide space between the Jordan valley and the eastern limit of crops; the heights of Idumea far to the south bear some corn, but it is significant that the stream which runs in winter down the long valley to Akaba itself is intermittent and does not flow after the winter ends.

It is surprising to note the figures of rainfall on the western part of the hills near the Mediterranean. At Jerusalem, for instance, you have a total precipitation for the whole year comparable to that of the western European capitals, London and Paris. At Beyrout to the north you have an even larger rainfall. The plains at the end of the hills and between them and the Mediterranean are less favoured; but until one gets quite to the south they still have enough water to sustain cities and men and harvests.

There is, however, this peculiarity about the Syrian rainfall. It is a winter rainfall. During the summer all is without appreciable rain.

When, after the equinox, the northern hemisphere begins to dip towards the sun the rainless area extends northward under the increasing heat and includes the whole of the Syrian belt of heights, the central valley, and the narrow sea-plains at their feet.

The rains begin to fall again with the opening of the autumn. In the greater part of the district, especially on the fertile sea-coast, you have what are called the "first" rains of October which furnish an opportunity for sowing, and a little later the "second" rains of December and January on which the growth of the harvest depends. But after March the moisture is quite insufficient and with the beginning of May the supply ceases.

This lack of rain in summer has affected all the history of the land. It means a heavy strain for immigrants from temperate and well-watered climates. It was a factor in the defeat of the Crusaders. It was a factor in the decline of the Greek Seleucid kingdom. Those very dry summers affect the people of Syria themselves, lowering their energy and (some would say) their political capacity.

The absence of a sufficient rainfall there for a great part of the year is in some degree compensated for by two other characters in the Syrian hills (in which term I include, of course, the highlands of Palestine and Moab beyond). In the first place the great bulk of them are composed of porous rock which stores water throughout the dry season; in the second place at the centre of these highlands stand the very high summits of Lebanon and Anti-Lebanon which store moisture in another form— that of snow.

This does not melt until long after the lower levels have been burnt brown. What with the water reserves formed by the snows of Lebanon and Anti-Lebanon and the water reserves formed by the limestone, Syria enjoys throughout its narrow length perennial streams. The Orontes, the Litani and the Jordan flow copiously all the year round and even the shorter torrents which come down the western slopes and fall at once into the Mediterranean have, the larger of them, water through most of the year. The torrents of the eastern side of the Anti-Lebanon towards the desert are so continually fed from the mountains that Damascus is plentifully nourished, though the waters fail so shortly beyond the town.

So much for Syria itself and the rainfall on its heights and flats between the deserts and the Mediterranean. Through these deserts run two great rivers which have added life and conflict to the land.

To the west and south of Syria is the valley of the Nile, cut off by a hundred miles and more of land which is everywhere desertic and is actually sheer desert almost up to the seashore.

The Nile, the near neighbour of Syria, attainable with some effort across the narrow intervening wilderness, is like no other geographical thing. For two thousand miles a broad stream of water flows across the worst deserts in the world. It not only maintains its great volume all the way from the well-watered Sudan to the Mediterranean, it overflows at regular periods, adding every year to the fertile soil of its valley. The banks of the Nile are for all that way between the tropical African rains and the European sea a ribbon of green: crops and the habitations of men and a culture stretching back far beyond history into the depths of time.

The connection between this human land and Syria is rendered the more possible by the spreading out of the Nile valley at its northern end into a great triangle of most fruitful land watered everywhere by the various branches of the Nile and their interconnecting channels. This "Delta" stretches its arms eastwards as well as westwards; and the easternmost mouth beyond which vegetation ceases is close enough to the southern habitable part of Syria for the gap to be covered in a few long marches, wherein is found at long intervals water sufficient to support the passage of armies and commerce.

From the Nile therefore there should naturally come towards Syria, sooner or later, some full influence through contact which began very early in this story. No strong effect, however, came upon Syria from Egypt till long after the first interchanges, but it came at last and, since it was established, between three and four thousand years ago, it has never ceased.

The other great neighbouring desert river, the Euphrates, performed for Syria a more useful function and one not tardily developed but coeval with the earliest story of man in the East.

The Euphrates rises in the northern mountains of Asia Minor, in what is still a temperate region and one with mountain rainfall and mountain torrents. It issues from that tangle of high hills already a fine stream so deep as to provide but rare and distant fords and some already established as great and broad. Its course as it flows through the mountain valleys runs westward as though it were to fall into the Mediterranean on the northern corner of the Syrian coast, but just as it is about to issue from the mountains and while it is still benefiting from the rains of the hills, it begins to turn southwards and then eastwards in a great bend. When it comes out on to the drier, but not yet desert, plain on the southern edges of the hills it is fairly set for the south-east. It enters the desert zone, and flows through it thus, south-easterly for three hundred miles.

Before falling into the Persian Gulf the Euphrates reaches upon a belt of fertile level soil the deposit of its own floods, and it also comes into the neighbourhood of another river not quite so great but of equal importance in the history of mankind, the Tigris, also rising in the northern mountains and running down southward along the edges of those great hills which are the wall of Persia: hills which also provoke rain and nourish torrents and rivers.

Very early indeed, in the days of the gods, a full culture arose upon the lower reaches of these two rivers, Tigris and Euphrates, and the fertile land between them irrigated by canals. The whole flat wherever water could reach it bore a dense population of great cities, temples and palaces standing in the midst of crowded harvest land. The Greeks, when they came to it so many centuries after its beginning, called it "Mesopotamia", "the midst of the rivers" and by that name it is to us in the West best known.

Now the effect of the Euphrates thus threading the desert from the habitable land in the north-west corner of Syria by the Mediterranean to the habitable land of Mesopotamia was capital. The Euphrates connecting the one with the other was a *bridge*. Men in numbers could follow that stream through the uninhabitable land between Mesopotamia and Syria. They could advance provisioned by vessels borne on the river, and were supplied by its waters in all the advance across the waste. Even great armies could march along that exceptional connection between the crowded land at the northern end of the Persian Gulf and the human liveable country between those fields and green hill slopes of Cilicia, of the Gulf of Alexandretta, and of all that country between the mouth of the Orontes and out beyond Aleppo which, with the more difficulty as one goes eastward, bears crops and sustains mankind.

If you make out upon a general map of south-western Asia the land made possible by the presence of water you will get between the eastern end of the Mediterranean and the distant mountains which are the buttresses of Persia on the Tigris, a sort of gigantic "N", of which the two uprights are the habitable coastal land of Syria between the desert and the Mediterranean, the habitable Mesopotamian land and especially the course of the Tigris, while the sloping stroke of the "N" between the two uprights is the course of the Euphrates.

But for the Euphrates the ancient civilisation of Mesopotamia, its wealth and its discoveries, its armaments, its social customs, its formative religion, would hardly have approached the West. Armies and commerce could advance with difficulty through the tangle of mountains to the north of the desert, and a more or less habitable fringe south of those mountains along the desert edge. With greater difficulty detachments or, as a rule, no more than small bands, might pass, from one well to another, from Mesopotamia to the hills above the Dead Sea. But it was the Euphrates which made possible great expeditions and permanent communications, commerce and communion of ideas, between the Syrian coast and that distant fertility upon which arose Chaldea and Assyria.

One may sum up and say that the whole district from the Persian hills to the Mediterranean would be one stretch of desert and would play no more part in history than the Sahara but for the rain caught by the narrow highland strip of Syria to the west, along the Mediterranean; the fringe north of the desert, and the diagonal junction formed by the mighty stream of the Euphrates making a precarious union between Mesopotamia and the coastal towns.

All the political powers which have controlled that land have depended upon, and have been effectively confined to, this "N" of water. They have never fully mastered the few nomads of the sands; and Syria means in history not the wide space between the buttress of the Persian mountains and the Mediterranean but the narrow exceptional coastal band where men may live. The Mesopotamian alluvial soil (now ruined), the coastal strip where habitation has been more permanent and civilisation has endured, are connected for travel, rather than as habitable land, by the northern "steppe" of this desert and by the middle Euphrates.

There is a last question on which, if we could answer it, much history would depend. Unfortunately we cannot answer it today and there seems little prospect that we will ever be able to do so. It is this: Have Arabia, and this Syrian desert which is the extension of Arabia to the north, have the desert of the Arabian peninsula and the desert east and west of the Nile, has the Sahara itself, been gradually drying throughout recorded history—that is during the last four to six thousand years? We have true history for four thousand, and nebulous indications carrying us back two thousand years before that. Is there proof within these limits of a change?

I have heard the matter debated, not without violence, by what are called experts on the two sides. From these debates I gathered that their science was, like nearly all modern things of the kind, a mass of affirmation lacking proof. Common sense inclines rather to the one side than to the other: it inclines to conclude that the climate has been much the same throughout the historic period: that there has been no appreciable desiccation.

That what is now desert was once well watered is plain enough; and from the evidences of this change one would naturally think it a continuous process. Thence it would follow that the change had carried on even during the last four or five thousand years.

One is tempted to affirm, for instance, that the journey directly across the desert from Mesopotamia to the region of the Dead Sea must have been easier in Abraham's time than our own; that wells were more numerous, and so forth.

But evidence of this is lacking. If it were true that there had been considerably more rainfall in the historic past than in the present there would be signs of it in the relics of human habitation and there would be traces of it in records. Such records as we have—for instance, the traditional records concerning Abraham and his successors—present landscape similar to that we have today save for one point: since the coming of Islam the trees have been massacred and, as everybody knows, trees preserve the soil of a country and store up its water. It is probably true that they also provoke rainfall.

It is just to remark that the cutting down of the trees on Lebanon was already excessive before the Mohammedan religion came and the Mongols followed to complete the ruin. The Roman governors were compelled to issue edicts restricting the cutting of timber. But it is still true that throughout Christendom, wherever Islam has overrun Roman land, it has destroyed the trees, for Islam cuts down but is too slack to replant. Sicily and Tunis are two outstanding examples. We may confidently ascribe the same results to the same cause in Syria.

To some slight extent then disafforestation may have affected the climate. But where the desert ceases today there approximately it ceased at the beginning of our records: where it begins today there approximately it began six thousand years ago. The frontier towns which could just maintain themselves on the edges of the inhuman land are still the frontier towns they were four thousand years ago, or, where they have been ruined by war, might again be rebuilt and occupied with much the same population. But, save in a rare oasis (as at Palmyra), men could not, within the historical period, live elsewhere than where we find them living today. Where they are constrained to be nomadic, there were they constrained to be nomadic six thousand years before our time.

III

The First Record

WHENCESOEVER or however men drifted first into that Syrian highland belt between the desert and the sea, we do not know. We know nothing of those origins at all. We have no records sufficiently numerous to create even the shadow of a picture, still less have we any continuous sequence of such records; we have not even monuments which so often suggest what preceded written things.

It is here as it seems to be universally throughout the world: man as we know him, possessed of the arts and the inheritor of the world, appears, as it were, suddenly with no background.

Our reason tells us that man must have, in some place or time, originated with, or developed, those powers which he is found enjoying in the fulness of being. But of a passage from some groping, half-conscious association to true political manhood, we have no witness. Here in Syria, as everywhere, there is evidence of very early human presence. It is furnished by ancient relics (how ancient we shall never know) of man's life and conflict. Here as everywhere there are fragments of bone and weapon; but fragments of bone and weapon are not enough, save to provide guesswork for unstable hypothesis. There is no more here, in Syria, than elsewhere any introduction to history through a gradation of ascending knowledge. When first we learn of men like ourselves, associated, established, Syrian mankind appears in maturity: fully grown.

What we do know is that, when evidence first appears, the society we find in Syria is of one group in language, and possibly—but not certainly—of similar blood. We do not know but that side by side with this general character there were not hostile exceptions, but we do find one stamp apparently present. Of the language, or at any rate the language of those who left any intelligible record thereof, there is no doubt; it is the sort called by the modern learned, in their special vocabulary, "Semitic".

The various dialects of that common tongue were, even in later times, after centuries of opportunities for change, so much akin that many main terms were identical throughout. It is so to the present day. The various forms of this "Semitic" speech are very much nearer to each other than are the various European languages which spring from popular Latin—Catalan, Castilian, Provençal, Portuguese, Romance, Tuscan and the rest. We may believe that a man from Babylon could understand an Arab, that a man from the Lebanon could understand one of the wanderers from Sinai, as well or better than a north country labourer today could understand a man from Devon. There is some evidence that (not at the origin of record, but much later) other forms of speech struck here and there—especially in certain towns on the sea-coast where foreign adventurers had come from over the waters. There is a possibility that in such spots as Gaza, Ascalon and Joppa, along the shores south of Carmel, the newcomers were European and therefore of our own kind. But, if they were so, they soon merged into the ocean of Semitic speech all around. It is possible, or even probable, that a very different tongue spoken by powerful societies living in the far north, in Asia Minor and its boundaries, had some early effect which also perished. We like to call them "Hittites" but we know nothing of their vocabulary. Egypt, though so near at hand, was of no effect, save perhaps for a few words borrowed in commerce. Syria was, when first we know it, what it is now in speech.

Of race, we can, of course, say very much less, or, more properly, nothing. Language is no test of race for language spreads like oil. It can be imposed by circumstances of every kind, religious mission, administration, social example from above; it can even be imposed by conquest, though such imposition is rare. But if there is one thing certain in the course of history it is that language spreads and disappears unconnected with the spreading or disappearance of a breed.

Moreover, race is the least certain (and therefore the most generally assumed) common factor in a nation or even in a culture. To explain everything by race is satisfactory indeed to the imagination, but it is not satisfactory to the reason: it does not correspond with reality.

In the case of Syria we may say that there is certainly something in common physically to many of those, though not to all of those, who speak, or spoke, Semitic languages; for instance, the high arch of the nose, though by no means universal among them, is widespread. But what one does find at the very heart and root of Syria and affecting the whole of it with one character is the *religious* motive. Now a particular religion is certainly the source and maker of every particular culture.

One common type of religion and consequently one culture is found in Syria from the very beginning. This religion was filled with the presence of a Deity protecting his worshippers and invisible master of their political unit—commonly a city. He was one of many gods, but, in each case the chief god. This god demanded sacrifice; a portion of tribute and loot must be set aside for him as also a portion of native wealth. To him were "devoted"—sometimes for destruction—the cities overcome by the national armies.

Sacrifice involved the conception of a special kind of man set apart for the service of the sacrifice, that is, an order of priests, and in that Order there constantly appears a Hierarchy so that the city or other political unit has its Chief Priest; the Priest being of such consequence his character is often merged in that of the King, and Priest-Kings appear throughout the ancient traditions of Mesopotamia and Syria. But it is not true that the two conceptions were originally one; that the King and Priest were a single office at the beginning and later differentiated into a lay King and the Priest of religion. The distribution is haphazard. Here you find priest-kings ruling a city, there you find a king and warrior assuming the office of a chief priest; and again, elsewhere, you find the two offices side by side. But everywhere in this Orient the Priest and the King are closely associated even when they are not mingled. The State is everywhere interwoven with religion.

The religion and culture of Syria are also that of a distant and separated land—Mesopotamia; the alluvial, habitable land of the lower Tigris and the lower Euphrates, fertile through the overflow of those great rivers, from the watercourses descending the high Persian mountains to the east, but much more through the artificial irrigation which men conducted in that dry land, which had in antiquity a canal system, connecting the seaward ends of the two great rivers that fall into the Persian Gulf. This canal system, and the high civilisation dependent upon it, were destroyed by vile Mongol invaders, Turks, very late in the story—only six hundred years ago. The greater part of all this alluvial Mesopotamian land, which was once, for thousands of years on end, populous, powerful and rich, has gone back to empty waste. Its enormous cities are heaps of dust. Its mighty temples and palaces—all its architecture—have gone. But while the Mesopotamian civilisation flourished, even in its earliest form, it impressed itself upon Syria; and that far-off business, stretching back beyond all that we know of human time, the business of Chaldea, had set its stamp beyond the broad desert, and through all those habitable hills which lie along the Mediterranean seaboard.

Now, how was this? How did a whole speech and manner of living and religious idea, native to the lands on the Persian Gulf, leap a vast stretch of howling wilderness hundreds of miles from side to side and take root in Syria far off to the west on the Mediterranean seaboard? Without water, men cannot live: and the region between the fruitful soil of Mesopotamia and Syria far to the west is rainless, or so nearly so as to forbid the growth of a human society. That immense desert could be traversed perilously and with special artifice, by caravans, dependent on rare wells, and coming in small numbers; it could be turned by following the half-habitable fringe to the north of it. But each approach is difficult.

The Syrian habitable belt of hills could be reached, it would seem, much more easily from the Egyptian south, where there is a sandy passage less than a third of the distance across the great desert to the east. Here, on the south, there is, as we have seen, a way along the sea-coast to the last southern fields of Palestine from the very fertile Delta of the Nile. The road skirted a mass of wilderness but was itself passable even by considerable numbers, by armies; for there is water at intervals not too long for provision from one march to another, and a week's advance carried troops across the empty gap of drought.

Egypt, therefore, one would have thought, with its most ancient, unbroken tradition of a profound civilisation, might have impressed the Syrian origins: but Egypt had no such effect.

Of what lay in habitable lands to the north, in the hills of what we call today Cilicia and Armenia, we know next to nothing. There have come to light recently certain undecipherable inscriptions which the learned ascribe to the people they have called Hittite; these inscriptions are broadcast far and wide, in Asia Minor, and more sparsely discoverable down into Northern Syria itself; they are accompanied sometimes by sculptures of a repulsive type, with violently exaggerated noses—proboscises rather—and these sculptures are presumed to represent a race, or culture or what not, which also invented the undecipherable inscriptions.

To the hideous human representations the title Hittite is also given. The modern habit of invention to supply the lack of knowledge talks of a "Hittite empire" in some remote past, and it is fairly certain that ancient Mesopotamian armies marching far westward came into conflict with other armies the names of which, "Khatti", suggest the word Hittite; but of all this remote story, we know hardly anything. It certainly was not from the north, though that was the most obvious entry, that there filtered into the first Syrian societies their way of worship, of dress and of speech.

There was indeed entry into Syria from the north by way of that fringe of the desert which, after rain, is less sterile and precariously supports a sparse population. That fringe unites the lands round Aleppo to the cities on the middle Tigris. Armies have followed it—though it is difficult to use permanently, for there are no sufficiently well-watered bases.

Besides land entry from Egypt, the desert and the north, there was a fourth entry: the entry by sea. Later, in recorded history, commerce from the shores and islands of the Mediterranean influenced Syria, and certain of her rare, difficult ports, notably Sidon and (later) Tyre, grew famous and very rich long after. But we know of no early impress coming upon Syria from the sea.

No, the kinship of Syria in its remotest origins is not in spirit, clothing, manner, gods, and the names of things, a kinship with the easily accessible north nor with the accessible (though less easily accessible) Egyptian south and west; it is from far beyond the desert, from the very distant Mesopotamian east, and we must ask again, why was this so?

The answer to that question, which lies at the root of the whole Syrian theory, the soul of Syria, and her vast effect upon the world, is found in that "bridge" of the middle Euphrates, the all-important function of which has been described. The Euphrates it was which permitted a diagonal advance to the north and west in spite of the intervening wilderness, and it was the Euphrates which maintained throughout the centuries that Mesopotamian influence on Syria which is discovered in the first records of that hill country and its streams, Orontes, Leontes (Litani), Jordan, and the brief rivers of Damascus.

Long before true history begins there are glints and flashes, as it were, of evidence upon the Syrian people. These are found in very sparse, disconnected and fragile records stamped upon baked clay in the Mesopotamian region. One late document, purporting to be the copy of a much older one but suspect from its magical character, speaks of a great monarch in the Mesopotamian east as advancing to the sea-waters of the west and even crossing them, so that some have imagined an expedition to Cyprus. In another more probable document, and in yet another, there is vague allusion to "Maru", the "West"; and one or two of the place names mentioned bear some similarity to the later place names of Syria.

But that is all. On such insufficient evidence there have been built, of course, very large but very flimsy structures of assertion; but there is no history, properly speaking, there is no firm outline, even in fragments, until round about the year 2000 B.C. It is, then, some four thousand years ago that something definite of Syria first appears. From that time onwards intermittently, but more and more frequently, something like a true history of Syria proceeds.

It is significant that this first piece of full evidence stands at the head of that great development which was to give Syria its full and final meaning: the development of the Jewish people through whom was maintained and affirmed the worship of the one true God and the prophecies of a Messiah, who saw at last his advent and heard in the climax of the affair the Gospel of the Incarnation. For this first full evidence on Syria is the still existing story of Abraham.

The document on which it reposes is one now as wrongly discredited as it was formerly overrated: the book called in its later Greek form "Genesis": the first of the sacred books of the Jews. The document as we have it is not contemporary; it was set down long after the events of which it preserves the memory. But it is strong, detailed and rings true.

It is natural that after the blind idolatry of the Old Testament text—especially in its English form—there should have come a reaction, and that today the sons of the Bible-Christians are the foremost in denying the historical reality of the Pentateuch. But natural emotions, though they explain, do not excuse bad history; and it is mere bad history to undervalue tradition. A man must be very ignorant of historical evidence and of man's nature who does not accept so firm and detailed a tradition as that which fills the Patriarchal Story from the first mention of Terah to the reception of Jacob in Egypt. The whole thing is clearly a true record of successive tribal ancestors whose names and habitations and burial places and journeys have been handed down many generations in an exact ritual; for thus do men in an early society preserve the common memory of their origins, and thus, for that matter, does each of us today after his fashion—at least, each of us who have great-grandfathers.

The document opens with the fortunes of Terah, the father of Abraham. Terah's is the first name* so far known in the Syrian story, and coupled with that name we find other names

* It is amusing to remember that it *may* mean "Wild Goat".

of two cities, one dead, the other still vigorously living: *Ur* and *Damascus*.

Ur is now a heap of mounds, like the rest of the dead cities of Mesopotamia. These heaps which once were Ur are called today Mugheir—the place of Bitumen. It stands in the dead flat plains on the right bank of the lower Euphrates, especially conspicuous when the floods are out and marked by the date palms which hence southward fringe the great river to its mouth. It may have been the oldest of the mud-brick towns, for its name "Urum" or "Uru" is said to mean "The City". It seems to have been of no very great size—rather more than half a mile across—but it was the capital of its district. Terah belonged to the place or its neighbourhood; a considerable lord rich in herds and with many dependents—for one of his sons alone could arm forty mounted men. What made him take that western journey with all his house and flocks we know not, but he settled at the end of it in Haran—that is, Hauran—the steppe district where there is still pasturage and tillage on the western edge of the desert near Damascus. There he died. Of his three sons, one, Abraham, moved off southward with his cattle, taking with him a nephew called Lot.

There has been a mass of conjecture as to the real site of this "Haran". The argument in favour of its being the Hauran is the habitable character of this district on the western edge of the Syrian desert, and its sufficiently close neighbourhood to Damascus and to Palestine to make it fit in; but the strongest evidence of all is that it is from the first called "Canaanite". Against it is the claim that the word Hauran is etymologically distinct and cannot be the origin of "Haran". Some identify Haran with a village and district with similar sounding name much nearer Damascus to the north. The older generation of critics made certain that "Haran" was a district of a similar sounding name in the north of Mesopotamia to which Terah emigrated from the south, going up the Tigris and remaining in the far east until, after his death, his son Abraham went off to the west.

That does not fit in with the character of the story. The whole spirit of it is that of a great change, of a journey cutting off a man from his origins. It was the beginning of a new state of affairs, and so struck the next generations that they saw it as the origin of a whole new phase in their culture. We had better stick to the Hauran until some new evidence appears: it is as good—or as bad—guesswork as any other.

Damascus, the other town mentioned in the story, appears as a place taken for granted: old established. The Herd-master Terah does not live there as a citizen nor does his son. It is mentioned because they stay in the neighbourhood and because one of their chief dependents was a native of the town.

The chief use of the story for understanding what Syria was when it first appears in our historical document is the state of affairs which the tradition takes for granted. Of Northern Syria we hear not a word. It looks as though Terah's trek had left the Euphrates high up and then struck down across the steppe for Damascus without coming near the Orontes: keeping outside Anti-Lebanon and the Homs and Hama country. There is still pasturage some little way east towards the desert, and flocks can advance along the fringe of it. It is not probable—perhaps impossible—that Terah and his large body of dependents and numerous flocks should have got westward as a camel caravan can do by risking long marches directly across the desert from one rare well to another. The Euphrates must have been the line of advance.

The south Syrian country appears in this first document as a district with plenty of towns, presumably small defended places, each under its local chieftain (called in our translation "kings").

It is evident that Southern Syria was then an admixture of open land, still only partly occupied, and fixed cities. It is easy enough to understand the cities, but the half-occupied land is a more difficult problem. Great chiefs of large herds roamed over it almost at will. They naturally could not do so without clashing with others similarly interested in the limited pasturage. There is no recorded tradition of customary boundaries, such as one finds in the later Western countries even at the beginning of history. *There*, where pasture is much deeper and more valuable and, in the west of Europe at least, fully settled, you have not always fixed property in it but always conventional rights sometimes varying with the season of use. In the Alps and Pyrenees, for instance, there is a seasonal migration of flocks to and from fixed areas, the whole regulated by a strict set of rules. But in Southern Syria four thousand years ago there were quarrels between the chieftains and their herdsmen, each complaining of the other's trespass upon land which had been occupied, for a time at least, by their sheep and cattle.

These masters of great herds were the peers of the city chiefs. They met as equals in combat. Their alliance as equals is desired and sought after, and there is even one source of tradition which represents these "Sheiks" (to use a modern word now familiar) as having occasionally ruled over a city as well as the open lands—the "king" of it, as we translate the term. Josephus records a tradition that Abraham himself was "king" in Damascus for some period.

Another political feature in these regions of early South Syrian history is the connection with Egypt which has never failed from that day to this and which must have been much older than Abraham's time.

It is particularly interesting to note its character. There is no trace of the Egyptian power pressing upon Southern Syria nor, as yet, of the so-called Semitic people (the people of Syria of the desert and of Mesopotamia beyond the desert) pressing upon the isolated high civilisation of Egypt. What we find is some slight allusion in Egyptian record to commerce, and a sort of sparse infiltration of the eastern populations into Egypt or perhaps into the eastern edges of the Delta, when there is famine on the stony hills and barren regions into which Syria fades off to the south. What this led to we will see when we come to the problem of the "Shepherd Kings". At any rate it seems clear that there was nothing like invasion and nothing like any considerable occupation of the land which the Nile makes fertile by people coming from the ill-watered land to the north-east of it.

Egypt was rather regarded as a source of supply. In time of scarcity some small body of herdsmen from the Syrian lands would ask leave to sojourn in Egypt. Abraham himself does so; but there is no permanent connection.

But, in this same story of Abraham, there is record of regular connection across the desert to the east, towards Mesopotamia. You have a journey undertaken by a man with ten camels and going apparently across the edges of the Syrian desert to the south, by long marches from well to well. There is also, unless the tradition has got warped or there has been some misreading, apparent evidence of an armed force from the foot of the very distant Persian mountains, the district of Elam, breaking in upon the hills above the Dead Sea. If that advance took place at all it cannot have come in large numbers but was rather a sort of raid.

Another historical point of the highest interest attaches to this first historical record of Syria. The central figure of the story, Abraham, "a father of peoples", is regarded as a common ancestor by several groups of tribes which we find appearing later in full history, particularly the "Bene Israel" ("children of Israel"), who later again are the highly distinct Hebrews.

There is no reason to doubt that traditional affirmation of descent from a real ancestor. A foolish scepticism has tried to rationalise it, making out the figure of Abraham a mythical one, imagined in order to explain tribal relationships. But there was nothing to rationalise. The story contains marvels, and marvels as we all know are a bugbear to dull minds, but there is nothing marvellous in the idea of a population growing from one stem in a very thinly inhabited country which was clearly only beginning to be developed at the moment to which the tradition relates, and genealogies are always preserved most carefully in such societies.

We find clearly described one of those skirmishes which are forever taking place between the heads of little armed bodies, whether nomadic or settled, in the Syrian world. A group of the petty city potentates quarrels with Abraham's nephew Lot and takes him prisoner. Abraham, arming three hundred men, presumably with allies of some sort, beats them and pursues them northward for 150 miles, freeing his nephew and recovering the loot which has been taken. There does not seem to have been any central authority exercising power over the place, but there is one allusion to a sort of tribute paid by Abraham to a priest-king of Salem (which was perhaps Jerusalem), a "tithe".

Moreover, the open pasturage country of the highlands on either side of the Dead Sea was not wholly without private property, in patches at any rate, for Abraham buys at a high price a burial ground, and when he himself at last settles in the extreme south round Hebron it is as in a kind of property of his own.

In connection with that purchase there is a valuable piece of evidence on the existence of money. Mesopotamian civilisation which had already given all its tone to Syria and made spiritually one thing of the whole land from Mesopotamia to the Mediterranean, had a currency. Abraham buys his bit of land at a rate measured in "shekels". Now the shekel was a Chaldean unit. It was a weight of silver: about half an ounce. Whether it were already a coin we do not know. It is customary to affirm that the first state to coin the precious metals was the State of Lydia in Asia Minor long after, but that is based on negative evidence. A shekel being given weight of silver must presumably have been guaranteed in some form. Of course the money was weighed when payment was made. So was coined money weighed much later, and weighing for the sake of accuracy does not exclude coinage.

As to the value of the shekel in Syria four thousand years ago, we again know hardly anything. We know that silver exchanged for gold in Egypt at a very high rate in the earliest times; we know that in Egypt at the beginning, when first metals are mentioned in a ratio, silver is actually half the value of gold. We know that after many centuries, towards the advent of the Roman Empire, silver had fallen to being in value by weight no more than one-twelfth of gold. Gold was plentiful in Egypt, silver was not, whereas in the nearer parts of Asia silver seems to have been the common medium of exchange which would argue that it was plentiful.

In the course of this traditional story, the story of Abraham with which the historical picture of Syria opens, there is a very striking recollection, the destruction of the Cities of the Plain.

The unthinking may put this down among the marvels, and on that account reject it as false. It contains elements that are miraculous and lend themselves to such treatment, notably the fate of Lot's wife on her looking back towards the doomed cities. But the main story as a whole does not exceed natural experience. The ascription to the catastrophe of a moral cause and a divine motive have nothing to do with the marvellous. If a man of evil life is struck by lightning we may call it accident or we may call it the judgment of Heaven. It may be either, and there is no one to decide. But in the fact of a man being struck by lightning there is nothing beyond the natural.

So it is with the destruction of Sodom and Gomorrah. A vivid memory was retained, and handed on in tradition, of a violent catastrophe in which two of the lower Jordan towns disappeared and the sites on which they stood were covered by the waters of the Dead Sea. If there is no element of memory or tradition in the matter, then it must be wholly unhistorical, but of the two it is more unlikely that such a story should arise without an historical basis of some kind than that a great cataclysm should have taken place.

There can be no certain solution of the problem thus set, and yet it is a question worth asking whether there was not some great change in the bed of the Dead Sea to which the tradition of Abraham refers. The story of the destruction of the Cities of the Plain points to such a thing. But of other evidence of it than this story there is none.

For the old-fashioned rationalist there was no problem. The Dead Sea is a very nasty place: the heat of it is fierce; the waters of it undrinkable, and unnaturally heavy; the shores of it blasted. Therefore (said the old-fashioned rationalist) a miraculous and impossible story was invented to explain such a strange climatic condition. But men as we know them do not make up accounts of this sort out of nothing. Such accounts are not hatched full-fledged. Something laid the egg. Cataclysms in nature are rare, but they happen; and accounts of this sort preserve the memory of them. No one doubts there was a Mesopotamian flood of exceptional severity in some very remote time, a flood exceed-

ing all ordinary floods in the Mesopotamian lowlands. But then
a flood is a recurrent natural phenomenon and a considerable
sudden change in such an area as the Dead Sea basin and
depression would be cataclysmic, not familiar, nor recurrent.
Supposing the land watered by the Jordan to have run farther
south than it does now and to have broadened after Jericho,
some part of it may have held cities destroyed in a great convul-
sion, and great convulsions are certainly phenomena familiar
enough to men of all times for us to accept them without undue
credulity.

The tradition is also of interest because it has a visual basis.
Lot stands on the high country of Southern Palestine where
one looks down now on to the Dead Sea depression, and he
sees a well-watered plain at the mouth of the Jordan with cities
upon it. When he parts with Abraham he goes down to this
plain as to a good pasturage ground not yet occupied. The
cities offer him violence and are destroyed. The land sinks and
waters cover the place where the two cities stood before the
cataclysm. All that is possible enough. It is remarkable that
apart from the destruction of the Jordan-plain cities, the geographical conditions upon which the whole story turns are
those of the present day. Abraham (going presumably down the
Yarmuk from the Hauran and crossing the Jordan a little below
the Sea of Galilee) comes up the right bank into the central
highlands of Palestine and then turns south by the hill which
later bears the city of Samaria. He comes through a narrow pass
which in the native language was called "the cleft" ("Sichem",
on which the Greek city of Neapolis, which is now called
Nablus, was to be built) and pitches his tents in the fertile plain
just to the south of that pass.

He proceeds southward along the high country west of the
Jordan ravine. He looks down with his companion Lot from the
high land south-east of Bethlehem towards the plain at the
mouth of the Jordan; he continues on to the south, settling at
last in Hebron. His visits to Egypt are made to and fro by the
same coast road on the fringe of the desert which is followed
today by the railway.

After the vivid episode of Abraham and his immediate descendants there comes a long gap in the story of the land.

We are given the tradition of these immediate descendants, of his son called Isaac, of his grandson called Jacob, of the latter's surname "Israel" and an explanation of that surname, the burial of the Patriarch himself in the tomb he had purchased near Hebron, the tomb of Jacob's wife Rebecca[1] on the north road out of Bethlehem, both of which sites are still preserved by tradition. We hear of one of Jacob's sons being sold into a sort of slavery in Egypt, of his rise to power there, of his sending for his father and his brethren and settling them under the protection he could give them as a high Egyptian official, so that their descendants, multiplied in the next generations into a large body, settled presumably in the Delta, probably on the northeast corner thereof, traditionally divided into twelve tribes, the descendants of the twelve sons of Jacob.

Of Syrian dates, of Syrian things happening contemporaneously with the growth of Jacob's descendants in Egypt, we hear nothing. After a hiatus of unknown duration, but certainly many generations, perhaps nearer seven hundred than six hundred years, the Bene Israel reappear—returning upon Syria in a horde after long wandering through the deserts to the south. After an interval of perhaps four hundred years from Abraham, say three hundred years or a little less after the death of the last descendant mentioned in the story—Joseph, Abraham's great-grandson—Syria appears in history again with the record of the first great Egyptian invasion. For this we have fairly approximate dates, as will be seen in the next chapter—a little after the year 1600 B.C. Abraham has been put at about or rather before 2000 B.C.* Joseph *may* carry us on till a generation after 1900 B.C. There is nothing more definite to be said.

[1] Belloc or his editor is in error here: The wife of Jacob whose tomb was near Bethlehem was Rachel.—ED.

* A comparatively recent discovery in Mesopotamia has made some authorities confident that Abraham's generation is that of the Mesopotamian king Hammurabi, that is, the twenty-first century B.C. The name of an Elamite king appearing in the story of Abraham is the same as that of a personage contemporary, in Mesopotamian record, with Hammurabi.

But the story of Abraham has a higher interest even than its interest as the first clear evidence on early Syria: I mean, the interest of Religion. For with Abraham's story begins the religion which changed our world and on which all the story of Syria is but a commentary.

In this all-important matter of religion that original and most ancient document presents factors which are, indeed, common to every religion throughout the world and in all ages: the recognition of the invisible but real powers in a world superior to our own, and the establishment of a link between them and ourselves, notably by the ritual of sacrifice: that is, by the offering up to the unseen power of something held valuable by the man who makes the gift in order to propitiate but also in order to adore.

Over and above what is common to all religions there is also in this story, of course, the colouring, the tone, of religion in that special form connected with the Semitic language, and which may have spread from Mesopotamia. That religion, we saw, recognised everywhere a God attaching to a group which worshipped him. He was their lord, and that Semitic word for "lord" (formed of the two letters B and L, "B-L", "Baal", "Bel") is discovered everywhere from the Persian mountains to the Mediterranean. He was also their King, and the term for King was formed with the consonants M, L and K, or the rough Ch in such terms as "Melek", "Moloch" and "Melchi".

Everywhere this Lord, this King is found, receiving sacrifice, praised and adored by the group, or city or individual attaching to him: for he is always local. Meanwhile there is for the idea of divinity in general, the conception "god" at large, a monosyllable based on the letter "L". It is a monosyllable appearing over and over again in all Semitic allusion to God or in names which include God: a monosyllable in which the vowel precedes the consonant so that it is rendered by the syllable "El".

This form of religion with its strong attachment to, and ceaseless praise of, a local or particular divinity attached to the city and its monarch has about it three characters which we must carefully distinguish, for the lack of distinction therein has spoilt most of the discussion upon it.

(1) *It presupposed a multitude of gods of which the local Baal or Moloch was only the chief, in the eyes of his local worshippers.*

(2) *This local and particular God, one, but the chief out of many, specially looked after his own.*

(3) *There was a vague, half-conscious memory of a supreme absolute God.*

We must get firmly fixed upon that last point lest we misunderstand the whole of the great message which it was the ultimate destiny of Syria to present to mankind.

The local God presumably began with beneficent characteristics, for it is the nature of man to love what he adores. But in their paganism these Orientals warped the original conception abominably and more and more lost the original idea of one supreme Divinity.

All human things grow corrupt through age, because all things tend through the passage of time to their own destruction. The last phase of any religion left to the workings of unaided man will be puerile or abominable or both, and there grew up in the last phase of religion in this most ancient Eastern world more and more that was at once puerile and abominable. Human sacrifice appeared and was especially emphasised in the very wealthy port-cities on the Mediterranean coast of Syria and their colonies. But there still survived, in lessening force, through all the religion of that world, the conception of a supreme divine essence, that is, of "God" pure and simple.

The local unseen Lord and King who demanded such abominable rites later on in luxurious over-wealthy Tyre, and for whom were set up the great temples of Mesopotamia; the unseen Lord and King who specially overshadowed this and that conqueror from Babylon, later from Asshur and Nineveh, and then from Babylon again, was vaguely supreme over all, though he were thus particularly addressed. It is not true that these men, from worshipping a great number of local deities, ultimately conceived the idea of one supreme God. What is true is that a supreme divine essence was everywhere locally worshipped.

So much of revelation was precariously retained. Now it was the peculiar function of Abraham—it is the whole meaning of his story and that of his chosen descendants—that of these three functions: (1) the tribal god, (2) the special power of protection ascribed to him, and (3) the general divine idea of which he was a manifestation, they, by emphasising such conceptions in a new order recovered the truth. It was a true restoring of revelation. For the God of Abraham was not the supreme god of many but the *only* God. He protected his chosen. He was indeed *their* God. But he was also the creator of all things; he, personal as any City-god, was also universal and alone.

Abraham receives the special revelation, the special promise of his God. These are given in a particular and definite occasion full of awe. He is set apart to be the ancestor whose descendants shall similarly be set apart and given unique protection under the inspiration of a unique mission. He is Chosen, and his descendants when they shall have grown to be a nation shall remain Chosen. But the Deity, who thus comes intimately and violently into the story is not only a particular god, but God Himself.

Modern efforts to deny this and to represent the tale as dealing with some local circumscribed tribal or less than tribal divinity, are compelled to torture the plain spirit of the text; the god who appears is indeed the God of Abraham, but He is also the universal God of the world and there is none with Him or like Him at all.

That was the great affirmation which began the business. But there went with it a lack: not a false doctrine but an hiatus. There was not in all this new theory the sense of human immortality.

We of the West always kept at the back of our minds the conception of a God supreme over all the other great unseen powers of whom we made particular divinities, but we had not that truth so vivid in us as had the Orientals. They gave us through Abraham's covenant and by insistence on his supreme God the essential doctrine of the Divine Unity. We of the West gave them back what they never had before—and they got it late—the doctrine of personal immortality. These two pillars upon which sane religion at last came to rest, and in the lack of either of which religion with us today can no longer be, came not from one Syrian source but from two—Syrian and other. Our religion—that which made Europe—came historically from a special emphasis laid upon these two doctrines combined, an Omnipotent creator and His immortal creation, man; upon the one by the men of the desert, upon the other by the men of the Atlantic. Not Egypt, not Etruria taught the Jews that the soul is imperishable, but the Gauls affecting the Græco-Roman world. In this early story of Abraham, the first record of Syria, you will find the Oriental contribution, the one True God. You will find nothing in Syria of the Occidental contribution, immortality.

IV

The Plough of Egypt

L ONG AFTER that flash, that sudden and limited vision of the past—the traditional story of Abraham—Syria goes back into the dark. It is lit up again fully and brightly after we know not how long an interval, but presumably something over three hundred years. When Syria thus appears once more, the light which falls upon it is not one of tradition but of contemporary record. That record is provided officially by those who govern Egypt, for it is from Egypt that the new light falls upon the story of Syria, a little after 1600 B.C., when the first Egyptian invasion of Syria begins a fairly consecutive story lasting till our own day. It is in this early sixteenth century before the Incarnation that the *regular* history of Syria begins its long ascent towards the Resurrection and Pentecost—whence we also inherit.

The story of Abraham is real history upon the face of it, though, being traditional only and set down long after, it may be warped; but in the new phase we are now entering we have more or less exact record, dates which we can fix within a small margin of error and a sufficient body of facts. Moreover, the Egyptian invasions cover, first and last, the greater part of Syria and the mass of its people. They are not, like the story of Abraham, confined to a limited field in the south of the country and to the fortunes of one minor chieftain.

The breaking out of the Egyptian power upon Syria came about as a reaction from a singular episode in Egyptian history, the episode traditionally called that of the "Shepherd Kings": the "Hyksos".

There was an older Egypt which goes back indefinitely to a time of mere myth and of gods rather than men. We have, on that older Egypt, both record and fragmentary, often confused, allusions; monuments innumerable which can be traced over at least two thousand years—from nearly 4000 B.C. But what we have not got is knowledge of two essential things— (1) the relations between Egypt and the outer world, and (2) a fairly true chronology—that is, the dates, even approximate, of the successive events presented to us.

As to relations of that older Egypt with the outside world, probably the reason we know so little about them is that there is very little to know. Egypt was of its nature the most isolated of all the ancient realms. It had indeed access to the sea, and had it used the sea thoroughly might have been in full touch with everything around. But the Egyptian was one of those cultures—the Slav proved to be another—which, for some reason, avoid the use of the sea. A certain trickle of commerce seems to have come in by the mouths of the Nile, but not mainly, it seems, in Egyptian ships. There is indeed allusion to sea-going ships, and some import (of copper in particular) is mentioned; but the sea plays no such Egyptian part as it did later, in the commercial nations, a Phœnician and a Grecian part. Precious stones were sought for in the peninsula of Sinai and there were certain slight exchanges between the lower Nile valley and the nomads who roamed the sands to the East. But no influence from Asia or from Europe appreciably influenced the strong and highly distinctive Egyptian culture.

The Egyptians themselves had a tradition that their science at least, and perhaps more, had reached them from a much older Atlantic civilisation which had disappeared in a cataclysm of nature. But, save for that tradition, there is nothing which binds them to any external source. They lived and worked in their millions from the beginning upon the narrow ribbon of green, hundreds of miles long and strictly bounded on either side by the cliffs and shelves of the desert which face each other across the river, never a day's journey apart and rarely more than a dozen miles.*

---

* At Cairo some eight miles: at the exceptionally broad flat by the mouth of the Fayum, sixteen miles: at another "broad", by Kouf, seventeen; at Luxor twelve, only half of which is fertile. Thence to the first cataract a mere strip of a mile or two sometimes narrowing to a few hundred yards.

Isolated in this strange form the Egyptian civilisation, very rapidly developed or learned, remained one thing for century after century, acquiring apparently nothing from foreigners and giving them nothing in return. It had a high continuous art in sculpture and fresco, a prodigious monumental architecture, exquisite craftsmanship in the design of ornament and implement. But it was so separate and unique that it had not fully organised the use of the bow for its battle-weapon nor known the use of the horse for its transport.

It is upon all this that there falls, some few hundred years before the sixteenth century B.C., the catastrophe of the Hyksos: foreigners whose rule—or, at least, the rule of whose leaders—appeared, to the Egyptians, as the one exceptional and abominable thing in their long history, cutting it in two and leaving a scar never forgotten. They spoke of that rule, when its worst effects had been set right, with loathing; they show in their traditions of that episode spiritual contempt as for oppression by something far inferior to themselves.

Now who were these Hyksos?

Josephus, writing as far off from it in time as we are from Republican Rome, and judging all from the sacred books of his own Jewish people, thought their power stood for the descendants of Jacob: the power of Joseph and of the growing settlement of Israel whom he protected. It is more than unlikely: but there is this truth in the idea, that the Hyksos or their chiefs were probably of the same blood as Israel.

All we can certainly say of this Hyksos business is that it was an invasion of the delta from the East, probably by nomads, certainly by Asiatics, presumably by the men of the sand, and these perhaps aided by contingents coming down from the north and Syria to share the loot.

The name Hyksos is best explained as "Lords of the desert-men"; the term "Shepherd Kings" came in later because the syllable "sos" or "shos" had come to mean a *shepherd* from the nomads and their flocks; but its original meaning referred to no more than the barren soil on the fringe of the desert over which those flocks wandered.

The Hyksos certainly began operations by garrisoning a large fortified town on the north-east of the delta, that is, on its extreme corner looking towards Syria; they as certainly extended their power southward up the Nile valley. There are traces of them on the extreme boundary of Egypt, but how far their real power extended, as tested by the collection of tribute (the principal object in any such invasion) and how far south their organised rule permanently reached, no one knows.

Some of the royal names which remain to us connected with that period are Semitic in form, but it seems clear that the invaders were only able to establish themselves, or at any rate to establish the power of their kings, over the north; perhaps not far beyond the delta. Even so they could only keep their position by adopting all Egyptian custom and title.

This was certainly so in the matter of religion. The sanction for political authority which religion gave was necessary to them at once, and used, apparently, from the original years of their effort. They were Pharaohs from the first; and though they were remembered as alien, they became native in that force of worship which is the soul of a civilisation. In that sense they merged with the Egyptians. But they were never fully accepted, and the desire to expel them never waned. When at last they were driven out the act was a national act of liberation.

The longest stretch of time over which this anomaly in Egyptian history lasted was once calculated at nine hundred years. It is an impossible figure, arrived at by adding reigns, many of which were not consecutive but contemporary. The shortest estimate gives them somewhat over three hundred; an intermediate one gives something like five hundred; but, save that we ought to incline to the shorter rather than the longer guess, we really know nothing. We only begin to touch firm ground with the national revolt which got rid of the Hyksos power.

That revolt had been growing for a long time before it struck this main effective blow early in the sixteenth century B.C., that is, shortly after the year 1600. It looks as though the lords of the south had long established an increasing independence and as though Hyksos power in the north disintegrated from within; but anyhow, it is certain that with the origin of what is called the XVIII dynasty, the expulsion of the Hyksos and their last garrison in the north-east seriously began.

The name of the man who started this conquering dynasty, the liberator, is given by Manetho, the very late Egyptian historian of his people, in the Greek form "Amosis". The learned have, of course, played the fool at large with that name as they do with all names and everything else which gives them an opportunity for displaying their erudition to the vulgar. They have called him "Amases", they have called him "Ahmose", they have called him "Aahmes". As this last is the form chosen by the greatest English authority upon ancient Egypt, Aahmes is perhaps the best form to use in English. It was Aahmes, then, who attacked the Hyksos in the delta itself and finally drove them out.

We have for this great soldier whose genius launched the first creative change in Syrian affairs, an approximately accurate date—the first fixed point in Syrian chronology. Abraham, whose story furnishes the first clear episode, is not fixed to within a century: Aahmes is fixed to within very close limits. We know that—subject to an error of very few years one way or the other—Aahmes assumed power over Egypt in 1580 B.C.

His first and necessary objective in the campaign was the great fortified town where the Hyksos still maintained their chief garrison. It was at once the symbol and foundation of their rule. The capture of that main fortress, which had stood in the north-east corner of the delta from the first moment of their appearance, was an action performed on Egyptian soil— on the extreme edge of it. It is part of Egyptian history alone. But it affected Syria, and the general history of the East, in the highest degree: for the storming of that city and the expulsion of its vast permanent garrison opened the way for an Egyptian army to march for the first time into Asia.

Egypt now rearmed and possessed of a clear policy—not only to get rid of the invader from the East but to make renewed invasion impossible—went forward, and did not halt until she had reached the Euphrates. That is the meaning of these years to the history of the world—the capital point is that Aahmes was not content with expelling the Hyksos but carried on the effort over the difficult dry seaboard eastward beyond the delta and pursued his enemies into Palestine.

In those first years of his reign—perhaps within the first five years, certainly the first seven—he had crossed the short desert and reached the Syrian land. He besieged and took Sharuhana. He pushed on into Syria proper, and got somewhere towards the far north for the utmost limit of his drive. And here, since what he did was to be followed by successive Egyptian invasions and their consequences for nearly four hundred years, we must take stock of the position.

The Hyksos had brought to the knowledge of the Egyptians the horse, the chariot and the disciplined warrior bowman; and with the bowman the use of the quiver which gave the fighting man his reserve of missile ammunition. It was with such an equipment, learnt from the invader, that Egypt began its first conquests on Asiatic soil.

Those Egyptian conquests in Syria were not intended for occupation. The new Pharaohs did not annex, still less did they colonise. They may not have had the aptitude, they certainly had not the desire to impose Egyptian things outside Egypt. They were not moved by the appetite for power or for the moulding of other men to their own image. Two things drove them to this novel action whereby for the first time the strength of the Nile appeared in the Syrian highlands. The first was the acquisition of wealth, the second (the original motive of the whole business) the determination to prevent the recurrence of invasions.

In pursuit of the first object they gathered tribute from the places they entered, tribute which, when it was accepted without resistance, was called "gift"; in pursuit of the second, they were so far successful that during the whole of the XVIII dynasty—that is, for 260 years—there was no actual invasion across the Egyptian limits. There was peril of it again towards the end of the XVIII dynasty after a successful rebellion, longer than usual, whereby Syrian towns ceased to pay tribute. The Syrian armed bands, joined with the nomadic tribes, reached at one moment the neighbourhood of the delta; but they never entered it, and the second King of the XIX dynasty, the first Seti, renewed the march into Syria.

This sort of intermittent Egyptian appearance in Syria, this sporadic series of campaigns, with their sieges and pitched battles, their bringing back of loot, their levying of tribute, went on till the neighbourhood of the year 1200, nearly four centuries after the first great reaction under Aahmes had begun.

In their first forms the successive Egyptian advances up the Syrian highlands and coastal plain swept over the whole oblong, from its last slopes on the southern wilderness beyond Gaza, to its broad northern root based on the mountains of Asia Minor. In the three generations after that of Aahmes Egyptian troops had appeared in nearly every one of the hundred and more cities, large and small, that were the strongholds or posts of the country. They reached the Euphrates. They even crossed it at Carchemish.

Of the Syrian town-lists appearing in Egyptian records in the following century, and later still in the despatches sent to Pharaoh from his Syrian vassals, the bulk of the names recur which are associated with the country for century after century—a half of them survive in our own day. There is Arvad, there is Damascus, there is Sidon, there is Aleppo, there is Jerusalem, there is Gaza, there is Magdala, there is a roll-call more. The Egyptian found there, in Syria, that loose jumble of townships large and small, most of them walled, each with its territory around it, which had been there since tradition began and remained there for centuries after he had departed. His energy passing there-through did not transform that condition; it did not give unity. But it gave Syria life, and it made all ready for new life as well.

In this first half of the four hundred years there was some considerable organisation by the invading power. Local "kings" were recognised or deposed, according as the tribute was regularly paid or not. There are traces of a set form, that of anointing, whereby these "kings" were confirmed in their little local powers. They give hostages where their submission is doubtful. After refusals to pay, especially after rebellions, they are severely handled when next a Pharaoh returns at the head of his army.

But the main point is that there was no Empire. There was no fixed policy of absorption or even of subjection. All that was aimed at was the reception of levies in bullion or kind, and the prevention of counterattack. A god of the great Egyptian ruler was formally worshipped on occasion, but so far from ousting the Syrian Baals he did not even leave a memory of himself behind him. Nor did Egypt build in Syria, nor did it found, even during that earlier half of its interrupted invasion, a permanent over-lordship.

In the second half it did still less. The strength of Egypt was failing after 1400 B.C. The ability to send armies beyond the frontiers was less steadily maintained and at last those armies were but accidental strangers appearing at very long intervals and hardly attempting to establish fixed relations.

The internal strength of Egypt waned in this second half of the affair, because the unity of Egyptian society had been shaken by a religious conflict at home. The resistance offered to a power thus diminished, was increased (perhaps) by a better-organised combination of the Syrian north, which is *guessed* to be Hittite, and by unrest among the nomad tribes of the eastern desert—whom another modern guess calls "Aramæan", and magnifies into a sort of wandering polity.

Therefore in the last generations of the Egyptian effort it does not overshadow Syria much north of Beyrout on the coast, or of the Litani sources in the inner valley between Lebanon and Anti-Lebanon. It comes to the Dog River—the Nahr-el-Kelb —and sets up a monument to mark its limit. It also leaves its mark on a rare stone in one place and another east of Jordan. But it will never again claim tribute from the cities and fields of the Orontes.

The effect upon Egypt of those creative four centuries does not directly concern us, as does their effect upon Syria. But it must be mentioned because it illustrates the general movement of the mind which was to fructify the time to come. For this new march of the foreigner into the unknown Syrian land disturbed and developed that foreigner within his own boundaries—and Egypt was not only greatly enriched by its Syrian experience, but filled with new ideas.

The same thing happened a thousand years later, when our own high civilisation of Greece and Rome came down from the north into Syria. The Macedonian Phalanx was followed by the Roman Legion, and from this invasion of Syria by our own people the transformation of all our world was drawn. Through the Macedonian Phalanx and the Roman Legion there came upon the West, upon Europe, the influence which first foreran, and next poured forth, the Gospel.

The same thing happened a thousand years later again when Europe reappeared from the extremes of the West, from Gaul. Europe returned once more in arms upon the Syrian hills— from Flanders under Godfrey, from Italy and Normandy under Tancred and Robert, his peers, from Toulouse under Raymond. As we know, there followed upon that crusading march the sudden flowering of the Middle Ages in Britain, France, Spain, Italy and the Rhine valley—the Ogive, the Universities, the Dominican philosophy, the Chivalric song.

Will our modern return to Syria begin, in the midst of our apparent decline, some great renewal? It may be doubted.

Egypt thus coming forth from its millenary seclusion, the new horizons presented to its soldiery, the new gods and the experience of new societies, provoked a desire for something universal in religion. Such expanding impressions, such shocks of novelty, breed rapidly in the soul.

The Egyptian had not known mountains; he had not well known the sea. He had not conceived of isolated, differentiated political bodies: each shut off from a neighbour by a ravine, a wilderness or a sharp ridge. All to him was new at the beginning of these campaigns. There was provoked at the core of his own civilisation a desire for generality in religion, for something greater and also simpler than his most ancient gods; for these had been but gods of one soil, the sacred soil of the Nile: now other gods worshipped in other tongues had to be considered, and some universal concept of the divine was demanded.

The Reform appeared—but it did not succeed. Its leader was insufficient to his task, and the millions of Egypt, who had not stirred abroad, were hostile to the change. The reforming Pharaoh, the very young monarch who proposed to substitute the simplicity of one God not even presiding over the Pantheon of his predecessors, and to praise one name only, shook and shocked all that ancient world of the Nile.

He was himself three-quarters a foreigner in blood, and had neither the influence nor the temperament to achieve so huge a change. Therefore the thing was but an interlude. Its value, to us, is the example and the proof of how much the invasions of Syria could have affected the Egyptian spirit hitherto unchanged from the beginning of man's record and founded upon such depths.

There was a material side to all this, more evident, much more enduring. The invasions of Syria flooded Egypt with new wealth. The populace of the great towns nourished by the Nile became accustomed to receiving loot and tribute in every form; the precious metals, rare woods from Lebanon, and troops of prisoners.

It seems also that such commerce as there had been between the delta and the outer world was multiplied. The invaders had come to know new seaports. In the greatest of the later invasions, they depended upon the support of a fleet. All Egypt was transformed, save in this capital point, that its original religion was restored. Those more than two centuries of great military chiefs, of Pharaohs who were also Cæsars, put into the story of Egypt a central point, a high summit, greater materially than anything that had gone before, and perhaps than anything that was to come later.

If there were more material wealth in the last Greek and Roman phase of the Egyptian monarchy (and that is not certain) yet there was never to be again under an independent government, full of national feeling, so great a time. Egypt, fully herself, had known pride approved by victory. It had been something much more than the old campaigns against an oasis, or against the negroid barbarians up river, alternatively feared and despised. The attempted religious revolution, the spiritual conflict, coming on such prosperity had done a further thing. It had begun to dissolve the granite unity which the mighty conquerors of the XVIII dynasty had welded; Egypt, beneath an unchanged front, was weakening from within.

If these were the effects on Egypt of the generations between her expulsion of the Hyksos and her breakdown in the face of Asshur, the effects upon Syria itself were of greater moment to the world.

I have called the thing a ploughing. It was exactly that: a turning over of the earth, a making of things ready for seed—a condition if not a cause of new life, whence proceeded the new ports of Phœnicia, the new cities of the Philistine coast, and at last—small, vague, hardly perceived—the beginnings of that Jewish thing which was far to outlast them all: perhaps to prove immortal.

The metaphor of the Plough is just. The instrument of Egypt that came thus up and through the Syrian field was of a different stuff altogether from that which it traversed, just as the iron of the share is wholly different from the soil it pierces. It passed and did not remain, just as the plough passes and does not remain. It returned and returned again to its function, as does the plough in the cutting and cross-cutting of the glebe. It was hard, as the plough is hard, working into softer medium which it comes to make ready for seed and harvest. It did not of itself fructify; so the plough does not; but it prepared for the harvest that was to follow.

Not only the character but the scale of the Egyptian effort in Syria must be grasped if we are to understand why it was of such effect upon what followed.

These armies of the Pharaohs were not large. Perhaps twenty or thirty thousand men, a division. But they were highly disciplined and they were a united command, with a method, a policy and an end. They came against a society which was a mosaic of little city states set (to the south at least) in a matrix of wandering men. Such opponents—if they could be called opponents, for they were not always so, but often allied with the invader against some local rival—offered no one resistance. Most of them yielded to a summons. Most of them sent gifts; and their rulers were glad to be confirmed in title by so powerful and permanent an overlord as the Pharaoh.

We saw how, in the north, later on, the successive Egyptian advances may have met something more organised, which is commonly identified with the Hittite name. But there was at first no empire to be challenged such as later spread from Assyria. There were Syrian coalitions from time to time and armies large enough to meet the Egyptian as an equal. But Syria did not become *one*. It remained a mass of chieftains and of kinglets over cities, such as had been found there from the beginning.

Against such material the Egyptian commanders advanced at will. One of these incessant campaigns, the most famous, may serve as a model to illustrate them all, though most are less thorough and less extended, and the later ones are reduced in scale. It is that of Tothmes III in the very height of the affair, about a hundred years after Aahmes had first ruled.

This main campaign of Tothmes was undertaken for the same reason as a dozen other such advances, to recover the tribute which had been refused during a gap in the Egyptian power over Syria.

The Pharaoh sets out from the delta boundary, the north-eastern frontier of Egypt, in the late spring of the year—it was the year 1479 by one calculating, the year 1482 by another, but not later than the one nor earlier than the other. He covers within ten days (in a working nine days) the 160 miles between El Kantara and Gaza by the coast road across the waste: long marches of nearly eighteen miles a day, for the rare water supply controlled him. He is under the ridge of Carmel twelve days later. Beyond the ridge the King of Kadesh on the Orontes (it lay just above the lake of Homs) had gathered allies and was waiting in front of Megiddo. The Pharaoh crosses the Carmel ridge by the middle road, fights his battle to the north of the hills, takes Megiddo and counts his spoils: over nine hundred chariots, over two thousand horses and vast hoards of silver and gold. He is back in Thebes by the autumn, displaying his prisoners and his booty for the glory of Egypt.

He comes again and again. In a later campaign, supported from the sea, he marches right up the coast, turns up the longest of the torrent valleys into Lebanon, crosses the watershed, and comes down on Kadesh again in the Orontes valley. In yet another campaign a main action fought near the same stronghold was indecisive: but the armies reappear and reappear and the Egyptian troops have again been seen far to the north.

The Egyptian effort in Syria, never continuous, grew weak after the great XVIII dynasty had closed. Before that the complaints of the governors set over the Syrian cities—their despatches, stamped in the Mesopotamian wedge-shaped lettering—remain to us. They show what the hold had become: a precarious one, exercised for tribute only, failing to recover it over long periods, and requiring renewed expeditions to enforce its payment. Of the highly characterised Egyptian thing nothing takes root in Syria nor is attempted. The strength of Egypt waning at last has not impressed itself upon that land. Syria was never Egyptian as it was later Assyrian, as it was Seleucid Greek, as it was Roman and at last Arab. Egypt has none the less done—not of set purpose—that which was intended in the long process of Syrian destiny. It has tilled by incursion. It has ploughed. That ploughing done, with the twelfth century of the old era, very new things were to be sown and to grow.

V

The Entry of Israel

WHEN THE Egyptian plough ceased from its ploughing, that field of Syria which it had traversed for four centuries showed the beginnings of a harvest: the diverse movement of many states appeared, and in that diversity was a new life. It is often so in History; a number of separate groups reacting upon one another breed fresh activities in letters and commerce and worship and vision. Their conflict is an awakening. It was so with the petty sovereignties of Greece, it was so with the feudal provinces of the early Middle Ages. It is so in Syria now during three centuries, the twelfth, the eleventh, the tenth of the old pagan world before the Incarnation—from about 1200 B.C. to just after 900.

I say "States", but the word is too precise. The multitude of separate polities which began to swarm in Syria were of every kind, from fixed and powerful cities centuries on centuries old, to wandering tribes of herdsmen and robber bands. And every form between these extremes was found. There were nomads who were still quite unrooted, nomads who had begun to settle, nomads who had recently captured cities and adopted their way of life. There were walled towns of considerable size and wealth, forming city-states with a ring of territory around each. There were ports and roadstead-towns with no fields, nourished by their trade alone. There were ancient centres, the terminals of caravan routes from across the Eastern deserts. There were large villages undefended yet leading their own lives or ready to change allegiance from one more powerful centre to another. There were allied groups of strongholds in confederacy. There were tribes of one name a-straddle of town and moorland.

Of these varied units many even of the settled ones interlocked: the wanderers naturally and necessarily interlocked with the settled people. That interlocking is the essential feature, a modern misunderstanding of which makes half the story incomprehensible: the fact that Southern Syria was not divided into fixed portions, but into *classes* of men who mingled.

We think today of a territory, however small, as one thing: inhabited and covered by one body of people. In the Syria of this vigorous renewal it was not so. Newcomers would establish themselves by force, or by a treaty of mutual advantage, on the lands of the older city-states: but without destroying or replacing them. The newcomers remained intermixed with their predecessors. As between wandering tribes coming in from the east and south some few boundaries grew fixed, most were fluctuating. With some you could hardly speak of boundaries at all so much movement was there and so frequent a remigration.

Whole communities are (though rarely) destroyed in combat. Many are merged with others by conquest. A strong group of cities will put governors into subject places in order to exact tribute. The subject places will rebel and re-group themselves into independent chieftains: for when we read the English word "King" in the confused and difficult records, traditions—sometimes mere memories—of that time, we must think of "King" as meaning no more than "Chieftain". The individuals of that world are marked less by a place of habitation than by blood relationship, real or assumed. A man is primarily an Amorite, a Hittite, an Israelite, a Philistine, rather than a citizen of such and such a district.

In all this fertile confusion three main divisions are distinguished. There are the old established city-states—strong towns; walled; many going back to before the beginnings of recorded time. There are the new city-states established, particularly, on the sea-coast, by recent colonisers. There are the migrant pastoral tribes, particularly of the south and east, coming in from the fringes of the desert to the better-watered hill country, and settled in various degrees of permanency.

Of these three main elements the first presents a long list of permanent names already established during the Egyptian invasions—Damascus, Beyrout, Hama, and a score of others.

The second, the colonies on the coast awakening to new life at the beginning of the new phase after 1200 B.C. are of two kinds: the Phœnicians to the north of Carmel up the coast all the way to beyond Lebanon: the Philistines to the south of Carmel and down in a line to the edge of the Egyptian desert.

The third are known by a whole list of clans fixed or shifting—Midian, Moab, Edom and the rest.

Of the Phœnicians we know the origins from a strong and acceptable tradition. These origins are extraordinary but too well founded to be denied. They came from islands in the Persian Gulf, reached the Mediterranean coast we know not how nor in what small numbers, and there founded maritime and trading communities on the model of those from which they sprang.

They may have come by a maritime-voyage round Arabia and by the Red Sea and so up northward by land: more probably they came by the caravan routes of the wells, or up the Euphrates. They cannot have been numerous, but they maintained a strict inheritance and continued in their new settlements the special aptitudes of their blood. They built ships. They fixed on island or half-island sites where they could be secure from interference; thence they traded far and wide, over sea, westward and northward.

They threw out colonies as by an instinct, reaching the farthest coasts, founding cities in Southern Spain and in North Africa where their gods were worshipped and their language endured till St. Augustine's Day. They named the headlands and the shores of the Mediterranean, and the later Grecian names are often a translation of the Phœnician.

Two centres of theirs became especially famous, powerful and rich—Sidon, first an island, later a hammer-headed little peninsula joined to the mainland by a sort of natural causeway, stood some little way south of the Dog River, beyond Beyrout: Tyre, a little rocky island twenty-five miles to the south again, half-way to Carmel.

The dates of early Phœnicia are unknown. The little island sites were occupied long before any remaining record. Sidon was apparently the eldest, Tyre the last. Their walls still show, especially in the ruins of Arvad, their northernmost settlement, these huge blocks which astonish us in all the primitive defences of this land. It is a form of building which argues immense antiquity, first undertaken by men when they could trust to no other art for the strengthening of a wall than the immovable mass of its lower courses to defy the battering rams. You have oblong stones as big as houses, and how they were put in position none can imagine. They appear at Baalbec, on the original fortress-hill of Jerusalem, and in these earliest Phœnician harbours.

Though the Phœnicians came thus early it is with the twelfth century, after the Egyptian plough had passed, that—it would seem—they began their chief adventures and expansion over all the Mediterranean. They set up depots in the islands of the Ægean; they sailed to the extreme west and out into the ocean beyond the Straits of Gibraltar. Through them Syria first began to look out westward and through them Syria became known to Western men.

The Philistines came apparently by ship. They seem to have been connected with the "war by (or along) the sea" which came at the end of Egyptian efforts in South Syria.

It is believed that they were of different stock altogether from the mass of the people already in the land, and it is guessed that they may have been emigrants from Crete. But nothing is really known about them except that they founded five towns strung along the coast and plain of Southern Palestine either actually on the sea or close by from the Carmel division southward, in climate that got drier as one proceeded until, at Gaza, they reached the limit of land where men can permanently build and live. Beyond that it was too desert and dry for a colony to fix itself.

The whole thing, like all these Syrian things, is on a small scale. The distance from their northernmost town to their southernmost is hardly eighty miles. The fertile plain on the north, Sharon, does not average fourteen miles broad, the drier Sephalah to the south is not twenty from the shore line to the rise of the inland limestone hills.

These Philistines were surely of a European sort, if, as is almost certain, the "P-L-S-T" of the Egyptian monuments are identical with them. But they soon merged, in language, with the people around them. Perhaps the most striking thing about them is that so small a body, and one that kept no separate existence after a few generations, gave its name to the whole region of Southern Syria. We talk of "Palestine" today because Egypt had known the "Pulasti".

Of the wandering tribes who entered into South Syria from the desert in this twelfth century one group was to prove of the last importance—to Europe and therefore to the world—the group which called itself the "Bene Israel": that is, the descendants (or "children") of Israel: twelve closely connected clans called after the twelve sons of Jacob.

That is of course; but what is half-forgotten is that the writings which the Bene Israel accepted as the record of their people is the *only* documentary evidence worth calling such which we possess on Syria during these three hundred years. The Old Testament is the *only* set of documents remaining on the Syria of 1200–900 before Our Lord, the centuries when the foundations were laid. Of contemporary record with which to compare it there are the fragments of early Assyrian inscriptions, very brief, an inscribed stone in Moab, hardly anything more.

The Old Testament is not only unique, it is also copious. Not only is it the sole set of documents (Exodus, Joshua, Judges, Kings and well into Chronicles) illuminating the new life of Syria in those critical creative three centuries (1200–900), but it is most ample and detailed, a full record.

That record regards only a part of Syrian territory, the south: of the north it tells us next to nothing. Also it is interested only in one group out of many—the Bene Israel tribes. Everything else that is mentioned—men, cities, clans, other than those of Israel—is mentioned in relation to Israel: their alien lives, their alien characters, are left undescribed. Thus Tyre was founded and grew great in that very time, yet of Tyre we have no account save one allusion to building material provided by one of its rulers for a contemporary ruler of Israel, and one other mention where the daughter of a priest-king in Tyre marries a chieftain who rules a section of the Bene Israel. The Philistine cities, again, must have had traditions of the highest interest. Their worship and culture would illuminate us on their origins. If they were indeed Cretan, what a mass of things to know! But the Israelite records tell us nothing of them except as neighbouring enemies of the sea-plain who overrun and occasionally subdue that hill country, a dozen miles above them, into which the Bene Israel had penetrated from their desert wanderings. But though this unique set of documents is thus limited it is manifold and from its ample body of stories we grasp the nature of the land, and the character of the time.

Yet the Old Testament, and especially that earlier part of it with which we are here concerned, does something much more. It presents us with a political fact unlike any other heard of in all history. This fact is the existence of a tribal body *convinced of spiritual supremacy.* The Bene Israel feel themselves to be the chosen not of a god, but of *the* God: Omnipotent, creator and ruler of the world.

This claim makes of Israel, from the moment it appears, something separate from the whole world. To this claim Israel owes the destruction of the Jewish State and the adamantine survival of the Jewish people. This claim it is on which the world is compelled most fixedly to gaze and yet to suffer repulsion.

Of all historical facts proceeding from antiquity, Israel is that which alone is permanent and alone always provocative. Israel has endured, still endures, and has every mark of enduring to the end. There is no trace of failure in that characteristic of assured selection by which it lives.

We find this claim present in the first memories, traditions and records. The Covenant is with Abraham and his posterity, and the spirit of the thing shines clear through all the racial consciousness from the moment that consciousness arises.

Every individual of the twelve tribes, the children of Jacob, the child of Isaac, the child of Abraham, had that claim in him. All felt it. It was kept vigorous of course by a minority only, as all national characteristics always are. It was guarded, enlivened, proclaimed by a succession of enthusiastic men filled with the inspiration of their mission. These insisted upon the revelation and its consequence, denounced all infiltration of other worship from without, cursed as an abomination the lure of the wealthy or powerful with whom Israel should come in contact. All worship that was not the pure worship of the One Omnipotent Creative power, which was also their own Protector and unseen Chief, was demoniac, a thing to be detested and destroyed.

Every effort has been made in the modern reaction against the past to rationalise the origin and the singular endurance of this mood. Every such effort has failed. This universal God who chose Israel out of all peoples and set it apart, has been called a tribal God. It is quite true. But there has followed immediately upon that statement the phrase "Like any other tribal God"— and that is quite false. The tribal God of Israel was *not* like any other tribal God, for it was affirmed of Him as it was affirmed of no other that He alone was and that by Him were all things made.

The similarities between the figure and actions of this supreme God of the Bene Israel and the figures and actions of the other Semitic deities have been insisted upon to weariness: the similarities of sacrifice, of devoting captives and captured cities, of exterminating enemies, of special worship in holy places and the rest. All those similarities are true, for everything however peculiar by itself and however astonishing must bear the colour of its environment—but there is that something more.

The universal God of Israel is made to begin as nothing of the sort; it is suggested that He arose as a mere local or racial imagination, likelier still a material object, a stone or what not, out of whose worship the larger idea gradually grew.

The process so suggested is wholly imaginary. It is a creation of the theoriser's brain. In the plain sequence of thought, in the record of tradition and tribal memory, Israel's God is the same God from the beginning. The records of Israel open, not with His special providence to themselves, but with His creation of heaven and earth.

The Old Testament being all this, the one record we have on any considerable documentary scale of Syria in its new birth and the statement of the Israelite claim which has stamped itself upon the history of the world, it is of the first moment that we should judge the books rightly. We must know what we are reading and how we should deal with what we are reading lest we should misunderstand the origins and discolour all that follows on them.

In this task the first thing we must do is to throw overboard the mass of fantastic whimsies which was spun out of the Bible text by scholars during the last century.

Of all forms of stupidity the most crass, the most tedious, and yet the most exasperating is learned stupidity; a pompous furniture of accumulated facts unrelated by the intelligence. We all know the symptoms. There is the use of a jargon to impress the gaping public and the substitution of specialist unfamiliar terms for plain English. There is the constant respectful allusion by one pedant to this, that and the other pedant, so as to present the whole herd of them as a sort of sacred college.

All these are the trappings of the thoroughly vicious method which came near to ruining history a lifetime ago, and which is still triumphant in popular manuals, though it is happily losing its hold upon the more highly instructed.

The soul of the error is a substitution of hypothesis for fact: the putting forward of what is in truth mere guesswork as affirmations, and the spinning of endless theories, any one of which is held respectable on condition that it contradicts traditional knowledge and the plain statements of the past.

The Bible has been made a playground, apparently inexhaustible in its resources for people of this kind. They are so lost to common sense that they solemnly present great poems as being the products not of poets but of committees. Splendid passages of descriptive prose they imagine to have been pieced together out of discordant fragments. They will talk in the most familiar way of wholly imaginary documents and by their aid dissolve all straightforward narrative, and incidentally all the dignity of just expression. The noble story of the Creation has at least two of these ghostly elements, a document "E" and a document "J", which are pretended to be "interwoven". There are a sheaf of Isaiahs; the more timid and primitive fools were content with two, but their bolder successors added half a dozen more.

The most comic of all this mumbo-jumbo (and, alas, it would seem the most successful) is the use of the word "Yahweh", applied to the Almighty.

The Israelite name for that great God who was their own God but also the God of the universe is constructed upon two consonants, Yod and Vav or Waw. Yod is I or Y used in a consonantal form, represented in some modern European languages by J. Vav or Waw is the sound of V which in many languages mixes with and may be replaced by the softer sound of our W. After the Yod and the Vav came an elided guttural, He, a nearly silent throaty "h". There were no fixed vowels in the original Semitic writing. A word was expressed in consonants only. At a late date vowel points were introduced to guide the reader, but in the mass of Semitic dialects, the vowel sounds are fluctuating.

What the original vowel sounds common among the Bene Israel for expressing the Supreme may have been, no mortal knows. They may have called him I.A. (ch), V.A. (ch) or I.O. (ch) V.O. (ch) or any other combination of vowel sounds; you might have, say, a dozen vowel sounds in this simple di-syllable consonant framework of Y and V.

The reason we know nothing of the way in which the early Jews pronounced their Sacred Name is that it was held too awful for common speech and was veiled, in general writing, by a substitute. The consonants were kept but the vowel points used when vowel points came into use were those of the word Adonai which means Lord.*

Out of this combination the late adapters of the Jewish sacred books constructed the word Jehovah, as it is spelt and pro-

---

* The four Hebrew letters making up the ineffable name, Yod, He, Waw, He, were left unpronounced as being too sacred. This was called in Greek "The four-lettered thing", the Tetragrammaton.

nounced in English. That name Jehovah became the biblical title of God in the English translation and has filled English literature since that literature in its modern form began.

As may be imagined, being of universal popular use and consecrated by hundreds of noble English lines, the learned made of Jehovah their special victim. "You common folk", they said, "may in your rustic ignorance speak of Jehovah, but we learned people, your superiors, know better than that. We call Him Yahweh." On hearing which, the gaping populace was so impressed that they gave up Jehovah, not without reluctance, and enthroned Yahweh in His stead.

The Bene Israel then are coming into history, and their strength (whether the Dons like it or not) is Jehovah. Jehovah did not come in later; He was not invented half a dozen centuries after the entry of Israel into the Promised Land; His awful presence was already there among them from the first, and while He was their God; He was also (they were very certain) the master of the whole world, being the Maker thereof. That He should be there and that they should be His was their strength, and so remained for a thousand years, and another thousand. It is their strength today.

Let us see what their fortunes were, and let us remember that in order to understand them we must take the Old Testament for our guide—and the Old Testament as it stands, not as it is imagined to be.

This document (or rather group of documents) has difficulties. Parts of the descriptions are contemporary, parts are clearly not so, for the writer speaks of this or that as long past. There are contradictions and there are repetitions which often do not tally, as is always the case with very early record when it is set down in multiple fashion. Much was traditional and handed down *perhaps* (not certainly) before the use of writing. But the general story is plain enough to show what happened.

The Bene Israel came into the habitable land which had been promised to them by a great leader who was almost their founder—certainly their second founder—Moses. They came in out of Egypt from the wilderness by way of the south and east, that is, not up the usual road from Egypt taking one up the coast to Hebron or Gaza, west of the Dead Sea, but round from the east of that depression.

Moses was recently dead, when, under Joshua as their leader for the conflict, they came down into the Jordan valley out of Moab and crossed it not far from the mouth of the river, on the plain where its delta opens into the Dead Sea. They took Jericho, the walled town of that plain, and then fought a re-markable campaign, quite unlike the mere aimless raids which are the common habit of the desert, and half-desert, tribes.

We must remember what the Bene Israel had in view. They wanted pasture, and they wanted a certain amount of arable land: they had neither the desire nor the habit of building walled cities. If they were successful they would come to mix with the people of the walled cities, and to settle within their boundaries as well as on the land outside. But it would be a slow process. Their immediate object was room for settlement as cultivators and for a more fluctuating habitation as herdsmen.

There could be no question of their tackling the wealthy and well-organised cities of the sea-coast; the Phœnician com-mercial ports were too far to the north; Damascus, the great "port of the desert", was beyond their scope. They were con-tent to leave alone the newly-founded five towns of the south-ern sea-coast between Carmel and the Egyptian waste, where the Philistines had a well-developed and well-armed civilisation. What lay to their hand was the hill country between the Jordan valley and the sea-plain, with an extension backwards and east-wards of the Jordan as well.

That hill country is for the most part a mass of limestone, with large pockets of arable land. It looks desolate enough now, but in those days, long before the devastation of the trees by the Moslem, it had forests and groves and presumably plantations and orchards, as well as a farming population amid its cities.

Joshua and his followers poured into the central section of these hills in great force, spreading over the highlands called "Mount Ephraim". (Joshua himself was of the tribe of Ephraim.)

In the midst of that country he set up the *Ark* or sacred chest which was the centre of Jehovah's worship, and thence the Bene Israel spread outward, assigning to each tribe territory which often it could not fill.

By the time he had achieved his purpose these children of Israel whom he led were so far established that although they only maintained themselves by continued fighting everywhere for many generations to come, they could not be turned out. The existing population whom Joshua and his armed bands had to meet—the Canaanites—were a people of much the same speech as Israel, as indeed was all Palestine. These original inhabitants suffered heavy losses during the invasion and, upon the whole, the invaders were the conquerors, but in no complete fashion; and from Joshua's great campaign onwards, Canaanite and Israelite mixing, now by contract, now by conflict, were always together till they merged into one.

But let us mark this: dominating what was externally a confusion stood the spiritual integrity of the Israelite mission. What with mixed blood and the attraction of superior and established wealth, and here and there civic life in the towns, there was a large and perhaps an increasing fringe of Jewish families who half forgot the ancient tradition which was their strength, groups and individuals who weakened in the service of Jehovah. But even these still had in their heart the pride and the peril of an invincible destiny.

The next phase in the business was the awakening of the Philistines on the west to the danger of such a spirit in coalescence with the Canaanites established on the hill country above them; and as the Philistines were better organised and their inter-city alliances far better armed and more firm, they were the masters in the early part of the business, although Israel had shown its fighting power in one great struggle at least, not against them but against sudden northern attack in the plain of Esdraelon, the wide fertile belt between the limestone hills and Carmel through which runs the watercourse called Kishon.

In the next phase, then, the Philistines marched up and over the hill country, fixed garrisons there, and kept it in subjection.

They seem even to have disarmed the combative Israelite tribes for a moment.

What were the dates of all this? We have no precise landmarks until we can compare events with the fairly well-known chronology of the Assyrian power, and this does not appear in South Syria until the earlier part of the ninth century B.C. and after 900 B.C. But we have a good deal to guide us in rough outline.

We know that the Egyptian Empire was no longer functioning in Syria when the Bene Israel came, for it does not appear as master in their traditions, save in one last raid which bore no fruit. In other words, the Jewish invasion came after the rough date 1200 B.C., or was, at the earliest, contemporary with that rough date. Further, the later rally against the Philistines—after the Philistines had for a time mastered the hill country, checked the push of the incursion and oppressively subdued its tribes—can also be fixed with a certain rough accuracy. The rallying of the hill-men for the recovery of their lands and the expulsion of Philistine garrisons was a good deal more than a hundred but less than two hundred years after the first invasion. It was somewhere well before the year 1000 B.C.; perhaps a lifetime before.

It was about then that there arose in Israel another of those successive religious exhorters and leaders whose strength was the mission of Jehovah: a "prophet"* (as their term went) called Samuel. We must put it down to his genius that the effort at independence succeeded. It was perhaps he who organised (there was at any rate organised in his time) a "school", or "congregation" of prophets, that is the grouping of enthusiastic preachers devoted to the ancient tradition.

It was through this organisation and through the character of Samuel himself that the reaction took form and strength. Thenceforward in the later part of the eleventh century, that is from shortly after 1050 B.C., perhaps about 1030 B.C., the prime institution of Monarchy arose in Israel. That institution was not

---

* "Prophet" is a Greek form, the translation of the Hebrew "Nâbi"; an inspired man.

favoured by the enthusiasts: it was with reluctance that it was introduced, but the peril of the nation had made it necessary.

It is often said that "War makes the King", and we see the process going on in our own time before our eyes throughout Europe. But the aphorism is not universally true. Rome, the supreme example of the military state, spread its authority throughout the Mediterranean world without having recourse to monarchy; and of course the aristocratic states, Carthage in her time, Venice in her time, England in hers, did all their great work not only without active monarchy but in contempt and opposition to its principle. Here, however, in the case of Israel, war (or rather the necessity for national survival against armed pressure) *did* make the King.

Samuel chose one who seemed indicated by his own inspiration, and to whom had been communicated also the enthusiasm of the prophets—a certain Saul. He anointed him with oil as a symbol of consecration (we saw how in the old days of the Egyptian Empire the subordinate "Kings" whom Egypt established received the same sacramental ceremony, anointment) and Saul gathered and led a sufficient force from among the disunited and oppressed people of the hills against the Philistine power.

He seized one of the cities of the oppressor near the confines of the hills; he was so far successful that after his time the Philistines cease to menace or administrate, or (what is always much the most important part of a conqueror's policy) *disarm*, Israel and those with whom Israel had mingled in the limestone heights between Jordan and the sea-plain.

But it was not in Saul's time (a little before the year 1000 B.C.) that the kingdom was fully formed. He stood only on the threshold of a brief period covering two lifetimes, in which the Jewish monarchy took root and enjoyed a strength, disposed of wealth and armament, sufficient to establish a fame which not all the divisions and disasters to follow ever obliterated. That period of real and great glory remained as yet another inspiration, a memory to strengthen the people of Jehovah from within, to carry them alive through the floods which again and again covered them, through defeat after defeat, through political confusion, savage conquest, wholesale exile and attempted extermination.

Why this comparatively brief period of great strength, unity, wealth and military glory should have arisen after Saul is a question not to be answered. We have not evidence to show what material conditions led to it. We only know that it happened. All is providential; but it is wise to see a special providence in whatever regards this fascinating people. We can only say that it was so.

The steps by which the thing took place were these:

It began by the defeat and death of Saul at the hands of the more powerful organised Philistine civilisation on the slopes of Mount Gilboa, to the north of the Palestinian group of hills, to the south of the cleft which divides them from the highlands of Galilee: but already before that defeat there had arisen in Israel a character who should take on and greatly increase the work which Saul had done.

This new man was from the south, of the tribe of Benjamin, the son of a certain Jesse who had lived in Bethlehem. We know that his name was made up of three consonants, "D", the "W" sound, and then another "D". One fair guess at it seems to be "Daoud". At any rate we have made of it the word David.

He was no one in particular, any more than Saul had been or than were any of those leaders who had risen suddenly in the loose tribal system of the past. But he must have had not only powers of leadership but skill in policy, and he must have impressed his contemporaries after the fashion of all those who found a great legend. He came in as an attendant upon Saul, distinguished himself in the fighting, was seen to be a rival, fled, headed a band of robbers, took refuge with the enemy (feigning madness), and then after Saul's death reappeared and imposed himself.

The men who had fought under him required him. He was anointed chieftain of the southernmost tribe, the tribe of Judah, which held the big rather badly watered patch which gradually sinks into desert and has for its last main town Hebron, where the tomb of Abraham remained a sacred centre for Israel. It was in Hebron that David began to be King. He got the northern tribes to acknowledge him—not without difficulty, and not without a succession of murders, after the general Oriental fashion. He suffered a renewed heavy attack from the Philistine plain below, and there was a moment when it looked as though the old subjection of Israel was to begin all over again in spite of the new name and leader.

Then, almost suddenly, the situation changed. The power of David increased prodigiously; he is found before the end of his life with Philistines actually enrolled among his guards. He takes their town of Gath, he masters Moab beyond the Dead Sea (where he massacres wholesale and by the thousand); Edom, to the south; and he becomes by far the strongest political power in Syria as a whole and dominating all the southern, Jordan, third of the country.

I have already said that we know nothing of the causes, and no guesses made at them are worth considering. All we know is that it happened. It could not have happened without military capacity and political capacity combined; but there must have been other causes besides these, of which we have no record. Something made the Philistine opposition of the coastal plain collapse; something handed over the north of Palestine right up to Mount Hermon and beyond to the rule of David. He had already by ruthless conquest seized the plateaux east of Jordan, and (what is most remarkable) before he had finished his business he had put a garrison into Damascus itself and levied tribute there.

As so far-reaching a success as this temporary occupation of Damascus is astonishing, we have of course the usual academic attitude in the face of whatever is vivid in history; the plain record is denied and the learned play the fool with imaginary reconstructions of the text.* But we need pay no attention to all that. David, by the only evidence we have, held Damascus; and there is no reason that a man who was master of all that he certainly did rule should not have done so.

* For instance, because the outline for "R" in Hebrew is like the outline for "D", we are told that "Aram" is a misreading of "Edom".

He made of the hill site of Jerusalem his stronghold, and the kingdom of which it was the capital and centre became in that lifetime of his in the middle of the tenth century (say somewhere about 990–960 B.C.) the thing it was. The new dynasty arisen in Tyre under the King called Hiram treated David almost as a superior and at least as an equal—they had no power against him by land.

There are indications that he organised much more thoroughly than anyone before him; he certainly took a census; he certainly set up a regular revenue; and he certainly established a good standing army in the place of the old tribal levies which melted after each campaign.

This episode of David, followed as it was by the still greater splendour of his son, was the third renewal of glory for the Chosen of the Universal God, for the Protected of Jehovah. Henceforward in the blood of David was to be fixed the undying hope of Israel; sooner or later there should spring from David a Messiah who should restore all things. On such a height did that name stand, during the centuries to come after this soldier's death.

His son, Solomon, raised the new kingdom to its summit. For about thirty years, from about 960 B.C. to about 930 B.C., Solomon's power was exercised in a way which has impressed itself upon the legends of three thousand years. All the East is still full of it; and the name is still a symbol of magnificence (through what was once our universal religion) to us of the West.

The new kingdom, though remarkable in its establishment, was small enough. It was not much larger than Wales—say 120 miles at its longest by 60 at its widest, and often much less—and we must make every allowance for the way in which the glamour of legend hugely magnifies some old original thing, as mist exaggerates the magnitude of one mountain among many. We must allow for the effect of the sacred books and for the branching out of fantastic imaginations in the Oriental mind. We must allow for the prodigious effect of the Mohammedan conquest, carrying with it its own adoption of Solomon's name. But after making every allowance, we must put down that lifetime between David's capture of power and the death of his great son as one of the capital phases in the story not only of Syria but of the world: for the world never forgot it.

The power which Solomon so conspicuously enjoyed reached the sea on both sides; he used a port on the Gulf of Akaba whence he sent ships through the Red Sea to the south; he sent ships from the Philistine coast also—from Dor perhaps—through the length of the Mediterranean. He was said to have treated with a district of Spain. Tyre was closely associated with him, as it had been with his father; and sent craftsmen to build the great Temple at Jerusalem of which Solomon made a centre of worship to Jehovah.

All that. It did not last in a material sense; but morally it was something founded for century upon century.

Solomon controlled the caravan routes which met in his territory; that from the east across the desert, of which Damascus was the desert terminal, and which went on through the Galilean highlands to the sea-coast; and that which came up from the Akaba Gulf on the Red Sea northward. Egypt, which was beginning to stir again abroad, preferred his alliance to his enmity; and supported his hold upon the sea-plain, instead of contesting it with him. And yet, immediately upon his death, this political edifice collapsed.

Solomon's son could not hold the northern tribes; they fell under one leader after another, military usurpers, making a new kingdom of their own. Whatever hold David had had upon Damascus was lost for good; and though the dynasty of Solomon endured, it endured only precariously over the little stretch which the tribes of Benjamin and Judah claimed in the south.

Less than one long lifetime after, indeed in less than sixty years, all that glory which still stands like a beacon disappeared. Solomon had not been dead half a dozen years when the power of Egypt raided Jerusalem, seizing its treasure. What lay to the east of Jordan was completely lost; the revenue sank to nothingness; and then (at a date which we can fix almost certainly, the date 876 B.C.) another era opened: Assyria began its long, broken, intermittent, but at last triumphant, march westward to the Mediterranean shore. For in that year a conquering monarch crossed the Euphrates for the first time since a military raid or march which had brought an army from the Tigris to the Gulf of Alexandretta 150 years before. With this new crossing of the Euphrates by the great force from Mesopotamia a new thing begins for Syria, and for all that we call the Near East.

VI

Assyria

EGYPT had made ready the field of Syria in a tillage of four hundred years. A harvest of new activity had followed for three centuries. The merchant cities of the coast had grown wealthy, and had bound up the land with all the western sea, even to the ends of the Mediterranean, with their colonies and trade. Syria had become known to what was to be in the future the chief civilisation of mankind: the Mediterranean world which Greece and Rome were to make universal. In such a renewal had also appeared the destiny of the land: they that were to give purpose to Syria for ever, the Bene Israel.

All this preparation was accomplished, when there opened this third phase which was to last three centuries more: the kneading and working of the land, the rolling of it, by the strength of Mesopotamia: of an Empire growing to fill all the land from the Persian rampart-hills beyond Tigris to the coast of Tyre and Sidon.

It was Assyria that now came forward with new power making gradually—and ruthlessly—one thing of whatever spoke with Semitic words between the Arabs to the south and the heights of Taurus and the Armenian mountains to the north. It has been guessed that in a remote past the great cities of the lower Tigris and Euphrates had appeared in arms for moments upon the Mediterranean. It is certain that their culture had affected all that Syrian shore and the highlands behind it since the beginning of history. But now there was approaching something hitherto unknown: a full organisation of Unity under one government determined on centralised power.

This story of the Assyrian Empire absorbing Syria is not a story of foreign conquest, exactly. Syria, from long before men could remember, had taken her character from Mesopotamia.

There had always been one culture on the Tigris, the Euphrates and the Orontes, the Litani and the Jordan, Lebanon and the towns of the seashore: one sort of speech in various dialects: one type of religion—until Israel declared its development thereof and its message of the One and Eternal. It had even, on the whole, one dress and one social custom, in the towns at least, and one script for communication among all its tribes and cities.

For, until the later alphabets arose, Phœnician, Palestinian and Greek (all from one unknown origin), Syria made its official records in the "wedge-writing" of Babylon and Asshur. The despatches sent by the governors of Syrian towns to the Pharaoh, their Egyptian overlord, 600 years before the first appearance of Assyrian armies in the west, 300 years before their permanent presence upon the Mediterranean, are written in what the textbooks call "Cuneiform" writing—and that learned-looking word "Cuneiform" is only Latin for "wedge-shaped".

It is thought that this script arose from the pressing of a chisel on to the damp clay, making a wedge-shaped, or arrowhead, dent, which became permanent when the clay was baked. But whatever its origin, it was, in all the early times, the official medium on the Syrian hills as it was hundreds of miles away beyond the desert to the east.

Of cultures really foreign only two have affected Syria, the Egyptian and the European, and of these the Egyptian imposed nothing—save, possibly, the custom of anointing rulers. The European—Greek, French crusading, and now mercantile—has done more to leave its mark. A third which is called "Hittite" *may* have been foreign. We do not know, because we are too ignorant of it to judge. But all the rest, Mesopotamian, Arabic, has been of one colour, one Asiatic thing. The Persian hold which succeeded the Assyrian and Babylonian was purely political, it brought no new speech or social habit to the masses.

The new and mighty power of Assyria, then, was not an alien influence. It was rather a tightening up of what had always been there—but it effected a great change. It set forward by one most marked step the advance of Syria towards that end whither all her history leads. For the crushing and rolling of the Levant

under the weight of the Assyrian armies, the mixture of populations by the deliberate policy of the Assyrian Kings left, in the
end, only one national unit alive, the Judæan: but that one
stands out the sharper in contrast against a society which—by
the sixth century B.C.—had lost all pride or even consciousness
of local freedom and local political soul.

The Assyrian Empire achieved unity of character by com-
bining two things: an official hierarchy in government, so that
local rulers felt a master above them, and wholesale deportation.

Whenever local resistance appeared whole populations were
carted away, whole cityfuls, whole tribes. Their fields and their
walls were filled by new immigrants driven in; they themselves
were transported hundreds of miles away by force to other seats
and often dispersed. At the end of such a process, repeated and
repeated again, the memory or possibility of patriotism—even
in its very attenuated tribal form—disappeared. The old homes
were forgotten: save by the last victims, that then tiny Jewish
nation which was to outlast them all.

Of the results this crushing of all into one Assyrian mould
achieved, the most remarkable and permanent was the creation
of the great armies.

Antiquity had not known these until the central power in
Mesopotamia produced them. The Egyptian Armies, often mercenary and always professional, had been small. The tribal levies
and city forces in Syria itself were necessarily small. But before
Assyria had completed her task she was able to gather troops by
the hundred thousand, and she handed on to the Persian power
an inheritance of such things: it was by the weight of numbers,
used on the scale of the Napoleonic wars, that our civilisation
was almost crushed in the years of Marathon and Salamis.

◆

A little before Saul was beginning that work which sowed the
first seeds of the Jewish Kingdom, the power of Assyria, under
a ruler whose name we have corrupted into Tiglath-Pileser,
appeared upon the upper Euphrates, on the edge of the mountains north of the desert.

He had advanced by the half-habitable fringe north of the

desert, south of the mountains, crossed the river and for the first time reached the sea, a few years before the date 1000 B.C.: less than a century before the death of Solomon.

I have already remarked as an example of the restricted horizon of the Old Testament and its exaggeration of local things and men that a northern portent of such moment to all the future of Syria passed unnoticed by those who set down the records of the Bene Israel in the south. Tiglath-Pileser and his host were at work not further from the last Jewish boundaries than York is from London; yet the men who were preserving by record the sacred tribal memories of the south were indifferent to or ignorant of what was appearing in the north.

It is true that this first advent of Assyria upon the sea-coast had nothing permanent about it; but it was a vivid foretaste of what was to come. The great Assyrian King sailed out to sea in the ships of Arvad, the northernmost of the Phœnician sea-towns; he visited the sea-slopes of Lebanon and hunted there. If he was not received as a master or a conqueror he was certainly received as a superior. He made no further effort and he went home; the forces from the Tigris were not seen again in the West for much more than a century. But the thing had begun.

Now, in 876 B.C. it was renewed, on a different scale and with a different method. A true conquest was attempted. It did not achieve its end for a long time. There was to be campaign after campaign, without permanent establishment of Assyrian governorships at so great a distance from the centre of Assyrian power; but a settled policy of conquest had begun, and after many checks was to triumph.

The man who in 876 B.C. crossed the Euphrates at the head of his army from the Tigris was called Ashur-Nasir-Pal, a name not easy to remember, yet to be remembered. He went over the river at Carchemish, the Hittite capital of the old days, took the submission of the town, marched on westward to the lower Orontes, garrisoned Aribua (near where Antioch was later to rise) and went on to the coast, marching southwards down it all the way to the Nahr-el-Kelb, the River of the Dog—which perpetually appears as a limit to conquests from the north or the south in the whole story of Syria—and he found there the carved stones which an ancient Pharaoh had set up to mark his own advance from the south centuries before. There he also set up his own carvings, to record his own progress.

The newly-rich cities of the Phœnicians, not only Arvad to the north but Gebal and Sidon, and even Tyre, right away beyond (now the chief of the trading cities upon the sea) sent what they again chose to call presents but what he called tribute. It was but one expedition, yet it was a foundation; for it began the organisation of Assyrian power on these far extremities beyond the desert. *For the first time an Assyrian King left behind him* (though only quite in the north) *permanent garrisons*; also an unwritten testament (as it were) of what his successors were expected to do. From the places where his soldiers remained and where his officials were set up along the northern mountains regular tribute was gathered.

His son Shalmaneser did much more. This son took over the power of Assyria sixteen years after his father had first crossed the boundary of the Euphrates; he himself crossed it in his turn a year after his accession, and reached it again and yet again in the next four years. Now let what follows be carefully marked: *Shalmaneser was aiming, when the time should be ripe, at the conquest of* DAMASCUS. It was nearly twenty years after his father had first appeared in Syria that the moment for this decisive stroke seemed to have come.

Damascus, already as old as old, understood what the success of the new advancing enemy would mean. He would burn and massacre and subdue; he would set up his governor within those all-important walls; he would gather tribute. Damascus would become but one city in the general sweep of his power, radiating out from the upper Tigris beyond the desert and with the fall of Damascus all Syria would become (as it at last did become) a province under the supreme King whose orders would be obeyed from the Persian mountains to the western sea.

Damascus is the symbol and the capital point of the whole Syrian belt of mountain and sea-plain, on the eastern desert boundaries of which it stands guardian. Today it is the possession of Damascus, not of Jerusalem, that decides in the long run the main issues of power in that land. When the Crusaders were to make their bid for the recovery of the Near East by Europe, it was their blunder in not first seizing Damascus which determined their final failure. It was their inability to take Damascus when they did make the effort which made that failure certain. It was upon Damascus that the lightning stroke fell when the new Mohammedan heresy came up in a storm to overrun half our civilisation. It was Islam's seizure of Damascus after so long a siege that was the starting point of Islam's triumph. From Damascus Pompey and the Roman power had negotiated in the days which first firmly established that power in the Syrian land.

From whence does this capital importance of Damascus proceed?

From all these things combined: First, it is the chief port of the desert, the direct goal upon reaching which by the shortest road from the habitable lands hundreds of miles to the east, a caravan comes again to habitable lands on the west. Next, because it is geographically central, standing mid-way to all the stretch of Syria: so that orders from Damascus, or to Damascus, from every point in Syria take less average time than from or to any other point. Next, because it cuts the trade route up from the south northward, which passes from the Gulf of Akaba through Edom and Moab and thence (still east of the Jordan) up to and down the Orontes by Hama; and so further to Aleppo in the north and to all the watered land and the mountains which overlook the west; while the other trade route continues the other caravan line westward through Galilee to the coast. Up the coast there is no uninterrupted road from south to north: each town is cut off in its own territory by spurs, hills reaching the sea. But *east* of the Jordan and the Orontes there is an uninterrupted run along the fringe of the desert, from this far south to the north.

But most of all is Damascus essential to any power that would master Syria for this reason, that nature has made it in itself wealthy, capable of supporting a great population and garrison and stores of munitions; and yet—what nature hardly ever does for points so favoured—it has given it a special defence. Damascus, standing on land made fertile and even luxuriant by the torrents from the great mountains behind it, has those mountains protecting it like a wall on one side—and all around it on the other the desert, where no armies can live. The two streams which nourish it and the chief of which flows in such strength and volume through the very midst of the city, die out in marshes, swallowed up by the sand close at hand. There is no other city nor can be within many marches from it which could be approached or which could be used as a base against it. Damascus itself is always a base, since whoever possesses it may strike round Lebanon to the shores of the Mediterranean, and cut off the north of Syria from the south.

On Damascus, then, marched Shalmaneser, in this year 854 B.C., showing sounder strategy than any man since his time. He went in his majesty through Aleppo (Chaleb), where he sacrificed to the god of the city; he reached to the Orontes on the south and west, passed Hama, and at last, in a place then called Karkar (it stood we do not know exactly where but, as it seems, nearer to Hama than to Damascus), he came in contact with the force advancing from Damascus northward, and battle was joined.

The King of Damascus had formed a coalition not to be despised, even by the power of Assyria, seeing that Assyria was acting so far from home. He had (so at least his opponent affirms) over sixty thousand armed men, serving in the federation at his side; his own nucleus formed one-third of this, with a force of cavalry as well, and over a thousand chariots. The King of Hama, who had fallen back southward before the invader, had more than half as many chariots and fully half as many infantry. The King of Israel was there, Ahab, with many more chariots than the rest, and a full contingent of ten thousand men; and there were detachments from Phœnicia and even from the nomad Arabs with their camels, which followed up at the tail.

Tyre, it would seem, sent no one—awaiting the issue secure upon her island and ready to follow the victor. The poor little kingdom of Judah may have been there, but we have not its name in the Assyrian inscriptions, our authorities for the battle. Perhaps its small contingent was present under Ahab, for we must always remember that it was the northern kingdom which was by far the wealthiest and had become the leader of the tribes of Jehovah. It was the northern kingdom which bore the name of Israel in especial and which isolated Judah and Benjamin had to follow almost as vassals. Further, Israel, to the indignation of the prophets, and against the august religious tradition which these conserved, was intermixed with the wealth of the sea-plains; and her King had at his side a Princess of Tyre itself, a daughter of Baal.

The might of Assyria lost that battle, though it was duly inscribed as a victory in imperishable fashion upon hard stone, when the Assyrian army had got back home. Damascus was for the moment saved.

Assyria returned to the charge only five years later, and Damascus was saved again. Three years later still, in 846 B.C., the greatest of these successive efforts was renewed, and once again broke down—so difficult was it to fight four hundred miles from home and with desert in between. Four years passed, and the vast resources of Assyria found it possible to attack once more.

This time the Great King had all but succeeded; the three successive efforts had exhausted the allies of Damascus; they broke up the confederation and Shalmaneser, having to deal with the great city alone, might think himself secure of victory. He advanced more methodically, less directly and with more complicated strategy. He went by the coast, and steadily moved south as far as Beyrout.

He was amply provided; Tyre and Sidon loaded him with the precious metals; he could gather what provisions he would, and even Israel submitted—for Ahab had been killed in a wretched little local quarrel of his own; his throne had been seized by yet another usurper, Jehu, who had defied Damascus and determined to secure himself by the friendship of the Assyrian invader.

But when that invader went forward for the last time to his supreme object and stood with all his men under the walls of Damascus beyond the mountains, he could not enter. He destroyed the glorious plantations and orchards and groves which made a garden all round the great city, but that great city itself held out; and at last, in the third year, thirteen years after his first crossing of the Euphrates and the initial Damascene campaign which had broken down at Karkar, Shalmaneser retreated for the last time. He went back to his palaces upon the eastern rivers beyond the wilderness, all that month and more of burning marches away.

For a century the Assyrian effort upon the coastal belt was abandoned; there was pressure upon Assyria from the north, from the mountains of Armenia; and one reign followed another without a renewal of that which still remained a traditional, inherited ambition.

There was a lesser effort, a mere appearance upon the coast in the extreme north at Arvad, exactly a hundred years after the great struggle at Karkar, but it was of no effect. We have to wait for one of those palace revolutions which are so often the beginnings of new energy in the East, before the noise of Assyria is heard again in force upon the Orontes, and echoing in Lebanon. One of the Assyrian King's Commanders usurped the Royal power, took on the old name of Tiglath-Pileser, as though to proclaim what lay in his mind—recalling by that name the ancient exploit of three hundred years before. This man it was who was to do the work, with a thoroughness no one of his predecessors had shown.

He began this new and complete business by advancing against a petty kingdom in the north (called at that moment "Yadi"), and there he carried out the earliest of those great transplantations of people which were to be the mark of the Assyrian Empire.

The records of these wholesale exilings stand out in a sharp phrase of the time "the daughters of the dawn did he bring to the evening light, and of the evening light to the dawn." It was a process as astonishing as it was horrible. The increasingly powerful Mesopotamian monarchy proposed to make itself secure not only by terrifying all those whom it had subdued, but, when there was the danger of reaction against the central authority, by lifting whole tribes and towns of people bodily, sending them off hundreds of miles away, re-establishing them in that foreign site and replacing them by immigrants of the conqueror's own choosing. In this case he drove thirty thousand of the people of Yadi off into Armenia and re-stocked with immigrants from the northern mountains the land he had occupied. This operation, steadily continued for centuries, was not only designed for the destruction of rebellion, but also for the creation of a level unity. By the mixing up of various tribes the whole might be reduced to a sort of hotch-potch where no independence even of the soul should remain.

This new Tiglath-Pileser, as he called himself, married the policy of transplantation to another corresponding with it, designing that the two between them should form a thoroughly welded administration. This second part of his policy was the putting in of governors over each district which submitted to, or was conquered by, his armies.

In the case of the Yadi he began by putting in his own son. Elsewhere, when he did not impose a governor he either confirmed the local kings, making them rule in his name, or put in a new king of his own; and he forged a strong link between each such local government and the centre upon the distant Tigris by requiring a regular annual payment upon a fixed assessment. We have record that he acted thus with the rich Phœnician ports of the Mediterranean shore, Gebal and Tyre. He acted thus with Samaria, the capital of the northern tribes of Israel under their separate king.

We have also a record of what happened in Israel among the other little states, and details of it from the sacred books of the Jews in which it is curious to note that this Tiglath-Pileser is called by his popular title of "Pul". For the King of Israel to be confirmed in his office by the supreme emperor (as we should call him) he had to levy fifty shekels upon each tenant of land. If the record is accurate it would show settled families to the great number of sixty thousand for this petty kingdom alone, but the figures may be exaggerated or wrongly copied. The point to note is rather the weight of the levy. The tribute was not a formality, or mere pledge of submission, it was drastic and exhausting, especially on the agricultural population. That is why there is recurrent effort at rebellion.

There was another character in this new universal Assyrian monarchy more onerous than tribute. It is, to us Europeans of the West, as amazing as it is repulsive in all these Oriental schemes of Absolutism—indeed it is present in all their methods of government even when absolutism was not attempted: I mean their disgusting cruelty.

We in Europe have been bad enough in that respect, God knows; worse of course when we were pagans. Even after that conversion to the Faith which filled the first six centuries A.D. we did abominable things. But we were nothing to these butchers of the East.

The European of today, with fifty generations of Christian philosophy in his blood, is appalled by the loathsome stories in the Old Testament, as when David set out against Midian and massacred close on thirty thousand men, women and children, indiscriminately, of his miserable captives. But the great Eastern conquerors, they who established themselves from the Armenian mountains to Arabia and from the Persian boundaries to the Western sea, were more horrible by far.

In a typical boast we have, for one campaign alone, a record which could not be equalled, I think, in the traditions of any other race than that of these Levantine Asiatics. The invader, provoked by resistance, glories in the impalement of his prisoners. Sculptures of that horror are preserved. We have them with us today.

He flays men alive and nails their skins to the doors of their own captured city. He walls them up alive into a tower specially built for that abomination. He burns their young girls and boys alive to complete the feast. But, let us mark it again, not the cruelty but the burden of tribute was the danger point in the system. The cruelties cowed men of a race which never understood what was meant by honour: a Western foible. But shekels were another matter. Tyre and Damascus rebelled in the great King's absence. In his absence also the Philistines from the west, Edom from the south, pressed on the great King's vassal, Ahaz the King in Jerusalem.

Ahaz called out to Assyria for aid. He purchased it by very grievous submission and the payment of masses of gold and silver taken from the treasury and from the temple of Jehovah. The great King answered and came. He rushed across Northern Israel and the plain of the Philistines destroying and carrying away masses, though he failed to take the walled city of Samaria.

The men of Israel killed their king and Tiglath-Pileser confirmed a successor. Then came the climax in which Tiglath-Pileser did what his predecessors had failed to do. He struck the final blow which he had designed all those years ago when he had first entered Syria. He made one last effort against Damascus, and Damascus fell. Its king was killed and whole mobs of its citizens were rounded up and driven far off to Kir. Tyre submitted in terror and paid gold—a mountain of gold—to buy off the Assyrian vengeance. The conqueror held his court at Damascus where the kings of the petty kingdoms came to bow down before him, and Ahaz, the ruler of the people of Jehovah, came near at last to idolatry from that subservience. He may not have worshipped the gods of Assyria, but he set up an altar after the Eastern fashion, had it copied and established in the holy house of the Eternal on the hill of Sion.

The great King died within half a dozen years of the fall of Damascus. That news led to further rebellion. It had no better fortune than the first. The successor of Tiglath-Pileser, his son, marched into Syria at will. He sat down for three years before Samaria and in the memorable year 722 before our era the city fell; there was no king in Israel thereafter any more.

As for the people who had been governed from that famous hill of Samaria crowned with its holy city—the twin, the wealthier twin, of Jerusalem of the south—he took them away captive. All their thousands, nearer thirty thousand than twenty-five thousand, were carried away to the Tigris and Euphrates lands and in their place came from the east and south men of alien blood. From the lower Tigris and from the Edomites came mixed immigrants of every kind so that Samaria henceforth was no longer in the Jewish tradition.

Something of that tradition filtered back. The mongrel Samaritans became possessed of the Jewish sacred books in a version of their own and carried on something of the worship due to the Supreme God. They too served Jehovah. But no Jew of the full tradition and of the unmixed blood thought of them as brethren, and after eight centuries you find the Jewish contempt of Samaria still echoing in the phrases of the New Testament.

To the south of the destroyed kingdom of Israel lay, still trembling but intact, the little territory round Jerusalem: its King still the guardian of the Temple wherein still lay the last sanctity of those who had come in so strongly from the south, from the desert, the elect of Jehovah, five hundred years before.

That poor handkerchief of a realm owed its despised security in part to its having been saved, early after the destruction of Samaria, by a plague destroying an Assyrian army encamped outside Jerusalem: perhaps also to its remoteness, far on the south: perhaps to its weakness. Perhaps to this, that, being right on the frontier, it could play Egypt against first Assyria, then the New Babylonian power, which for a brief interval inherited the decayed Assyrian Empire.

But little isolated Judah could not hold. All the Bene Israel had been destroyed and this final shred had, it would seem, no hope left at all. The last Jewish effort at playing one against the other the great powers of Egypt and Assyria broke down: Jerusalem was occupied; the last of the Bene Israel, the two tribes of Judah and Benjamin, went off into captivity in Babylon and disappeared, as it seemed, for ever. It was the year 586 B.C. They had survived the ten tribes and the northern kingdom by 156 years and now all was ended.

♦

At this moment in the story of Syria it behoves the reader and the writer to halt. Our generation has concluded firmly that things merely happen in a blind sequence and are not designed. Something had happened here, in 586: the end of the Bene Israel and the failure of their Jehovah.

They had appeared upon the immemorial stage of Syria, a loose coalition of tribes coming out of the southern desert, as the chosen of that God who was not only their God but the God of all things; and this singular claim had been kept intensely alive meanwhile by a minority of enthusiasts who had represented, though a minority, the inward image which the Bene Israel made of themselves: their soul.

They had splashed over only a part of Southern Syria indefinitely and without boundaries. They had maintained themselves with difficulty among people of a similar speech with whom they should normally have merged. What was more fundamental by far than any question of speech or race, they had lapsed into the general and repulsive worship of the tribes and cities with whom they mingled. They had had a brief moment of glory with something like unity, but over a restricted territory. I say "glory"—but the glory of Solomon himself did not seem of great moment to the vast administrations, Assyrian and Egyptian, which in turn dominated their land. Such unity as the Chosen had achieved broke down. Much the greater part of them—who kept the name of Israel peculiar to themselves because they were so much the greater part—so much more wealthy as well as more numerous—had been utterly wiped out. Their capital, Samaria, had been taken, destroyed and pillaged by aliens: they had been driven like cattle from their infertile lands; and their stony fields, such as they were, had been given to immigrants of all nations.

To the south one poor remnant had remained, that other kingdom of the Bene Israel, the tiny kingdom of Judah. How small it was can best be seen in this: that a man walking out from Jerusalem eastward or northward, or westward, would have reached its boundaries in a morning. It was not a dozen miles in any direction before he was out of the district which the chieftain, the so-called petty "King" of Jerusalem, claimed to govern.

Even if he had gone southward where the increasing aridity of the land prolonged the boundaries towards the desert and made them vaguer, one long day's excursion would have put him beyond the news and administration of the old sacred city. The last agglomeration to the south was little Hebron, not twenty miles away. Another ten miles and the wilderness began.

That was the Judæan "kingdom". That was Judah and Benjamin, the obviously dying fragment of what had never been of much consequence by the standards of this world, even at its highest: the little territory of the Bene Israel. That was the end of all their little raids and forays, restricted provincial glories, and now of their collapse.

At the price of every humiliation, especially at the price of effacement, that minute, decayed, doomed fragment survived after a fashion for two lifetimes only. Now it was over.

What remains today out of all that Syria of long ago: now, after two thousand years and half another thousand? Only Judah.

THE PERSIAN SPHERE OF INFLUENCE

VII

Persia

THE CARRYING OFF of the Jews to Babylon was the last of those great inhuman crimes of transportation which the Asiatic Paganism of Mesopotamia had committed. Assyria had broken down, Nineveh had been captured and destroyed; a new direction from Babylon, from the south, had succeeded to it. It was a King of Babylon who had ruined Jerusalem and taken away its population captive.

To this renewed rule from Babylon, by yet another change, the rule of Persians succeeded: Orientals from the further depths of Asia, the high plateaux beyond the mountain ranges which overlook the Tigris from the east and which we call by the general name of "Persia". But whether the monarchy called itself Babylon or Nineveh or Persia is indifferent to the history of Syria; Syria was still under the full control of Mesopotamia. This control was to continue, though in a somewhat different form, until that great turn-over, the creative and fundamental change of Alexander's Greek invasion.

The somewhat different form in which the control of Syria from the East continued was that the monarchy of the Tigris and Euphrates and most of its higher officials and the leaders of its Army ceased to be either Chaldean or Assyrian and ceased to be what is today called "Semitic" in speech. Nor were they quite of the same blood. What had happened was that the immemorial high throne of Western Asia had been seized by a conqueror from beyond the mountains, different in speech, different in religion, and somewhat different in race, shifting his capital somewhat farther to the east as well. The Persian, ruling from Susa, was established over all those lands, and the great name associated with that change was the name of Cyrus.

Though the transfer of power was important, it was not so

important as the scholars of the nineteenth century made it out to be. You have only to look at the surviving monuments to understand that the substitution of a Persian overlord for an Assyrian or Babylonian one did not break the continuity of that civilisation.

Its building, still more its art (as in sculpture), remained the same. The same spirit flowed through the administration of the new dynasty as had flowed through the administration of the old. There was the same establishment in much the same provinces—save that the Governors were now called by the Persian name of Satrap; there was the same adoration of the King, the same conception that everything, human and divine, flowed from one supreme Oriental crown claiming authority over the world: a human God.

The change in language among the minority of those who thus began a new Government over the East was superficially the most striking, but morally the least important change. Cyrus, the new conqueror, spoke, as had his predecessors who had undermined the power of Assyria before Babylon was at last taken, a language of the group called by scholars "Indo-European", or, by some of the more old-fashioned, "Aryan". Therefore new forms of speech were present at the Court, in some part at least of the Army (especially its higher command) and in the official places.

Of far more importance than the court language was the change in the religion of those who governed. The Persian religion, the religion of Cyrus and his soldiers, was of a temper strongly contrasting with the temper of what are called the "Semitic" religions: that is, the religions of the Baals and the Molochs with their terrors of murderous gods. The religion of Persia was a saner and a nobler thing. It was an inherited worship of the forces of nature, and though it recognised, it did not adore, maleficence. In the culture founded on that religion there was less place for cruelty, and the abominations that disgust us in the savage massacres and still worse human sacrifices of the older time, though they do not disappear, are softened.

A Government has influence even over immemorial custom; the Baals and the rest were still receiving their tribute of panic and torture; Carthage, a Syrian colony, was still burning young children alive in honour of its god for hundreds of years to come; but there was not a little change in the spirit of the Syrian gods and their worship after the Persian conquest of the central power—that is after the middle of, or a little later than, the middle of the sixth century before the Incarnation.

The advent of Cyrus to full power in Babylon was the year 539 B.C., but with the passage of the years the absorption of the Persian spirit by the Babylonian became complete, and with it the massacres and the tyranny returned.

Cyrus himself, in his formal worship of the conquered gods and the example he thus set to his officers and officials, had begun the process. In little more than a hundred years it was so far advanced that the late Persian power in its struggle against the Greeks of the mainland beyond the Ægean is exactly like that of any other Oriental or Semitic power—as ruthless, and as rapidly undermined: above all, as dependent as the older Kings had been upon mere mass and numbers.

Two main effects of the new Persian Empire are to be marked. The first is the extension of its rule from the East to the Greek world on the Ægean; the second the liberation of the Jewish exiles and the return of so many to their Holy City.

Before his final triumph in the capture of Babylon, the conquest of Cyrus had already spread westward, based upon those of his predecessors, the Medes. He had marched through Asia Minor and attacked the dominant power in the West, the kingdom of Lydia, the heart of which was an inland plain with its capital at Sardis, about fifty miles in a straight line from the Ægean coast. In mastering Lydia, Cyrus would be mastering also the Greek cities of the Ægean sea-board, and the nearer islands; so that, when, later, he became universal monarch, ruling from Babylon, he could for the first time extend the great Oriental Empire to the Greek seas. The cities of western Asia Minor had paid occasional tribute to the Mesopotamian Emperors, but there was no true extension of direct rule, no mastery of Oriental over Western man, until the new Empire of the Persian rule.

Cyrus then, previous to his establishment at Babylon itself, had led his troops across the Halys, the farthest point of direct Assyrian rule in old times, and marched on Sardis, taking the town. By conquering Sardis and its King (that Crœsus round whom legends have gathered) he (and still more his successors) became masters of the Greek cities upon the Asiatic shore of the Ægean. There was a direct contact which later would mean a necessary conflict between the Greek world and the Orientals.

The indirect consequences for Syria of this extension westward of Eastern power were great and were to increase in the next two centuries, until the Macedonian troops were launched across the Dardanelles, with power to transform all that world. For those two hundred years—from the middle of the sixth to the first third of the fourth century, say from 539, the moment of Cyrus's first triumph, to 333, the crashing blow of Issus, Syria was governed by men who at least had come to know the West, though they did not make Syria Western. But communication with the West, the Syrian knowledge of Western things, was more founded in the new Empire upon the Phœnician fleet than upon the land armies. The Persian generals and the Persian officials who were masters of the Greek cities of the Asian shore and inland were one with those generals and officials who were masters also of Syria. But the armed ships which sailed from the Phœnician ports were in continual, much more direct, touch with our Western race.

For it was one of the marks of the new Persian Empire that it used the Phœnician ports as the older Assyrian Empire had never done. The Kings of Asshur and Nineveh and Babylon could depend upon that universal sea-power of the day as an auxiliary, and even as an occasional instrument; but with the new Persian Empire the armed ships sailing from all the harbours of the Levantine coast, Arvad, Sidon and Tyre, became a direct instrument of rule; and they were used more and more in this fashion, as the two centuries of Persian power proceeded. We shall see in a moment what that instrument was to mean, and how nearly it achieved the conquest of Hellas itself, beyond the Ægean; since, but for the Phœnician sailors, neither the attack at Marathon nor that at Salamis on the eve of the high Greek time would have been possible.

The power of the Oriental over the Greek, even over that mere fringe of the Grecian culture along the western coast of Asia Minor, was not to be patiently endured. There was something stirring in the Greek blood, revolt would come, and the great reaction which flooded the Orient from the West. But even so the new Persian Empire had done its work towards the ultimate fate of Syria by thus bringing together the Levant and the Ægean Sea.

The restoration of the Jews was a separate thing; and one of at least equal moment to the story of the world. It was, as everything in Jewish history had been from the beginning, including even the brief glory of Solomon and the brief local strength of David, a restricted provincial episode. As the Pharaohs of Egypt for century upon century in the oldest time and during their renewed appearances in Palestine, as the Assyrian Kings in the moment of their highest domination, so also the Persian Kings could not think of Judæa and its fortunes as anything of importance. Indeed Jerusalem had owed its precarious salvation, after the rest of Israel had gone, to its remoteness, lying to one side of the main sea-coast road to the west, and of the two main caravan tracks—the one ending in Damascus and thence reaching to the shore, the other passing south of the Dead Sea.

To the rulers of the day the return of the Jewish deportees among so many others was a very small affair. But we know today what the restoration of Jewry was to mean; that imperishable seed had survived its generation of exile, and under the pressure of that exile had been hardened in its power of resistance. The coming of Persian power had been welcomed with lyrical cries by the prophets of Judah, the fall of Babylon was for them the act of Jehovah, and when Cyrus lifted the ban and allowed such as would to go back to the home Babylon had ruined, they knew in their blood what a great thing was toward—and they were right.

This second exodus became exaggerated by tradition as to its numbers. It may have been only a few thousand, at least in this first movement. But it could not be exaggerated in its ultimate value to the story of the world. We do not know the line of march, but from the length of time it took from one point to another we may make fairly certain that it was the only road whereby considerable numbers can cross the desert, that is, the banks of the Euphrates. For the season of starting on this expedition was what we should call the late spring—April or thereabouts, after the barley harvest had furnished grain; and the journey occupied pretty well all the summer. Thus Ezra's group in 458, about five thousand in number, took all the time from April to August.

The train of the returning exiles was led by a man who was of the old Royal blood, a descendant of David, and they brought with them all the old hope and all the old claim—but intensified. Indeed the effects of the exile, short as it had been, only forty-eight years, from 586 to 538, was so great that it has been exaggerated by modern scholars out of all measure. It has been thought convenient by those who will not accept the plain records of antiquity (and particularly by those who desire to weaken the authority of the Bible) to imagine all manner of things originating in that half lifetime; and the more extreme among them suggest that the mass of the Scripture was put together then.

That of course is nonsense. The documents of the Old Testament are what they claim to be; they are (within certain limits) reliable as history, they are certainly reliable as a tradition of the religion and the special mission of a chosen people, centuries older than these last catastrophes of Israel and Judah.

But it *is* true that the exile crystallised and strengthened, as by a sort of case-hardening, that conception of which the prophets and leaders of the Bene Israel had from the beginning been the conservators. The new little State that was to be founded became passionate in its sense of unity, and that unity was based upon the sanctity of the Law.

In one way the development did harm; it began that exaggerated formalising of the Jewish religion which went to such lengths as almost to deaden the thing it protected; it is responsible, humanly speaking, for the failure of the Jews to take their unique opportunity, and to know the Messiah when he came. But so far as mere history goes this clasping together of the Jewish remnant, this squeezing of it into an unalterable nucleus by the pressure of captivity and bonds, was the saving of the Jews as a people.

Note that they alone were saved. Not they alone returned home; all the other gods that had been exiled and all their followers were free under the new Empire to go back to their old homes; but of such released prisoners none but the remnant of Judah *remembered.* Query: May not all the Jewish story be expressed as tenacious memory?

It was the boast of Cyrus that he had granted this general emancipation from the cruelty of those universal transportations of which the old Empire bears the guilt. We have remaining the record of his pride in having done this: "I restored the gods to their thrones, I gave them a habitation for ever; I gathered their worshippers and gave them back their homes." Cyrus, moreover, after the fashion of all universal sovereigns, was compelled to tolerance, and evidently had no personal reason for practising its opposite. The Jews of Judah and Benjamin were nothing in particular to him, perhaps he hardly distinguished them; but of all those whom he set free no other group held fixedly to their past.

There were left behind in Babylon great numbers who were content to continue their lives in the place where they had taken root. They were the wealthier part of the people, and the more cultured; it was they who had during the exile founded the new and intense school of religion, and it was they who morally and materially supported the section which had returned. This settlement of the Jews in Babylon was the beginning of that capital phenomenon in history called the Diaspora, which is Greek for "The Scattering"—but may also be used to mean "The Broadcast Sowing": that is, the growing up of Jewish communities, isolated in the midst of Gentiles, all over the ancient world.

The Babylonian Jews and the new Jewish colonies just beginning; the groups of Jewish merchants and the rest to be found, now, in more and more towns of the Persian Empire, bred, coupled with the new and stricter religious enthusiasm, a certain conception which was to prove of the highest effect; it was the conception of the Jews as a people bound by special custom and especially by religion rather than by attachment to any territory. It was a new cosmopolitan conception which has endured from that day to this, and has been of such profound and permanent effect in the story of Europe and the world. This conception did not contradict the twin conception of a territorial centre—Jerusalem the Holy City and the Temple built therein.

The universal exiles, held together by their highly individual code of life and worship, the exceptional sojourners, were still always exiles, and still remembered Jerusalem. They still demanded for some central portion of their blood the original home. They are demanding it clamorously today. The return of the exiles and the re-establishment of Jerusalem was as important a thing as the Diaspora itself, and it was the two together which built up the resurrection of the Jewish power in the succeeding centuries.

When the exiles got back to the old territory of Judah and Benjamin, they found it half deserted and more than half wild. Even in Hebron, the Arabs were established; to the north, where had been the kingdom of Israel, the very mixed blood of the Samaritans was established, and beyond these again to the north the district of the heathen—"G'lil Ha Goyim"—of which the Greeks made the word "Galilee". So thoroughly had that hill country been colonised with new blood that it remained, and now still is, of a very different kind and spirit from what those hills had been when they were first ruled from Jerusalem and later from Samaria.

In the neighbourhood of the Holy City itself (by this time more than half in ruins) there were brigands and wild beasts; a very poor labouring population which had remained during the exile, hardly holding on, were all that could remind them of what Judah had been.

There were heavy labours before the returning exiles; it was eighteen whole years before they found the energy and material for the rebuilding of the Temple; but, once begun, the task was accomplished in five.

It was later still before there could be any question of re-building the walls of Jerusalem. The neighbours were jealous, notably Samaria; they represented the rebuilding of the walls of Jerusalem as a prelude to rebellion—and there was something in what they said. It was one thing to let the exiles (or such of them as chose to) return; it was another to give them the opportunity of a stronghold and a garrison. But there were arguments on the other side; for the Jews the rebuilding of the wall was a guarantee against Arab and other raiding. To this the central power was indifferent; but what they had to consider was the value of Jerusalem as an outpost against Egypt. Egypt was subdued and was part of the general Persian Empire by the time the question of rebuilding the walls arose. But there might yet be and in fact were rebellions in Egypt; and it was worth while considering the value of Jerusalem as a frontier post in case an independent Egypt should arise again. Anyhow, a century after the return of the first exiles the thing was still being debated. When Nehemiah began to build the wall, thirteen years after the protest Samaria had made, the work could only be done with great difficulty and by men ready to stand to arms as they laboured.

The Babylonian Jews continued to send help, money and advice; and after a lifetime they sent also new leaders, who began the setting up of a full though exiguous State; a real political unit, very small in area (as the old kingdom of Judah had been) but perhaps even more compact.

The most important of these delegates from the rich Jewry of Babylon was Ezra the Scribe. We may take the year of his advent in Jerusalem to be 458 B.C. That is the Jewish traditional date, and tradition is here as always a much sounder guide than modern academic imaginaries. But whether Ezra came as early as that date or fifty years later, the essential thing is that he and a Persian official, also of Jewish birth, also from Babylon, one Nehemiah, built up Jewry again under a form which it has never lost.

Two elements joined to create this form. The first was the principle that a gulf must be dug between the Jews and the rest of the world, a spiritual boundary, within which the supreme claims of the Jewish race, the Chosen, should remain secure. Within that spiritual wall were the people of God, the Elect of Jehovah; without, were the lesser breeds. This conception had always run in the Jewish blood since first they had been told in splendid rhetoric what things their God had done for them— how He had brought them out of the Land of Egypt, and what a Lord He was, how He had set them apart. But it now took on an intensity which was to the old sense of a supreme mission what the clear flame of a blast pipe is to an open fire.

The second element was the Torah, the Law. This special and segregated people was to be founded upon a Book, available to all, unchanging, detailed and particular; prescribing every action of life. Those obedient to such a code and only those obedient to it could be called Jews; but those who would be called Jews, those who were worthy of the sacred title, were not only separate but spiritually supreme above the masses of this world.

Nehemiah (who may be called the lay side of this spiritual movement) had been a favourite with the Persian court in Babylon—for let it be remarked that the antagonism between the Jew and his environment did not arise, in spite of the Jewish claims, for many generations. It was not to be distinguished from the friction which always arises between neighbours of different blood or creed; it did not become a sort of universal and necessary thing, full of tragic consequences, until that date which is the turning point of all our history, that major event, the violent Death, Burial and Resurrection of a certain Leader, just outside the north-eastern wall of the city, on some spring day between A.D. 29 and 33.

Nehemiah, therefore, with a high court position, under the title of cup-bearer to the universal Emperor and Great King— the Lord of all the East—came twice to his compatriots to forward the movement, and is bracketed with Ezra as one of the twin founders of the new thing. He came first in 445, next in 437; and we may say that before the end of the fifth century, that is before the year 400 B.C., the new Jewish people were working under that full inspiration which they have retained throughout the centuries and which marks them now before our eyes.

Politically the structure of that State was for the first time a theocracy. The old loose Jewish confederation, lying between the coming of the Bene Israel and the leadership of Saul, knew no King. But then neither did it know any organised rule by a hierarchy. It had priests, it had great spiritual leaders, it had its college of "prophets"; but it was not properly speaking a theocracy. After the return from exile and the exceptional effort of Ezra and Nehemiah had done their work the Jewish state *was* a theocracy; it had a monarch, but that monarch was not a King, he was a High Priest. He was political, and had the vices of your political man; he could bribe and on occasion would murder from ambition; but he remained a High Priest and not a King. And that state of things, peculiar in its time to Jerusalem, though inherited in instinct at least from the very beginnings of the Palestinian civilisation, went on until the rise of the Maccabees, nearly three hundred years after the days of Nehemiah.

There is one point of especial and permanent value to be remarked about this period of the early restoration after the exile; there worked through it as a leaven a strong demand for equality—what is called by those whose sympathies are egalitarian "social justice".

Now with the experience we have of the Jewish temper as it has been retained through these three millenniums, that is very significant. The Jewish feeling in this regard may be connected with the general feeling of equality that must always run through nomad populations of armed men. It is not only Jewish, it is Arab; it is not only Arab, it is Mohammedan.

But the Jews in this as in everything else were at once more intense and more highly specialised; theirs was not a vague sense of equality, it was a particular, strongly affirmed, policy, based on a vivid political emotion. It is true that the returning exiles were for the most part poor men, among whom the beginnings of new private fortunes or the presence of a few wealthy leaders come from Babylon would arouse envy; but the thing was much greater than that: it was a creative impulse affirming social justice. There had already appeared in the Jewish temper, and there is present in the Jewish temper today, not only an intellectual contempt for social inequality, but a hatred of it. Renan, who said many foolish and untrue things about the Jews, said many true things as well; and perhaps the truest thing he ever said was that of all nations they are the *least aristocratic.*

Here, in the period after the exile, the cry for equality took active form and appeared in laws and institutions. Side by side with this determination to make of the Jew something quite separate from the Gentile—to forbid intermarriage, to make the Law the test of Judaic citizenship—went positive enactments for the redistribution of property at fixed intervals, and a fragmentary but powerful scheme for safeguarding the process of redistribution and guaranteeing its renewal.

There was also, be it remembered, something military about the whole conception. The Jews had fought from the beginning, as invaders, as colonists, and were now in Jerusalem, even in their subjection, a little nation of armed men. Now war and the military spirit make for equality. Not only within their own boundaries, but occasionally as mercenaries and as a sort of conscripts for the Diaspora in the Imperial Armies the Jews of that old time were soldiers. But when they ceased to be soldiers, much later, and especially when, after the triumph of the Christian religion, they were at enmity with the society in which they found themselves immersed, this sense of equality not only survived but was intensified.

It may be thought a paradox that such a feeling should go side by side with the accumulation of great fortunes in commerce and especially in the most oppressive form of usury; but there is no contradiction. The Jew today in the slums of our great cities has kept intact this sense of equality which is coincident with the feeling of human dignity—for human dignity is a product of religion where religion binds the individual to a supreme God; and the Jewish millionaire does not, like *our* rich men, mistake his wealth for excellence, nor do his fellow Jews think him the greater for it, but only more fortunate.

But note a consequence. This profound, active and undying passion for equality is also, in the presence of an alien society, subversive. When later the Jews found themselves organised as isolated communities, scattered among people of another culture and with other traditions, their sense of equality could not but make for the disruption of social bonds other than their own. This "least aristocratic" of the peoples must of their nature protest against a hierarchy of rank in the structure of any society which at the worst oppressed, or at the best was alien to, them. And that is why the Jew has always been a revolutionary and has both suffered and triumphed in that capacity. It is not for nothing that the revolutionary prophet of our own day was a Mordecai, for Mordecai is the real Jewish name concealed under the pseudonym of Marx.

♦

While these things were happening in Palestine under a Persian satrapy which included all Syria, the main Persian power was suffering from a false step which was ultimately to bring it down. It had found itself at issue with the fringes of the rising Greek culture; it was to be entangled in heavy conflict therewith; it was to attempt further conquest, and to fail.

There was passing through the Greek city-states on both sides of the Ægean a spirit of renewal such as breaks through the surface of society from time to time, and affects the whole of a culture or race as the spring affects vegetation. The causes of such things are, of course, unknown to us; speculation is free to search for them: it will never reach its object. Forces of this kind are never to be discovered wholly among measurable or even among mortal things. They come from within.

At any rate, whatever may have been the explanation, this creative stirring of the blood was going on through all the Greek world; in Hellas itself, upon the Ægean Asiatic shore, and in the lively colonies which Greeks had founded far afield, such as Marseilles in the south of Gaul, Syracuse in Sicily.

The Persian Empire, after Cyrus had been dead a lifetime, was morally absorbed into the old Mesopotamian model; it was, as much as its predecessor had been, a majestic but fixed and very cruel despotism based upon the strength of numbers and destructive of political action and inquiry. Where it was found that the Greek cities upon the Ægean were recalcitrant to Imperial rule, it could conceive of but one remedy—suppression. There were violent struggles, accompanied by the usual massacres and burnings; and those struggles, had they been confined to the mainland of Asia Minor, might have ended in a complete Imperial victory. What turned the scale and ultimately let loose all the spiritual forces of Greece against the huge but more inert body ruled from Mesopotamia and beyond, was the risk which Persia undertook by crossing the sea.

European Greece had sent ships to help its kinsmen in their vigorous rebellion against the Emperor across the Ægean; Athens in particular had sent twenty ships of war.

So long as there was an independent Greece which could thus support the Greeks subject to the descendants of Cyrus, those monarchs were condemned to continual peril on the western extremities of the immense territories which obeyed them. Elsewhere they were secure. Egypt was incapable of successful revolt. It had attempted it more than once under native leaders, but always sank back into the position of a Persian satrapy. The active and very wealthy Phœnician sea-ports, with their almost inexhaustible supply of ships, accepted their position with content, and were ready to provide an almost permanent and very large battle fleet, which might have been thought sufficient to control the Ægean. The ulcer weakening the Persian Empire lay on the Ionian coast. The Greek settlements to the eastward (notably in Cyprus), the rest of the enormous body stretching from India to the Mediterranean, seemed sound.

But it should be the very first rule in the conduct of an Imperial power to consider its frontier. Had Persia remained on the Halys, as the older Mesopotamian Empire had done, abstaining from any movement into western Asia Minor, it might have maintained itself indefinitely. Not only in war but in Government, especially in the government of aliens, to go too far is fatal. Men were not yet old who as boys could remember the Great Cyrus, when the chief of his successors, Darius, moved for the attack upon Athens and the independent Greek world beyond the Ægean. The whole of that world was his final goal, but Attica and the town of Athens his immediate objective.

Darius sent an army directly across the Ægean, landed it on a flat shore in the narrow waters beyond Eubœa and Attica, where a wide plain between the mountains and the sea was called Marathon, after the fennel which grew there. The Persian Army thus transported over the Ægean cannot have been large; a guess has estimated it at twenty thousand men—perhaps rather more. The Athenians met it with a force rather more than half its numbers, and achieved a complete victory.

What the superior intelligence of the Greek, and probably his superior morale, almost certainly his superior physical powers, could not have achieved against the great forces of the mainland (where numbers overwhelmed the advantages of individual character) they could achieve against a force limited in size by the necessity of sea-transport.

As a military episode Marathon was but a retarding action, and a small one at that; but it was a pivotal point in the story of Europe, for it was the first halt called (even if it were to be only a temporary halt) to the apparently inevitable advance of the Great Empire into the disunited little states of our race along the Mediterranean Sea.

Ten years later, Darius being dead, his son Xerxes (the Greek form of an unpronounceable Persian name) planned and launched an expedition on a very different scale from that which his father had proposed. It was to be a victory by massed numbers—numbers so great that the little Greek states awaiting his attack could have no chance against them. Modern criticism has, true to form, belittled the effort and denied the statements of antiquity. There is no reason why we should disbelieve antiquity, but even if we accept the reduction of its figures the odds were still overwhelming.

A force of this size had of course to march by land; but it was accompanied by the large fleet which Phœnicia and the other tributaries had put at the service of the Great King. Athens made an effort extraordinary for her limitations; she put hundreds of triremes upon the sea; but could not hope to match this oncoming maritime host; while as for the land army, there was no comparison—it must necessarily sweep forward and prove irresistible. Another retarding action, necessarily doomed, was fought by the Spartans, who had come up late in the common cause of Hellas; they held for such time as was possible a narrow pass between the mountains and the sea within a few marches of Athens itself—but their position was of course turned. The invaders occupied and burnt Athens, the main population of which had been evacuated; and the Persian fleet came up in all its strength past the shores to the south of the city, where the harbour of Athens, the Piræus, lies to the narrow waters between the Attic shore and the island of Salamis.

What followed was a naval action in which the larger force was destroyed by the smaller. The hundreds (even thousands) of Phœnician boats were cramped for sea-room, lost order, and were thus at the mercy of the Athenian attack.

Xerxes, watching the battle from a height, knew that a fleet so crippled might be called, for fighting purposes, destroyed, and there could now be no maintenance for his very large land force. It was drawn back into Asia, and the Great King got what satisfaction he could by the wholesale executions of the unsuccessful Phœnician commanders. The remnant which he had left behind him on land to hold what could be held was defeated finally in the following year, and thenceforward, that is from the year 479 B.C. (Salamis was fought in 480 B.C.)* Hellas was free; and not only Hellas, but the Greek colonies far to the west in Sicily, against whom Xerxes had launched by alliance the Phœnician colony of Carthage. There also the European had defeated the Oriental.

There followed three generations such as Europe had never yet known and was never to know again—three generations of Greek activity in the arts, in science and in the orderly development of beauty. The greatest names of Europe are marshalled in that time; its all but greatest verse, and certainly its

* Some argue for the date 481.

greatest triumph in sculpture. Stone lived; not only in the representation of living form but in the use of architectural ornament and proportion. Greece threw out full beauty, with such confidence and vigour that the canon was maintained for century after century; she taught, moulded, and established the people of our blood.

That full beauty and that fulness also of life hung ready to transform the East, and was soon to make of Syria a new thing, worthy to endure, as it did, for close upon a thousand years. For close upon a thousand years after the appearance of the Greek clarity in mind, the Greek splendour in ornament, and the Greek norm in architecture, these things occupied the Orient; and during their occupation framed the last preparation which was to introduce the Godhead. In those three lifetimes of the original Greek splendour in Hellas itself and the Ionian cities beyond the Ægean, conflict between the city-states had ended in one general rule. The kingdom of Macedon having become master, but also leader, of the Greek civilisation at its heart, was ready to land new armies beyond the sea into Asia.

The task of thus calling the Orient into life fell upon a very young man, Alexander, the son and heir of that King Philip of Macedon who had made one the strength of Greece. He and his Macedonians, in no very great force, were to be seen in Asia: their marching could already be heard. Alexander was twenty years old when Kingship and the power over his Army came into his hands; before he was twenty-three he had challenged and overthrown the garrisons of the Great King from the Ægean and along the road to the east. He had passed the Cilician Gates, he had come to the Gulf of Alexandretta on the northern ends of the Syrian shores; and the thing was about to be accomplished.

VIII

Greece

BEYOND the borders of the Cilician plain, where it is
bounded on the east by mountains, the thing was decided.

The hills ring round the shores of that gulf (then called the
Gulf of Issus), which is the northern corner of Syria; and at their
feet, between their steep slopes and the shore, the shock of
Europe against Asia came—a short march north and east of the
place where little Alexandretta (which takes its name from the
new Greek invader) stands today.

Alexander, marching from the Ægean, had reached that point
towards the end of the second year of his advance—November,
333 B.C. Here the great hills, green for the greater part of the
year, nourished with rills that fall from their melting snows,
stand round the gulf as guardians.

I have compared that landscape to one of the larger Scottish
sea-lochs. The parallel is striking when one steams in-especially
in the earlier months of the year—from the outer sea into the
gulf, and sees the mists covering those heights and coming far
down them, hanging low above the waters.

Here there runs a stream somewhat larger than the rest, yet
short, for the range rises straight up from the shore. The Macedonian Army, no very great force (say, in modern terms, a
couple of divisions), strong in cavalry (one-eighth perhaps of
its total), stronger still in its compact and disciplined body of
spearmen on foot, the phalanx, had already crossed the river,
when it was cut off by the host of the Great King—yet another
Darius, the third of that name. His army, arriving from the north
and east, lay across the road by which the Greeks had come and
cut their communications. Alexander had no choice but to
attack the enemy's greatly superior numbers.

Until they thus met, contact between the invader and the

main body of the Persian monarchy had not been taken. Until that autumn month, in the year 333 B.C., which was to fix the fate of the East, Alexander had attacked the Persian outlying forces only. Now the time for a decision had come.

The numbers in the Persian command may have been exaggerated by their enemies, but they were certainly very much greater than those of the Macedonians who now turned at bay, with the Asiatic crowd of Darius between them and their own far land. The action, therefore, was fought, as has been more than one such decisive conflict in history, topsy-turvy; with the invader facing back in the direction from which he had come. Jena and Valmy were of that kind.

The triumph of Alexander was complete. See that very young lion-like man, with his thick mane of hair and his flaming eyes, his face alight with battle, charging at the head of his horsemen on the right wing and grasping the mastery of the world! The roar from the lines in grapple rolled up those green hills into the mists above as the Greek cavalry on that right wing did its work; it destroyed the Persian left, thereby exposing a flank, while the central phalanx thrust back the broken and disordered Orientals into what became first a confusion and then a rout.

Then the Macedonian horse wheeled round to their left against the exposed flank of the Persians and destroyed the enemy formation.

Darius fled, his mother and his sister and son fell, with the camp, into the hands of the conqueror; and with the broken Emperor there fled also the remnant of his troops, which would be swelled with further contingents as he made at full speed for the East.

Alexander did not pursue. There was still in full power behind him, on the waters between him and Greece, the great mass of the Phœnician fleet holding the sea: master of the Ægean and of all the country between the Gulf of Issus and Europe. It might provoke rebellion in his rear. He had no instrument for meeting it; but he could paralyse it by occupying from the land side the Syrian ports, notably Tyre and Sidon, on which it was ultimately based and from which it was

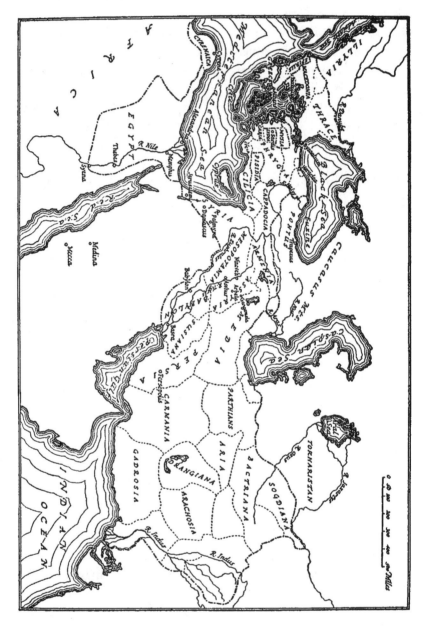

THE MACEDONIAN EMPIRE OF ALEXANDER

recruited and provisioned. The orders of anyone mastering those ports the fighting ships would obey. Therefore the young conqueror swept down southward upon those coastal cities of Syria, while his best general, passing to the east of the mountains, seized Damascus.

The string of Phœnician sea-ports surrendered at once; Arvad in the north, and Sidon and the rest. The Tyrians were ready to follow suit, but, for some unknown reason, though they would accept the new rule, they would not admit Alexander himself within their island.

Some think there was a religious scruple; some think that it was a piece of national vanity based upon such long invincibility and the fatal lure of sea-power. Tyre stood siege for seven months, and was only taken at last by the Greeks building a great mole, outwards, towards its island city from the shore. On that advancing mole clanged the new Greek siege-artillery which Asia did not yet know: hurling its stones against the Tyrian walls. The Tyrians, so captured at last, were destroyed; killed and sold into slavery. Alexander went on southward, he sacrificed in the Temple at Jerusalem, he met a check at Gaza which also stood a siege, stubbornly resisting but carried after two months. Thence he marched on for Egypt at the rate of twenty miles a day. A week after breaking camp before the ruined walls of Gaza, he was on the edge of the delta.*

Egypt, which had twice attempted to shake off its Persian governors, called him to deliver her, and received him with glory. There also he worshipped the Egyptian gods, and proclaimed himself a god through the oracle in the oasis of Ammon, the sacred oracle of the Lybian desert to the west.

Alexander might now have sat enthroned, the undisputed ruler of all the Levant with Syria for his centre of strength. He felt sure of Asia Minor through which he had passed to his victory;

---

* All through history, until the railway was built the other day, advance along this nearly desert shore has had, as I have said, to be rapid and by long day's marches from one water supply to the next. The Egyptians of old allowed nearly twenty miles a day. So did Napoleon. Alexander did the same. Now twenty miles a day is rare going for an army; even in a short bout. Rome allowed twelve or thirteen.

Phœnicia and Palestine, all the coast and coastal ranges were his, and now also the wealth and the human millions of Egypt.

Darius offered to compromise. He was willing to return eastward and to give the Macedonian the frontier of the Euphrates. Alexander refused. Those crushing successes, and above all Issus, final and complete, were to him the proof that his command of less than forty thousand men could master the Orientals at will. He determined to pour Greece into Asia as it were—spreading everywhere the glory and the order of Hellas, its beauty and creative thought and the full presence of Europe.

The oldest and wisest of his father's counsellors, who was his own chief lieutenant in arms, was for peace; Alexander would have none of it. He would fulfil his vision. The young man turned back northward, following the fringe of the habitable land; crossed the Euphrates just above the point where the desert begins, crossed the Tigris near by the mounds which marked dead Nineveh, reversing the march which the old Assyrian conquerors had taken. There, east of Nineveh, in the plain beyond the Tigris, on the flats that lie between the river and the eastern mountains, he found Darius rallied with his vast hordes of Eastern men.

Here again the numbers quoted are perhaps too great to be true; but they were overwhelmingly greater than the Greeks. It was here, near Gaugamela,* that Alexander fell upon them, confident in the weapon he had in hand—the Macedonian phalanx and that unconquered cavalry which he himself would lead.

There, by Gaugamela, on the 1st of October, 331, not quite two years after Issus, the second decision was achieved and that great Oriental Empire, inherited from the Assyrian, and counting in all more than three thousand years, going backward beyond known time, was at an end.

The huge crowd of Orientals again became a rabble in rout. Once more Darius fled, eastward into the recesses of what had

---

* "The Camel Station". The battle is traditionally known as that of *Arbela* because from that town as a base—a day's march to the east—Darius had advanced, and thither was he pursued after his defeat.

been his kingdom, taking refuge with a dependent governor far off in Bactria—and there was murdered. As for Alexander, he and his, supplemented by levies from home, they, the young god having assumed the throne of Babylon, passed right on into Asia, marched to the Indus—where his name is still remembered. He would have gone further, to the Ganges itself, but that the army could do no more—and its retreat was disastrous.

Still, he had already grasped all that Assyria had ever held, and all that Persia had held as well. He was now a Divine Power over the Eastern world and had joined to it Europe and the new creative life of our Western blood. The flood-tide of Greece followed in. Then, in the height of his triumph, ten years after Issus, Alexander died.

How had this astonishing feat been accomplished? It is not enough to say that the white races can always overcome any Oriental body; for the races he dealt with as enemies were of every kind, and how often the men of our blood have failed against the mountaineers of Asia and the fierce Arabian spearmen from the desert! Perhaps the chief factor in the breakdown of Darius was his reliance upon mere mass; and certainly a chief factor in the victory of his opponent was a commander of genius handling a perfect instrument, highly disciplined, mobile, and possessed of a new tactic. Alexander reads like Napoleon.

The great Empire which he dissolved—and more than reconstituted—had deadened the spirit of its original various states; they had lost civic power; they had become a unity such that the removal of the head and the substitution of another master was enough to transform the world.

As wonderful as the victory, and the astonishing pursuit, and the lightning marches, was the policy. Alexander had determined to let all Hellas into Asia, and he succeeded. From his day onward it was we that pressed upon Asia, in Syria, the boundary, rather than Asia upon us for nearly a thousand years (333 B.C. to A.D. 634). Coastal Syria, the test and the pivot, the hills a hold on which is a hold on the Orient, or at the least a bulwark against it, was now Greek and would remain Greek till the Mohammedan blight fell over it.

In this triumphant policy the settlement of Greek cities did the work. Alexander and his marshals founded Greek cities everywhere; seventy at least, of which after every destruction and ruin forty can still be traced; many still live. He also had the wisdom to mix the Greek with the Asiatic blood. He himself married women of that old world, a daughter of Darius, a daughter of the Satrap of Bactria, and perhaps another. His officers followed his example.

Greece could not have come into Asia in any other way. It was not in the genius of Hellas to be a bully or even a mere master, and indeed all those who have permanently impressed themselves upon the world have freely intermarried with the governed.

So strong was the structure thus raised, in the western part of Alexander's Empire at least, that it has never wholly fallen into dust, and for century upon century Greece continued to shine throughout all the Orient. The heavenly sculpture, the not less heavenly proportion between erect and horizontal line, the rank of the Grecian colonnade, put the mark of Greece upon everything. Greek letters—in science, in high verse, in chronicle and in religion itself—were at once the medium and the inspiration of everything in hither Asia.

Particularly did Greece renew and invigorate Syria, taking root there and making of coast and hills a Grecian thing; so that even now, after so many centuries of Moslem ruin, you see, throughout that coast and those hills, the structure of Greece remaining even far into the desert, in the oasis of Palmyra.

In Baalbec the Greek columns so remain; and you see them, fresh from the hands of Constantine's workmen, still standing above the stable grotto where Our Lord was born. I have said it was a thousand years of Greece and of Europe clothing Syria: were it not for mortality, that garment should have been worn perennially, for it was the best.

This impression of Hellas upon the East did much more. Through it the Gospel transformed mankind. Never should we have known that mighty change had the Oriental been left to his insufficiency. On the contrary, in so far as he has returned he has ruined the Message. It was in a Greek world that the renovation of our race began; and that to which all the history of Syria was leading, the Divine Event, the Theophany, was (under Providence) proclaimed and illumined through the Greek tongue.

It is a common, shallow and therefore false thing to say that Alexander's realm fell to pieces. It is true that there was no continuity of single government; the huge dominion was partitioned among rival generals, the frontiers between whose jurisdictions long fluctuated. But the Greek spirit therein remained one, if not in all Asia, at least from the Tigris to the Mediterranean. And when the governments of Alexander's marshals had become kingdoms, those kingdoms, Ptolemy's descendants in Egypt, the descendants of Seleucus in Syria, were of one culture.

The chief of many cities founded for the attainment of the conqueror's object was Alexandria, on the sea-coast of the Egyptian Delta. It rapidly became the chief port of the Orient, and the chief centre of its intellect as well. There was another city founded (not by Alexander but by Seleucus, his general) rather more than twenty years after the Hero's death—this was Antioch, on the lower Orontes, in the plain which lies beyond the Amanus Mountains, just south of the Gulf of Issus. The Syrian coastal range rises immediately above the last stretches of that river Orontes, its northern summits overlook Antioch, and thence it runs southward for its hundreds of miles till it is lost in the desert beyond Palestine.

Each of those two high cities, Alexandria, south of Syria, Antioch in the north, were beacons of civilisation and strongholds thereof; and each was a new creation, as all this Greek thing was a new creation. For each had been deliberately planned, made out of nothing, and erected into splendour. Such was the power of the spirit at work when Greece conquered the East: the best piece of temporal good fortune, perhaps, that ever befell our civilisation.

Alexandria, the chief Greek city of Egypt and of the Ptolemies, concerns Syria only indirectly: but it was an adjunct to Syria. It gathered up into itself as a main sea-port all that the

Phœnician cities had once been; it was the very capital of the new Greek civilisation in the East, the place where all men met and the place where, when the Christian religion grew to absorb mankind, that religion was most active and most fiercely debated.

Alexandria was also the chief city of the Diaspora. The Jewish communities, already widespread and already growing rich at the end of the Persian Empire, increased quickly in numbers and in wealth with the coming of Alexander; they welcomed him, as the Jews have always welcomed every great change (save One)—for their Messianic temper always expected of old some betterment for the world from any change, and later on, their suffering gave them a right to expect almost any change to be a chance of betterment for themselves.

The Jews, then, welcomed Alexander. They welcomed the new culture of the Orient, the "Hellenisation" of all that land; nor did they welcome it only as a change—a new chance—they welcomed it also through their appreciation of a higher civilisation. They welcomed it as so many of them welcomed the Renaissance in Europe and as so many more welcomed and aided and took part in the great modern advance of physical science.

It was in Alexandria that the sacred books of the Jews were translated into that Greek tongue which was now the universal medium of all the Eastern Mediterranean: a long task, not completed till the eve of the Christian Movement which closed the old era. Through this version of the sacred Hebrew books (called the Septuagint from the story of its compilation by Seventy Elders) all that world became familiar with the singular and very ancient story, with the claim and the mystery of those hill tribes: once no more than the Bene Israel, now dispersed throughout all the Greek world—and yet more closely bound together and more individual than ever.

Such was the one Egyptian centre to the south of Syria, Alexandria. The other, Antioch, in the extreme north, became by far the greatest town in Syria; the town of the Court, and the heart of all the country, the expression of the land.

Antioch was splendid, after the fashion of Alexandria, its wide paved streets stretching straight for miles, colonnaded and statued. The site chosen gave to Antioch in its glory a certain character of landscape like no other new city. It was built upon ground which rises from the left bank of the Orontes up to a jagged ridge standing hundreds of feet into the sky. In the river itself an island bore the Royal Palace, and beyond the river on the right bank the town had also extended.

Like Alexandria, its population was enormous; it may have been the third (as Alexandria was the second) city of the Roman Empire; it was (at least now, in its original design) equal with Alexandria in numbers and in wealth.

But unlike Alexandria the wealth of this northern capital was not mainly commercial. It was too high up the river for a port; a special harbour had to be built to serve it at the mouth of the Orontes, some miles to the west of the town; and this harbour, artificially made, was with difficulty kept up. The river would be always silting it, although its current had been diverted with great labour. Today that harbour has disappeared, filled up.

Small craft could come up from this sea-port to Antioch bridge; but the river was not large (forty yards wide); and above the town the Orontes would bear but boats for transport. Its valley bent round southward, not far east of the capital; and the Orontes in all its upper reaches, though it fertilised fields and gardens, nourished a lake of some size not far from its source, and watered at least one considerable town, was never a stream sufficient to create a province. Rivers were never the making of Syria, and their absence forbade such unity as marked Egypt and Mesopotamia.

But the concentration of large incomes and of the Royal Syrian revenues in Antioch made it famous and infamous for its luxury. Later on there grew up a sort of legend throughout the harder Western world. Antioch became the symbol of sensuality, of display, of the loosened zone and soft degradation. It stood for corruption after a fashion never attached to Alexandria.

There was a Syrian goddess presiding over these things, and imposing upon men her mystery and her spell. The groves of

Daphne, for which the neighbourhood of Antioch grew famous, were a symbol of all that. The Goddess had many names, but they were all the veils of one spirit, best called Astarte, Ashtaroth. All down the coast that influence lay; she and her lover Adonis, were most ancient in Byblos, and on the river which in the spring runs blood-red. Nor has the worship of Astarte wholly disappeared, though there is no more chanting of her hymns.

Antioch did not lose splendour until the Moslem came. It was ill-placed, far to the north, hemmed in by the mountains; it was discovered to be founded on perilous ground; one shock of earthquake after another fell upon it, century after century; it was half destroyed over and over again—once almost wholly levelled; but it re-arose, in its miles of streets and myriads of freemen and slaves.

For the moment, then, Antioch was the capital of the house of Seleucus, and of its great kingdom established over one chief department of the new Hellenistic world in the East. That house had also another capital in Mesopotamia, far off beyond the desert, called Seleucia, but it never played such a part as Antioch did.

One may say that Greece, pouring into the Orient and flooding it with the speech and manner of the West, was more and more merged into Asia as one went eastward. The Greek blood and tradition tended to ebb westward, in the direction whence it came. The stamp of Greece remained fixed upon the Syrian hills and in Antioch. Though some Semitic speech must have been commonest with the mass of the people, Greek was the dominant tongue; and it remained the dominant tongue of all that was noblest between the Egyptian desert and the mountains of Asia Minor throughout the Syrian sea-plain and highlands.

The city names were disputed between the two idioms, and the native Semitic idiom, that which had been inherited from so many thousand years, has upon the whole conquered, though even today the Greek survives. "Chaleb", for instance, is still Aleppo, and Berœa, which was the Greek title of Aleppo, is no longer heard. The river Hieromax has become once more the

Yarmuk; and even the Greek names of the Decapolis were in part lost.

Yet some of those new sounds have withstood the passage of so many years and armies; Laodicea is still Latakia; and Antioch will, of course, maintain its title so long as its shrunken relic survives—to the memory of the father of Seleucus, after whom it was called.

The Seleucid dynasty took Greece into Syria more thoroughly than did the Ptolemaic dynasty take Greece into Egypt. In Egypt the very ancient thing, with its innumerable inheritance in symbol and every convention of man, stood strong, even till the Mohammedan conquest—that is, for nearly a thousand years after the first enthusiastic welcome given to Alexander. But in Syria, city after city, groves and gardens, palaces and grottos, got Greece into their very soul. Such was the work of that Seleucid dynasty, which has borne so much contempt through its later decay.

The dynasty did not maintain itself from the beginning throughout the Syrian range; all the southern part was claimed by the Ptolemies. It was not till a conclusive battle, fought on the midway of the Syrian belt, in 198 B.C., that the southern half fell for good under the government of Antioch. Thenceforward Palestine also was Seleucid and ruled from Antioch until the whole came under the shadow of Rome and at last under the full power thereof: then the Seleucid name and its remnant of authority were extinguished.

It would seem as though Syria had cast over those who professed to hold her, even the Greeks, some subtle influence making for a decline of energy. It cannot have been wholly climate, for even in the parched, rainless summers the higher hills are long fresh and green; and though the torrents dry up before the heat is over, the snows linger on Lebanon.

It is easy to ascribe it to blood; but there is something more. What was to happen to the Crusaders, more than a thousand years later, what may happen to us of the West when our latest incursion since the Great War has borne its fruit, happened also to the Greek in Syria. It did not prevent great verse or glorious building everywhere; but it did prevent the continuance of strength.

Those isolated little sea-plains between the spurs of the dry hills, that cutting up into small particular regions through the tangle and isolation of the mountain groups, played its part. But whatever the causes of the decline in the Greek Syrian power that is in the authority and strength of the Seleucid house—and those causes we shall never fully know—one fruit thereof is especially memorable: the resurrection of a Jewish kingdom.

It was not a mere new Jewish survival, astonishing though such had been throughout the ages; it was the setting up once more of a separate Jewish political unit, just when all small states had ceased to be.

Judah did not come to life again, for Judah had always been alive. The fire rekindled upon the Holy Hill by the returning exiles, the work of Ezra and Nehemiah, was a proof that the Chosen would endure. No; it was the reappearance of Judah as a *State*; the emergence once more of a little kingdom which was to spread somewhat beyond its strict boundaries, as the ancient kingdom of David and of Solomon had once spread; which was to have its own dynasty and to form a special thing among the many city-states and separated districts of the long Syrian strip. This upheaval of a Jewish island, as it were, above the general waters of Grecian Syria bears in history one name. That name will remain as great as the field in which it worked was small—the name of the Maccabees.

The Maccabees it was, the family of the Asmonæans, to whom we owe the thing; not consciously, but as instruments of that purpose which had maintained its course through every vicissitude since first the Bene Israel had broken into the land from the desert, and which made of the Maccabees an instrument sufficient to tide over the last great change. The little Lion of Judah lived on fiercely, oddly indomitable, until Messiah came indeed, and its task was accomplished.

IX

Maccabeus

THE RISING of a curtain; the unexpected scene appearing; the entry of a small negligible force in arms upon the stage—and from that tiny spring rises a flooding force of disruption which has flowed from that day to this: something permanently at issue with the civilisation of the West: an undying feud, an irreducible alien solvent in the midst of our Greek and Roman things.

Religion, lying at the root of all human affairs, determined it. The great part which the Jews were to play in the newly extended Greek world did not proceed from their very wide diffusion nor from the heaped-up and organised wealth of their chief money dealers, acting as bankers, from the Nile to the Black Sea and from the Mediterranean to the Persian hills. It proceeded from the inward exaltation of a very few poor men and their tenacity.

Rome had defeated Macedon. The kings descendant from Alexander's generals had to find money to pay a heavy indemnity. During the next few years after the defeat of the Macedonian power on European soil by the Roman Army, just on the turn of the second century (197 B.C.), the Greek power in Syria was straining all its society to recover, by taxation and levy, the wherewithal to pay the indemnities of the war. It was at the moment separate from the Greek Kingdom of Egypt. It had to work within its own limits of Mesopotamia and of the long Syrian belt united with Mesopotamia by the narrow ill-watered line south of the mountains and north of the desert, and, across the desert, by the river line of the Euphrates.

The "Exactor of Tribute", acting under orders from Antioch in each district of Syria, was hard put to it. Among other accumulations which the "Exactor of Tribute" could drain in

Syria, was that of the Jewish Temple in Jerusalem to the extreme south of the Syrian realm. The Royal Seleucid power had levied on the Temple Treasury, and on private funds held therein for safekeeping. The sacrilege had led to bloodshed, confused by the faction fighting to which the Jewish character necessarily led; but no economic cause, even when mixed with sacrilege, could be sufficient to provoke what followed. With the separation of Syria from Egyptian rule, little Judæa, a fragment of hill country hardly more than one long day's ride from end to end, had become a frontier post. The heights upon it, and particularly its chief human agglomeration, the walled town and citadel of Jerusalem, its capital, were a watch-tower and an advanced post. They were not this of their own will, but they could not but be regarded by the great Seleucid Kings of Syria as having this function—to observe and take the brunt of any advance against Syria from the rival Egyptian kingdom of the Ptolemies to the south.

Jerusalem and Judæa around it did not lie, as is so often said, upon a main line of communication. They lay to one side and they did not of themselves seriously menace the main road which ran to the west of them and below them along the seacoast. This road—*not* passing through Judæa—was a highway for the nations; but in case of invasion from the south, those who ruled Syria would necessarily use the high bulwark of the Judæan hills whence to come down and get on the flank of an invader from Egypt. So the invader on his side must see to it that Jerusalem should be taken before he could proceed northward.

All this we have seen in our first consideration of the military position of Jerusalem; but in the past that hill town had not possessed the importance which now suddenly fell upon it by the isolation of Syria and the menace of that Greek Kingdom by the other Greek Kingdom of Egypt to the south, for in the past the Judæan tangle of high land and the fortress town in its midst had interrupted advance from the north or from the east, which in any case could flow round it, as the tide flows round a rock. But now it was what has just been described, a bulwark and a watch-tower against the menace of armies from the south.

As first the Grecian King of Syria had thought to save himself by invading Egypt and having himself crowned there. But the growing Roman power had given him an ultimatum. He had been ordered out of Egypt and he had yielded. All the more did the making sure of his remaining realm and of its southern boundary become imperative to him.

Now for resistance, and especially for resistance in a supreme effort, *Unity* is the essential. In the year 167 B.C. Antiochus* the Greek King of Syria, now mainly Greek in its externals of architecture, in its beauty and order, largely in its speech and thought Hellenised, prepared to enforce *Unity* in his realm. It was the year after the menacing power of Rome from the West had spoken so emphatically that he set out to attempt that which every governing power when threatened must attempt, whether to succeed or to fail. He set out to draw together, to cement, to make one, the political body which he had to secure and through which he had to exercise his power. He did not achieve his end, but he only failed through stumbling against that force incalculable—the Spirit.

For political *Unity* religious unity was needed; some general similarity of public worship throughout the State from the Gulf of Issus on the north and the Cilician land, Tarsus and the rest, down to Gaza and the edge of the desert through which ran the road to Egypt on the south.

Syria already had, in great matters, a common administration, in lesser, local matters, an elastic city rule; a dense and wealthy population on the sea side of the hills, on all the habitable country of the hills themselves and even along the edges of the eastern waste. On its chief eastern city, Damascus, it would be an easy task to impose and strengthen a general unity of religion as it would be with Tyre and Sidon and the rest: the rites of each place were its own and so were the names of its gods, for that was the unquestioned practice of pagan antiquity all around and had been so for all recorded time; but the fruitful and beneficent

* This is that one of the Seleucian line of Greek kings over Syria who is known as Antiochus IV and surnamed *Epiphanes*, that is, "the God apparent": a very Oriental and fantastic title.

air of Greece had blown over that land for now very long and the gods of Antioch were part of a general custom in worship. Much of the vileness in the older rituals remained, yet Greece had humanised those shores and there was now more of loveliness than of cruelty between Lebanon and the Great Sea and in the deep secluded valleys of the Orontes and the Litani. Greek beauty and order had stamped itself also upon the cities farther to the south, in Galilee and on to the Judæan hills, thus making a string along the sea-coast of Phœnicia and on southward to the Philistine plain, and there were new Greek cities beyond Jordan, founded in the high and fertile land, the Hauran and Moab.

Pagan antiquity held towards its gods an attitude which must be understood if we are to see how easy it seemed to establish the generalised worship which the Greek statesmen had in mind. The citizens were devoted to the gods of the city, but in their hearts they recognised how much there was of human imagination in these gods. They worshipped the unseen powers under various titles which might be taken as translations; the title of another city's god was equivalent to one of their own. Thus the Semite god Melkarth, of Tyre, was equivalent to the Greek Herakles. They would not brook an attack on the ritual, each of his own society; but they were willing to see, in the ritual of their own society, something consonant with and in cousinship with the ritual of a neighbour, even of a distant neighbour. The reverence given, and the powers invoked, could be recognised under forms other than those most immediately familiar, thus that power which even the doubting Lucretius almost worshipped, and which moves all the world, might be called Venus or Astarte or Aphrodite, it was all one. So with the strength which is apparent in the sun, beneficent or terrible; so with the conception of the Chief God, whether he were called Zeus or Baal of the city. It needed but the common government to give a common initiative for a religious fusion to follow in the nature of things.

It had been observed, no doubt, that in the south a sort of isolated spirit survived and that among the Syrian gods one of them, the Jehovah of Israel, had a sort of unneighbourly jealousy about him; but all that could be arranged; good fellowship was in the air. Moreover among these Jews, who stood somewhat apart, the majority were already international. Only a remnant of them remained isolated in their original villages and towns; the rest were steeped in the surrounding pagan sea which Greece and Syria, and Rome too for that matter, and even Egypt, took for granted.

Moreover the Jews themselves were of all opinions in this matter. The most cultivated, the wealthiest and perhaps the most *politically* national were by now in tune with the Greek mind; with the Greek language of course, but also with something of the love which the Greek felt so strongly for the manifestation of the Divine through proportion—and beauty, which is the flower of proportion.

Many Jews, perhaps most Jews, were already absorbed in the Greek manner; many others, touched by tradition and perhaps by pride of family, compromised between the two ideas, holding indeed to the ritual of the Law, to the circumcision, to the sacrifice, to the Temple, to the sacred Books, but holding them under the conditions of Greek life and manner. Many of the Jewish Priests themselves were of this temper.

But there remained a nucleus of ultra-Jewish Judæa; almost certainly a minority and perhaps a small minority, which still stood in fierce opposition to Grecian things. Not only would they maintain the ancient soul of Israel intact, but they would *kill* all Jews that were not aflame with that tradition: they would extirpate all innovations and all innovators. The new beauty was hateful to them because it seduced the Holy One of Israel from his Jehovah. Men of this sort acting at a potential so far higher than that of their neighbours, were the men against whom the project of Antiochus made shipwreck. They withstood unity— and they succeeded. The succession of events whereby the thing was done makes up one of the most extraordinary stories in the record of mankind.

I say we do not know the number of these recalcitrants: those enthusiasts who refused to be moved by one inch, who contrariwise hardened against all pressure from aliens, who hated every graven image and treasured only that inward image which might never be in stone or bronze, which inhabited only the vivid mind. The Almighty creative God who bore with no rival; their God: the God who had made of them His chosen, out of all the world and who would never fail them, Him alone would they serve. They saw Him sometimes in the dark storm cloud when He came up from the hills beyond the Dead Sea, northward, strongly destroying. They knew that He had made the far-off snows on Hermon and that every high place was His own.

But in this year 167 B.C. Antiochus the Greek King of Syria, not weighing what he did (for how could he know its gravity?) set up the Olympian Jove in the Temple Court and with courtesy explained to the less lettered of Jerusalem that this god was also their god, for he was Baal Shamin the Lord of Heaven. It was all one (said he) whether they called him by the one name or the other, but meanwhile those things which too much separated men should be forbidden; the unnatural rite of circumcision in particular and the quaint punctilios of Torah—the Law. It became a criminal offence to keep this or that ancient tradition in its fulness.

Towards the end of the year, on that Feast of Light, when the Oriental heathen also welcomed the passing of the shortest day, a new altar was set up in place of the old Altar of Jehovah upon the Sacred Hill, in His Temple enclosure, and the ancient sacrifice ceased.

To how many among the Jews was this Royal act a murder, an intolerable thing? I have already said to a minority, perhaps to a small minority. The High Priests wavered, or smiled at the now advancing culture of the world. The bulk of men must, as they always do, have drifted with the tide; but whether those who found the new thing intolerable were few or very few, it matters little. The story of the world is not built by majorities. The zealots of Jewry were working at a voltage which was deadly to everything of lower pressure around them; they refused obedience, and the inevitable persecution began.

Now persecution, when it falls upon the few and these few not powerful and apparently of inferior culture and, what is more, stupidly obstinate, refusing to see and to follow the comfort which all their fellows see and follow, does not feel like persecution to the persecutor. To the persecutor it is only enforcing reasonable law. It is the persecuted who know what is toward and it is *their* martyrdom which sometimes (rarely, and only if Heaven favour them) can turn the tide.

For there were martyrs, such as the famous "Seven Brothers", and groups of men here and there took up arms. They were, in their own eyes, the Light Infantry of the Eternal, the hallowed skirmishers of God, and when they killed the renegades or when they stormed the houses of the isolated pagans in the wild, they were but the sword-bearers of justice. To the government they were a petty nuisance which had to be suppressed.

The High Priest sent off a contribution from his funds to subscribe to the games of Hercules of Tyre. The King, in whose eyes these little risings were at first negligible, went off to meet a more worthy adversary in Mesopotamia on the frontiers of his dominions, the great Eastern attack. In Judæa the resistance, during his absence, began to grow: yet even as it grew it long remained hardly observable.

There is, on the older of the roads between Jerusalem and the sea-coast, one very long day's journey from the capital, in the foothills before the Philistine plain is reached, a little place about on a level with Lydda on the southern road; it is called Modem or Modin. There lived here one, Mattathias, of the House of Asmon or Hashmon, so that his family are called the Asmonæans. This man was already of mature years, with five vigorous sons ready for all trials, for he and they were determined to resist.

This man watched the pagan priest sacrificing at the pagan altar. He rushed at that priest and killed him; then, flying before the officers of the King, he and his sons made for the wilderness.

Antiochus, marching against the Persians, had left behind him officials to govern in his place and keep custody of the little son who was still a child and who should be the future king. As the troubles were spreading, and the groups of those who were fanatics in the eyes of the government seemed to be increasing in vigour and perhaps in numbers, an army came out against them. Perhaps no very great force but one which seemed overwhelming to the small body whom the Asmonæans had gathered round them when they returned to take up the fight.

There stand on that old main road from Jerusalem to the seacoast and to Joppa, but north of the present road, two villages, the one lower down the foothills, the other higher up; they are called the Upper and Lower Beth Horon, that is, "place of caves". There the zealots assembled. Mattathias was dead, and his third son led the little host of enthusiasts.

Not a few of them complained that it was impossible to fight against such odds. To him, the third son of Mattathias, a warrior, the natural leader of them (by name Judas) answered, "In the sight of the God of Heaven, there is no difference between saving the many and saving the few."

The year was the year 164 B.C. The abomination in the Temple Court, the desecration of the Holy Place, had lasted nearly three years. Judas, whom they called "the Maccabean" (maybe because they likened him to a hammer, for the weight of his blows, maybe because they thought him "Named of the Lord"—the derivation is doubtful), hurled his little group like a spear, with himself as the spearhead; and he halted the official force that had come against him. The exploit became a great victory in the eyes of those who had charged. When further government forces came round by the south of Jerusalem to Beth Sur, a long day's march beyond the Holy City, Judas, with an increased band (for victory breeds victory), checked the Royal General again, entered Jerusalem and claimed to rule it.

But it was impossible that under such disability of strength even the most devoted should succeed. For the moment there was a compromise because the lieutenant of Antiochus hesitated how to act in the King's absence. The old Jewish temple-worship of Jehovah was re-established on the third anniversary after they had attempted to supplant it, that is, at the Feast of Light: that 25th December, 164 B.C., was the date of the return. It has never been forgotten.

It was but a breathing space; approaching defeat by the main armies of the Seleucid King was certain; unless Jehovah . . .

Far off in Persia before, or towards the middle of the next year, 163, Antiochus died and his death saved the rebels because Syria fell under divided powers.

Antiochus had named Philip, the General who was with him in the Eastern war and who was now on his way back, to rule Syria. He left the little boy his son under the custody of a Regent. Each of these two men, the General and the Regent, felt Royal power to be attainable; each intrigued for that power, and in the conflict between them, in the growing anarchy, the champions of Jehovah, these determined few, were able to strike.

They struck at random, but they struck deep. The Royal garrison in the citadels at Jerusalem, against the Temple and on the north-western corner of the city wall, held out; but it was hard pressed, and beyond Jordan the Maccabean forces or bands (they who called themselves "The Godly") cleaned up with their knives and torches the heathen, the backsliders and the indifferent. They killed, they burned, they raided, they made themselves terrible all the way down to Idumea. The garrison fled for immediate help and so did the same Judas Maccabeus who was defeated in the field, but again Philip from the east arrived in time to save him; not that the General of Antiochus favoured the rebels, but that he must play for time until the regular forces of government should be assembled and the quarrels of the Greek authorities should cease.

Thus a compromise with the Jewish zealots was maintained; the ancient religion was still fully observed upon the Holy Hill and in the Temple Court, for a new source of weakness appeared on the government side to comfort Judas Maccabeus and his train.

The nephew of the dead Antiochus, son of his elder brother, appeared in Syria, landing at Tripoli, and proclaimed his right to the throne, in the second year after his uncle's death. He was called Demetrius, to which, when he had defeated the usurper in Mesopotamia and recovered the Greek cities there, the inhabitants added the surname Soter—"the saviour".

The slowly advancing but overwhelming power of Rome was concerned to keep up these divisions in Syria lest a powerful kingdom should stand on its frontier. Judas Maccabeus saw the opportunity. He appealed to the Roman Senate to help him. Rome was far off and deliberately tardy in its decision, yet this diplomacy of Judas Maccabeus bore fruit. Young Demetrius (he was only twenty-five) was not yet in power. With the spring of 160 B.C. in the month of March, the Greek General was met by Judas Maccabeus on the main road, a day's march to the north of Jerusalem at Adasa. Once again the Maccabean charge caught him, and in the mêlée the Greek Commander was killed. They cut off his head and hung the bleeding thing up to adorn the Temple of the Most High.

But this first essential chapter of the adventure was coming to an end. Hardly a month had passed when, in the same place, Judas with a handful of eight hundred men still true to his Faith (for the Eternal could give victory as easily to a few as to a myriad) charged and was destroyed, he and his followers. His brothers bore him back to their home a day's march off down the hills to their old home where their father had begun the strife.

The words in which that last action (if the skirmish could be called an action) is described were written down later, but they preserve a battle-song which keeps its strength over the gulf of more than two thousand years. The epic quality, the ballad character, of these small battles gives them greatness.

> The earth was shaken by the shouts of the armies and the fight was from the morning till the evening. Many fell, Judas fell—and the rest fled. Jonathan and Simon took Judas their brother and buried him in the home of his fathers in Modin and all the people of Israel wept for him with loud wailing for many days, saying, "How has the mighty one fallen! He who had saved his people Israel!"

It is of profound interest that after each reverse the inflamed defenders of Jehovah sank in destruction—and were never destroyed.

Over and over again in the next lifetime, and onwards beyond that, it should have been a matter of course to destroy them: a simple matter and an easy one. They were no more than a nuisance—a small, alien, irritant body in the midst of the increasing Western civilisation which was already established in Syria, and which was to make of the Mediterranean the origin of all our own Europe, that is, of Christendom.

The attempt to set up an independent Judæan state in so late a day ought, by every calculation, to have broken down, even in its absurd, fantastic origins. It was worthless in the numbers of those who fought, still more worthless in their lack of judgment: for they were fighting Heaven knows what odds. Yet their effort not only bore fruit but that fruit grew and grew: the Judæan State was at last established. Jerusalem was to be once more a capital (and the Capital of the Most High) after five hundred years: five hundred years which had begun with a wholesale capture and deportation and which had been harried throughout by every kind of interference and misfortune. When the great Judas was dead, and buried in the tomb of his fathers down the hillside on the Joppa road, he died certain that his religion would now stand. There was no further attempt to impose pagan gods upon the Temple Hill.

The Maccabees, the unsubdued and absolute swordsmen, fought on in their scattered little bands. It was not enough for them that Jehovah should be tolerated. He had made the heavens and the earth. He must rule, and all His enemies must be crushed. Though He had but one man left to suffer in the divine cause that man would still fight on.

The bands of the Maccabeans fought on in what small numbers we know not, but with a fierceness undiminished, though now they could only act beyond Jordan in the uplands, in the wilderness, on passing through this in the better lands of Moab to the east and of Idumea to the south.

Of the three brothers who survived, Dan was killed by the Arabs; Simon and Jonathan alone remained. The zealot rebels grew in power to the annoyance of that great body of Jews, the wealthiest (and most enlightened in their own eyes) who were for receiving Greek civilisation and watering down the fiery essence of the old religion. The head of the rebels was tolerated at last: the regular government allowed Jonathan to settle north of Jerusalem.

Once more fortune—or Providence—served the unchanging Maccabean drive. The Syrian monarchy was again in dispute. Demetrius, the true heir, was faced with a usurper. The one was played against the other. Within half a dozen years Demetrius was killed in battle; and as the exhausted Greek parties wore each other down in civil war, the steadfast vision of reestablishing a Judæan State increased. Jonathan annexed Ashdod (which the Greeks called Azotus) and Joppa and Ascalon, and as the chaos of government among the Greeks continued he annexed three districts of the Samaritans to the north.

Jonathan, caught up in one of the factions, was put to death, his brother Simon, who had already been given the title of local General by one of the rival Greek governments, took charge and the sovereignty of an independent Judæan territory was at hand. An assembly of the people was summoned. Simon was given the title of High Priest and Commander. During the quarrel of the Greek leaders one against the other he accepted the further title of "Prince of the People".

The last Greek King with any strong personality attempted to recover Judæa, but he was beaten by Simon's own sons on the family fields of Modin. It was twenty-six years since Judas Maccabeus had fallen at the head of that handful within a few miles of the place whence his family had risen and where he himself lay in the tomb of his fathers.

At last Simon, the last brother of Judas, the High Priest and the real ruler of the new Jerusalem, also met with his death.

The manner of his death is significant.

There was drink in the family. It is a defect which sometimes accompanies genius, and, still more often, enthusiasm. It was in his cups that he was murdered. None the less the Maccabees had achieved their object, and Israel was again a nation.

The son of Simon, John, seized upon the high priesthood after his father's death. The Greek sovereign power besieged

Jerusalem for a year till the city surrendered to famine, and once again in this reiterated story came the apparent certitude of extermination. But that small, hard, indigestible pebble, the zealots, those who still maintained the impossible dream of Judah's survival, were not crushed. They were not crushed because there was beginning to press more and more against the Greek generals of Syria the power of Rome. The Jews were destined to challenge that power also in turn, for they were destined to challenge all powers, and are still challenging them: and Rome was to destroy Jerusalem—but not the Jews.

Rome, whom all feared, would not as yet take sides in Syrian quarrels, but the Greek King Antiochus VII * who might now have made an end of the Judæan thing was compelled by the advance of Rome to hold his hand.

Antiochus VII hesitated to exterminate. He was more afraid of the power of Rome extending through the East than of anything else. Then he went off to what was, for him, as for all his house, the much more important business of defeating his Syrian rivals and, fighting them, he was killed.

Another Greek king succeeded, only to be assassinated in three years. Full chaos followed. The Seleucid power was really at an end. It was thirty-four years since the great attempt at unity of religion in Syria had been made. It had wholly failed, and now in the welter the new Jewish State still grew.

John, the son of Simon, might not yet call himself king, prince only; but he spread the power of Jerusalem northward. He took Samaria, a city mainly Greek, and destroyed its temple. He seized upon Idumea to the south and there enforced the Jewish religion and circumcision.

So thoroughly had the Greek kingdom broken down, so completely had it turned into a turmoil of Syrian cities acting independently, of Arab brigands, of bands calling themselves

---

* He was called the Seventh because between Antiochus IV, "Epiphanes", the man who had attempted to destroy the Jewish worship thirty years before, and himself, there had been two claimants to the throne bearing the same name: the little boy who had been put to death and who was the son of Antiochus IV, called Antiochus V, during the period of struggle between the Greek generals, and the son of Aristobulus, who had been called Antiochus VI.

Seleucid armies, that the further establishment of the Jewish
State went forward unimpeded, although the men presiding
over that progress became more and more base. Judah, who was
also called Aristobulus, murdered three of his brothers and
starved his mother to death: but he conquered Galilee to the
north. His brother Jannai also added to his name the Greek
name Alexander, and openly and for the first time used upon his
coinage the word "king" in Hebrew and in Greek. He put on
his head the Greek emblem of sovereignty, the diadem. He held
his own in face of invasion from Egypt and the last degraded
efforts of the Seleucid power. He held his own. He showed the
taint in his blood, for he also was a drunkard—but he held
his own.

He could boast, in the confusion of his dreams or visions,
that, after five hundred years, since Babylon had wiped out the
old royalty of David, there was again a king in Jerusalem. Under
him the insistence upon Judaic power, the execution of the law
of circumcision, were enforced everywhere. He made secure his
hold down the sea-coast right down to Gaza.

The Maccabees had restored Israel. They were High Priests as
well as Kings. But they were a temporal power and therefore
against them the Spirit rose again.

It rose in the shape of a new set of zealots—the Pharisees. The
new Puritans presented what the Puritan has everywhere presented, a claim to special sanctity against the mass of mankind:
for the word Pharisee meant "a man apart", separate from
others. The Pharisees were behind a Jewish rebellion which
Jannai, that last strength of the Maccabean house, had to meet
and to overcome, as he overcame at last all his enemies. To the
rebels who withstood him he was not merciful. He crucified
them by hundreds and in ranks. He gloated over their deaths
from his palace walls in the north-west of the Holy City.

Such was the fruit borne by that tree which his great-uncle
Judas had planted, when he died at the head of his forlorn hope,
restoring the Kingdom of Jehovah.

After a long reign, Jannai, he who called himself Alexander,
died in the tradition of his family, drunk. His widow, Salome by

name, allied herself with his enemies, the party of the Pharisees, and carried on for five years; but the Maccabean rule was nearly over.

There entered upon the scene a new character—unexpected, well poised, determined, following his ambition with clarity. This newcomer was one Antipater.

He appeared just as the Roman power was at last deciding to play the waiting game no longer but to manifest itself in Syria and to take possession. Antipater was the ancestor of the Herods: the last kings over the Jews: but they were not to be kings of the Jews as the Maccabees had been. They had no tradition of battle nor any glory behind them. For them the right name was found, the name "fox". They were manly, but using their manhood ill. They were intriguers much more than they were athletes.

Antipater was from those high plateaux to the east of the rift valley between the Dead Sea and the Mediterranean—the country of Edom, in the Greek form Idumea. He inherited from his father, who had been made Captain General over that conquered land by the power of Jannai Alexander.

When Salome was dead this Antipater intrigued his way forward between the quarrels of her two sons and the now manifest Roman power in Syria to which they each appealed for support.

In the year 63 B.C. the Roman General Pompey, coming from the heart of the Roman governing classes which everywhere led to a new organisation of the world state, was himself in Damascus and received in person those two rival Maccabean brothers. He concluded for neither (though he took plenty of gold), for he had in view a Syria that should be a province of the now almost completed Roman Empire which was absorbing the Eastern Greek world. That Syria must be one thing, undivided and undisturbed by local factions. Therefore Pompey determined, as less powerful men before him had determined, to flatten out the new Maccabean Jewish kingdom in the south. He marched against Jerusalem.

It took him three months to reduce the town, or rather the hill on which the temple stood. When he had conquered he entered, as Antiochus had done before him, the Holy of Holies. He sold many thousands of his Jewish victims into slavery and of the two brothers who had appealed to him, Aristobulus, the titular King, the last of the Maccabees, was led captive in Pompey's triumph in Rome. The Greek cities of Palestine were liberated. The Jewish State no longer lived save as one division in a province of the Roman world.

In that province one man still remained, retaining the personal advantages and wealth of a titular king—it was Antipater. He, keeping the balance, juggling without error, stood watching to serve whatever power should emerge victorious from the enormous struggle which had arisen between the Roman generals for the mastery of the world.

Now it should be Cæsar, now it should be Pompey. He watched the fluctuations of that civil war between the rival Roman generals which was not to end for twenty years. He was never at fault. He achieved the unworthy award. His son Herod the Great, and Herod's line, are remembered through that hollow achievement.

See how the fortunes of Syria, layer by layer, phase by phase, are leading up to an Event. See how the drama of fifteen hundred years unfolds, act by act, to its climax. The ageless original mass of Asian things, half-conscious. The stirring of that mass by the Egyptian armies marching through. The harvest of new port-cities and little living states. The coming therein, strangely, from the Desert, of Israel. The rolling and mixing and crushing of that soil by Assyria. The bare survival of one small seed, and Israel, in the issue, still surviving after the return from exile to its Holy Hill, a ruined fragment. The resistance and peril of death. The Kingdom restored, and a king still crowned in Jerusalem. A Herod living on till the opening of a new day wherein was consummated in a world now one, and in a Jerusalem now frontier town of Rome, that Sacrifice whereby this same newly united world was to be rekindled and transformed.

If all this be but a blind sequence, never was chance more like design.

X

Rome

ALL SYRIA was now part of a state which covered what we call the ancient world: the whole of that mixture of Italian and Greek influence which made up the civilisation of the Mediterranean.

To that unity we give the name, "The Roman Empire". There were still a few years to run before an Imperial Governor should stand in the place of the local kinglet over Jewry, Herod the Great. He had still some years to live, and it was not until a couple of years after his death that the last nominal title of a separate Jewish State, the last symbol of Jewish nationality, disappeared; and that the so-called Kingdom of Herod the Great (already in reality the mere fragment of a Roman province) was taken over for direct administration by the central power.

Even so, there was a shadowy sort of resurrection permitted by the Emperors. A grandson of Herod the Great was allowed to call himself King over some part of the district; and even after the temple had been destroyed forever a great-grandson of Herod was calling himself "King" on his coins and inscriptions—prudently adding "Friend of Cæsar and of the Romans".

As the times are accomplished for this coalescence of all our world into one great State, and as all that follows—the Passion, the Crucifixion and the Resurrection, the birth of the Church, its progress and its ultimate triumph—takes place within that State, we must ask ourselves of what nature it was. Why had this word "Rome"—no more than the name of one Italian city—come to mean so much? What is signified by that later term, "Roman Empire", wherein we express the achievement of unity by our race? What was that which set out the scene for the Incarnation and was called in the end Christendom?

We must not be deceived by that word "Empire". Seeing

how fixed the unity of our civilisation became, how strong was the authority at its centre, that is in Rome itself; and reading of the perpetual wars through which the whole thing had developed, men cannot but imagine the Roman Empire to be the result of a continuous fixed purpose, a sort of tyrannical conspiracy against those who were at last all brought under one rule. We think of some highly localised and distinctive thing called "Rome" proceeding to "conquer" the world. That misconception is one more example of an inevitable error, the most difficult of all to avoid in judging the past—the error called "reading history backwards".

Because we who live after know that Napoleon Buonaparte came to be what he was, we can hardly prevent ourselves from imagining him plotting the whole affair. But Napoleon, the young Lieutenant of Guns, was only concerned with immediate promotion. Napoleon, proving by good fortune the victor of Marengo, was not yet determined upon autocracy, still less upon the title of a Monarch: not at all upon the conquest of Europe.

Because we, living after, know that England became wholly and intensely Protestant, we cannot but imagine the origins of the Reformation in England to have been designed to that end; and we think of England under Elizabeth as though it were already what it only became nearly a century after Elizabeth was dead—and after a fashion which Elizabeth herself never dreamed of.

So too with the Roman Empire. Because we who come after know that it was universal, spreading from its centre the town of Rome and retaining the highest political authority in that centre for centuries, we cannot but imagine that which was a destiny planned by Heaven to have been a scheme planned by men.

It was not so. There was no fixed purpose in the mind of any man to call this Roman order into being. It came into being through perpetual necessities, based first upon a very small group, then upon a larger and still larger one; necessities of defence, necessities of alliance, necessities of choice between extinction or expansion. Rome was an organism that grew, and that grew by the action of forces not consciously aimed at the end which was reached.

As it grew it did not crush, it absorbed. It did not become the master of discontented and embittered victims; it became the expression of their common lives: all the lives of the millions who were proud to be at the best Roman citizens (and at last all free men became so) but proud at any rate to be part of that universal policy the grandeur of which inspired all its members.

The first stages of this growth do not directly concern the history and divine fate of Syria. "Rome" (to use that general term) does not concern us here directly till the shadow of its wings was first thrown over that hill country of the Orient. But we must have some idea of how it grew in order to understand its spirit, and above all that high military tradition which it permanently preserved.

The beginning of the affair was the coalescence of certain little tribes in mid-Italy round their principal market; it was not so much one city as a group of hamlets crowning detached portions of hilly ground on the left bank of the Tiber, a day's march inland from the sea. The site was a natural centre. The only river of Central Italy navigable for a few miles up from its mouth was here marked by an island; the island made easier the throwing of a bridge from shore to shore. With such a crossing place established, high enough upstream to be free of the marshes at the river mouth, traffic came from north and south to the bridge and by water down the current and up from the sea: the Bridge of Rome became a nodal point.

Fairly central to the group of hamlets was a depression where men could meet, lying low and therefore at first rather marshy, but later drained and made firm for the purposes of assembly and market. This was the Forum.

Among the separate heights was one more easily defensible than the rest; upon one side it was actually precipitous, though of no great height. This was what the Greeks would have called the Acropolis of the little group, and which the inhabitants called their "Head Hill"—their "Capitol". Thereon stood the temple of their chief god.

Upon another low summit close at hand, the Palatine, the first square enclosure had arisen. Soon the whole group of hamlets was conscious of its unity, and acted as one city. It had Kings drawn from the high Etruscan culture immediately to the north, whence also came the mysteries of its religion. These Kings were expelled and their old authority was taken over by an arrangement which was not peculiar to this town, for it was of a sort that one would find in any other of the Italian centres; but it was an arrangement, or local constitution, the fortunes of which have made it famous.

This constitution was not (as has often been pretended) aristocratic. Authority did not lie in the hands of a class of wealthy citizens accepted as a matter of course by the mass of poorer people: it was much more complex and vital than that. There was indeed such a class, and it has been conjectured that this class (the "Patricians", that is, the men with lineage: "Descendants") represented the original owners of houses and land, who only admitted as inferiors later immigrants taken into the growing city. But the mark of Rome from the beginning was the activity of all, Patricians and non-Patricians, in claiming their share in actual government.

A large standing committee of Patricians, called "the Elders", "the Senate", very soon came to be—perhaps was from the beginning—mixed. As the town increased it was necessary that this committee should exercise more and more power; but at the same time this governing committee, the Senate, took in men who had passed through the higher official positions, and these were of every class. The Senate was not an aristocratic thing, still less had the people whom it governed what is called the "aristocratic spirit"—that is, a distaste for political power in the mass of citizens: that desire in the poor to be governed by the rich which is the mark of aristocratic states. Offices were in part elective, and the sense of patriotism in the common life was stronger by far than the sense of social difference.

The source of this spirit, which was the special strength of the Romans, was their character of a *Peasantry*. They were a confederation of free farmers, and such yeomen—"freeholders" as we

should call them in modern English—had to defend their possessions against other small groups, other neighbouring villages,
even organised little towns not far off from them; and also
against brigandage.

Therefore from the beginning these peasants were also soldiers. They were only quite intermittently soldiers, coming in to
serve when the necessities of defence summoned them; but
those occasions were so numerous that a military organisation
arose among them, and with it that sense of equality which the
military habit breeds. For though the officering of the little
bands during their few days or weeks of service was largely
drawn from the wealthier people, command was not a function
of wealth. It was a function of military efficiency; it had to be so,
otherwise they would not have won the little battles in which
they were ceaselessly engaged. The higher command, the control of the whole force, was merely official and continued to be
so for a very long time, long after the Army had changed in
character and the Roman State had become a great Mediterranean power. But the company, and what we should call the
battalion, were wholly military in discipline and command.

This little military peasant state was the market and the largest
town and natural leader of a broad plain on the edges of which it
stood. A considerable territory, some two days' march across
either way, say seven hundred square miles, much of it arable
and all of it open save for an island of hilly land in its middle.
The men who lived in and tilled this plain called it "The
Broad", *Latium*; and themselves the "Inhabitants of the Broad",
Latini, Latins. Rome became the natural leader of all these, and
though the term "Roman" was kept, it really stood for the mass
of men in this agglomeration.

Things were in this state when a violent incident shook all
Northern Italy: the Gauls came pouring in over the Alps—a
people still half barbaric. They sacked Rome, and, very unfortunately for history, the old records were destroyed. Though
it nearly engulfed that society, the tide receded. The disaster,
perhaps, led to the building of walls round the now closely
inhabited and large territory of the city, perhaps only fortifying

walls already built. Anyhow the military strength thus added made for further increase in the body, which under the title of "Roman" was to come to mean "Italian".

The time during which all this was going on, the coalescence of the hamlets, the fortifying of the first square enclosure on the Palatine, the Gaulish invasion, was the three hundred years, or rather less, corresponding to the Assyrian and Persian rule over Syria. The traditional date for the founding of Rome was half a lifetime after the date when Tiglath-Pileser crossed the Euphrates and began his final conquest of the Syrian belt. The invasion of the Gauls came towards the end of the Persian power in Syria; fifty years before Alexander struck his first blow. But as yet what was happening in Italy meant nothing to the Orient.

The Roman State threw out agricultural colonies of its citizens, groups of farmers migrating to settle elsewhere and to organise themselves on the model of the place whence they had come. Thus there were villages, and towns with their surrounding territory, called "Roman", though they were beyond the Central Italian mountains, the Apennines, and settled on the eastern side of the country, while Rome is on the western side. The hill tribes between felt themselves to be hemmed in.

They attempted to check the growth of what menaced them with absorption, they even tried to call in the Gauls (who in their retirement had settled in Lombardy, to the north); but the Roman State was already too strong for them, as it was for all the sporadic efforts at disassociation within itself: and before the end of another hundred years these hill tribes had been forced into the growing coalition. Though they were Italian their dialects were not the same as that of the Latins; but they soon fitted in, and, a few years after the time when Alexander's generals were dividing his Empire among themselves, ten years after Seleucus had founded Antioch, the mass of Italians grouped under Rome and, organised by her, included all middle Italy. That group had now a very large recruiting field, a first-rate military tradition and the consciousness of being a State. It had, in spite of different classes and varied elements, a rooted sense of unity.

Meanwhile the Greek civilisation had been expanding, not

only, as we have seen, all over the East, but long before that in the foundation of Greek cities westward.

There were many such in South Italy, which men were to come to call "greater Greece"; there were some in Sicily; there was even one far off near the mouths of the Rhône. Of those who had inherited from the great Macedonian traditions, the Hellenistic world, one Pyrrhus, King of an Albanian realm on the Adriatic opposite Italy, proposed to unite all that western Greek colonial world into one. Here again the Roman thing (it would be by this time wrong to think of it as a town or even a city-state, it had become something like a nation, though under the organisation of the city and its officers) had to defend itself. It did not set out to conquer, but it had to survive, and could only do so by defence and counterattack against the designs of Pyrrhus upon Italian soil.

It succeeded, although it had no fleet and although Pyrrhus had inherited and used the Macedonian military formation. It could not have done so perhaps if Pyrrhus had aimed at Rome for his one objective; but he had not done so, he had aimed at uniting the Greek cities—and Rome survived the shock. Pyrrhus won battles, but they bore no fruit, he had to go back home. The Roman State, to prevent the recurrence of such a peril, took over by consent and sometimes by violence the Greek States of the Italian mainland; and after Tarentum in the extreme south had been absorbed you may say that all the mainland from as far north as the Arno, that is, from where Pisa and Florence now stand, southward to the end of the peninsula, was *Rome*.

Now this was a formidable extension in revenue and recruiting power. "Rome" was now a really large State, having behind it a prolonged and well-exercised military tradition. On this account another apparently greater power, long since present in the western Mediterranean, inevitably became the rival of Rome.

The city of Carthage had been founded by Syrian colonists from Tyre, the Phœnician port, somewhat before the beginnings of Rome. The traditional date for the foundation of

Rome (which it is wise to accept, as it is wise to accept all traditions until they be disproved) was 753 B.C. Carthage was apparently founded about a century earlier. That was their traditional date, and the Phœnicians had a high civilisation at the time, which gives solidity to the tradition.

Carthage, unlike Rome, was aristocratic. It was a merchant city, again unlike Rome, which was military; it had to hire soldiers to fight for it, though the governing class were patriotic enough and themselves would fight on occasion, and produced good leaders and *one* supreme general. But Carthage had not the military temper, still less the tradition of a peasantry, as Rome had. It was immensely wealthy through exchange, and it was, at this moment when Rome was welding all Central and Southern Italy into one State, three times bigger even than Rome itself in area and numbers. It had founded emporiums and counting houses far from its own site, scattered on the shores of the Mediterranean Sea, commercial centres of the sort which Phœnician cities established everywhere.

The contrast and the corresponding latent conflict between Carthage and Rome went much deeper, however, than a contrast in the political system; it was even deeper than the contrast between merchants and soldiers; for there was a profound antagonism in *religion*—that is, in all social structure and morals between the Phœnician and the Græco-Roman world.

What the Phœnician religion was we have seen: and its horror. The mind that made it and was made by it was odious to the mind of our race; the one could not live in permanent contact with the other. That was the true root of the quarrel; not commercial rivalry, still less the mere desire for domination. For Carthage did not desire domination, but the occupation of naval key-points in order to exploit territory and to make money. And the many merchants of the new enlarged Roman State, though active for gain in the parts they knew, were not yet hungry for fresh markets. They had even an arrangement with Carthage, each set of traders keeping to their own ports.

Nor did the Roman State aim at domination. It acted as it did because it could only continue to live by the incorporation of groups which were not natively hostile but similar to itself. The Roman State was further the natural protector of those Greek west-colonial cities which, not being on the mainland of Italy, had not joined it. For those Greek cities, particularly in Sicily (Syracuse and Messina) for instance, were pressed upon by Carthage; and the Carthaginians, like not only all the Phœnicians but all the peoples of Oriental blood, were quite ruthless. They would destroy and massacre at large. It was not for nothing that their god was Moloch.

Carthage, then, was threatening the life of the Greek civilisation in the west before Rome had taken over that civilisation on the mainland of Italy. Carthage was now, about ten years after the retirement of Pyrrhus, threatening the life of the Greek cities in Sicily: and this at a moment when Greek culture had begun to penetrate, transform and ennoble the Roman power. Sicily was on the point of becoming Carthaginian; and with Sicily Carthaginian, considering the strength Carthage then had, the newly enlarged Roman State could not hold.

Carthage menaced in particular Messina: that meant the control of the Straits and the destruction of the first of the Greek cities. Carthage, during a quarrel between Messina and Syracuse, threw a garrison into Messina. Rome had no fleet nor had as yet dreamed of one. The Carthaginians boasted that the Romans could not wash their hands in the sea without Carthaginian leave. But now, for the first time in history, a Roman Army crossed the sea; and a duel had begun in which, as invariably happens, throughout history, the power which trusts in command of the sea ends in defeat.

The Roman Army which thus first crossed the sea was a very different thing from the strong but primitive little peasant force which the Rome of generations before had created. Not only was the recruiting field vastly larger and the numbers correspondingly larger also, but the qualification of a soldier was no longer his yeoman position on the land; the Roman recruiting officers would now take pretty well any freeman whom they thought sufficiently established. In fighting the Macedonian phalanx of Pyrrhus (which had badly defeated them) the Romans developed a new and elastic formation. The *Legion*, which was the Roman military unit (of about six thousand men), and which had originally been conceived as a solid body, like the contemporary phalanx of the Greeks, fought in three lines, that is, a front line with reserves behind it; and each of these three lines was subdivided into smaller units with spaces between allowing for lateral movement and for the unhampered filling of gaps in the line by the reserve body behind it. Moreover Rome, in spite of her distaste for the sea, now added to transports a fighting fleet.

That fleet had varying fortunes; it began with victory, it suffered defeat which ended in victory again; and indeed the close of the war and the defeat (though only the partial defeat) of Carthage in the struggle (it had lasted twenty-three years) was due to a naval battle. It was a very great effort, and only just successful; but it was successful in the end. Two hundred of the largest men-of-war were created by private subscription when the public finances of the Roman State were almost exhausted.

The Carthaginian fleet upon which the very life of Carthage depended was destroyed by this last thrust. Carthage consented to the payment of an indemnity and to the abandonment of Sicily. Rome, with the sea now open to her, occupied Sardinia and Corsica lest they should become for the Carthaginians what Sicily had been. By land, the Roman power rounded off all the Italian territory, taking over the Gauls of Lombardy, as it had taken over the Greeks of the south.

There had been in this first of Rome's Mediterranean wars a victory, but no decision. Carthage still stood, and began to build up again the foundations for a new war. She established a solid occupation on the shores of Spain, and it was there that one of her young nobles, a boy from one of the highest commercial families (the Barcas), by name Hannibal, whose father was Governor of the Spanish coast, prepared a revenge. He was one of the young conquerors, like Napoleon Buonaparte or Alexander, a lad of twenty-four. He gathered a host of hired men, drawn from every source; and, not having the sea open to him, he made for Italy from Spain by land.

He crossed the Alps, won victory after victory over the armies of Rome sent to defend her territory, and even persuaded some of her allies and subjects on the mainland to rebel. He destroyed one Roman Army after another, threatened Rome itself, but had no siege train for the attack. He urgently needed reinforcements in spite of his triumphs; the Roman Army, perpetually renewed after defeat, intercepted these reinforcements and Hannibal was compelled (as Pyrrhus had been) to abandon Italy, but not until the Romans had themselves invaded the territory of Carthage in Africa. There, at the very end of the third century B.C., the mercenary army which Carthage had gathered and in which there fought, for once, troops from the ranks of the wealthy Carthaginians themselves, was destroyed at Zama in 202 B.C.

Rome allowed the commercial city to live on, but she doubted the wisdom of her toleration. For the commercial genius of the Phœnician blood survived even these disasters; and its wealth—which is one form of power—increased. Hannibal, exiled, and without an armed man to use, continued the struggle.

He urged those Greek generals who had inherited the Empire of Alexander to withstand this new overwhelming power which had arisen in the West; for the Roman State, having won its great duel, was without a rival outside the Hellenistic East. Macedon, the old leader of the eastern Greek world, attempted the task and failed. A Roman Army triumphed over the phalanx at Cynoscephalæ in Thessaly, and Antiochus Epiphanes, the same that had provoked Judæa and its religion, acting in Asia Minor, attempted to stop the tide. A Roman Army met his close on the coast of the Ægean, at the edges of his territory, outside the town of Magnesia, below Sardis; and Antiochus had to fall back beyond what had been the old boundary of Assyrian rule, the river Halys.

Thus during the time of the Maccabees the shadow of Rome was already thrown over the Orient. It was certain that Roman influence at last, and perhaps Roman direct power, would appear in the Greek world of Syria and in the Greek world of

Egypt, though the issue was delayed for more than a hundred years by the changes and perils through which the newly expanded Roman organisation was to pass and the civil war in which the newly organised and vastly increased Roman Army was to engage.

What happened to the suddenly expanded Roman area was this: violent internal strains and the threat of dislocation through its very success in expansion.

The organisation called "Roman" had come to cover all Italy, the old historic Greece of Europe, the Grecian Ægean coast in Asia, and the islands of the Mediterranean Sea. There had been an immense increase of revenue, a corresponding increase in the places open to prominent men of the Roman Republic; these had now opportunity for making rapid fortunes as local governors. There had been a corresponding increase in the large class of tax-gatherers who could and did enrich themselves by their office, in the money-dealings of rich men, in distant trade enterprise and in the sums paid to contractors for the Army. In every direction there was this cataclysmic pouring in of wealth to the advantage of a privileged class, comparatively small.

With that change in the social affairs of the Western world, and particularly of Italy, went capitalistic enterprise, the growth of a large destitute class, the increase in the proportion of slaves to free men (for all ancient civilisation was based upon slavery) and, what was more disturbing than anything else, the impoverishment of the yeomanry who had been the basis not only of the Roman Republic but of all the Italian world save in the Greek cities of the south.

Those now impoverished Roman farmers who were also Roman citizens found it intolerable that they should be growing poorer and dependent, just when the State of which they were members and of which they were proud was entering such great new destinies and gazing upon an horizon so widely enlarged.

That was the economic side of the revolution now pending. The political side of the disturbance lay in this, that the political rights of Italian men still lay in separate categories. There were

THE ROMAN EMPIRE AT THE DEATH OF DIOCLETIAN, A.D. 305

the full Roman citizens, there were the associated states and cities allied with the Roman citizens and furnishing the armies with numbers at least as great as the citizens themselves, and yet not enjoying the same full political rights.

Another separate trouble, going on side by side with all this, was the increasing tension between the governing committee called the Senate, largely patrician and in general wealthy, and the mass of the Roman populace. All these things combined led to a hundred years of internal violence—133 B.C. to 30 B.C.— which did not end until all our Western society from Syria to the Atlantic had settled down as a monarchy under one military head. There was violent fighting between the Italians with full citizenship and the Italians with lesser political rights, between the faction of the Senate and the faction of the populace. There was oppression in the newly occupied provinces oversea follow- ing upon gross abuses; and on the top of all this there was the threat, against Western civilisation as a whole, of irruption by barbarians from beyond its frontiers.

It was this danger which provoked the turning point in the whole affair. Roman administration had triumphed every- where, even in Greece, because it was military; now a general who had sprung from the people and who, in the quarrels of the time, represented the popular party, Marius, successfully met the irruption of the barbarians and at the same time trans- formed the Army.

Two great mixed hordes of Germans and Slavs poured in, the one down the Rhône valley, the other across the Alps into Italy itself; Marius destroyed both of them utterly, as the barbarians were always destroyed by the Roman Armies from the begin- ning to the end. Both because he was the leader of the popular party and because of his victorious record, he was given power to do what he would; and what he did was to make the Roman Army a long-service professional force on a new model. It was divorced from the elective machinery, which still clumsily creaked on in an attempt to continue the politics of the old and simpler peasant days. The Roman Army henceforward was a body of men highly disciplined, permanent, mobile both for rapid strategical movement from place to place and for tactical movement upon the field of battle. The distinctions of social rank and the distinction between various strata in the service disappeared; there remained only the function of command and the hierarchy of officers.

A Roman Army henceforward, in the last century B.C. (roughly from the time when Marius had defeated the barbarians, 102 B.C., to the establishment, in 30 B.C., of one commander-in-chief as master over all the Roman world), was a thing living its own life and dominating every other factor in the State, because it was a perfectly united organism and its commander could handle it at will.

But there were more than one such Army, because Rome had to take action now over so wide a territory. An Army sent to fight in the East would have its own commander; a man fighting on the borders of Italy against the barbarians would have *his* own Army; a provincial governor occupying a still-disputed district was independent master of *his* group of forces— the civilian power faded in the presence of such realities. It was inevitable that those who showed the greater military skill or who commanded a larger group of legions should establish their superiority over rival generals.

Individuals had come to control what was vital in the State: Armies—and Armies now disassociated from the mass of the population through whom they moved and whose fate they decided.

In the conflict of appetites, political passions, and lingering traditions of ancient local independence, there followed a whole century filled with the clash of armies under leaders, each the general of his own force.

The welter of revolution and civil war which seems to fill the whole story has led historians to forget the much more remarkable point that the Roman Empire not only survived but was the field wherein all this disturbance took place. The legions met and fought each other in the interests of this leader and that, the victory of each group serving the interest of its commander who rewarded his soldiers with spoils and subsidy. The story appears to be one of mere chaos. But it was not so; for if there had been chaos there would have been dissolution—and on the contrary, the new universal Roman State, founded on the victory over Carthage and the advance to the East, stood firm in spite of all internal violence.

That is the true note of the time; not the struggle in Italy which ended in the recognition of the allied peoples as equal to the Romans, not the quarrels between rival commanders and their victories, but the survival of the Universal State.

The old rules of election, the passing of laws by the traditional authorities, the granting of commissions from those authorities to command armies, even the establishment of the successful dictatorships, popular and aristocratic, with their accompaniment of massacre and civil turmoil, still kept alive an unbroken tradition. The Roman State, enormously expanded, was taken for granted. Within its framework all these whirlpools turned outrageously, but without disturbing its boundaries or its unity—any more than the fiercest storms disturb the boundaries or the unity of the sea.

But within the internal welter of that revolutionary century, when the sudden expanding of one great State over all the Mediterranean world had so violently strained its structure, there was a natural and permanent division to be distinguished. To the west of the Adriatic, Italy, the official Latin language, the Roman system unbroken though enlarged, ruled everywhere. East of the Adriatic that Greek civilisation which Rome revered, which instructed Rome and informed all its spirit, continued with its own language, its one high culture, the architecture and philosophy of which was to permeate in time the West as it had long permeated the East.

The Greek rhythms in verse, the Greek column, Greek sculpture, were to be universal; and meanwhile the Greek language as a medium, and the external aspect of the Greek world, ruled throughout the East of the Mediterranean Sea. The whole air was Greek, in old Greece itself, in Asia Minor, in Syria, in Egypt.

There was also this difference between the two halves of this world, that if in what has been called "The Revolutionary

Century" the West was torn by wars, those wars were the protests of the men who demanded to be Roman. But the wars that took place in the eastern half of the new domain were nothing of the kind. They were the protests of men who were determined to be not Roman in speech or manner but of their own Greek kind.

About half-way through that revolutionary century, after the proscriptions and the massacres of rival dictators, the popular dictator Marius and the senatorial dictator Sulla, the central power had to undertake a struggle of a special kind—the maintenance of its influence in the East. On the southern shores of the Black Sea, the State of Pontus and its King stood out for independence against what was rapidly becoming the one necessary State common to all civilised men. This energetic King, Mithridates, gives his name to the three wars which had to be fought before Rome could be moderately certain of security on her Asiatic frontiers.

The man who triumphed in the East against such a peril was an able general who had risen in the service of the Senatorial Party during the Civil Wars: that Pompey whose name we have heard in the final annexation of Syria to Rome. Pompey's campaigns in Asia Minor, his ultimate victory, made men think of him for the moment as an Alexander. It is remarkable that he went so far as with his own eyes to look upon the Caspian. But his object, and that of the Roman order which he served, was not mere extension of territory—far from that. The Roman temper in the East was much more for consolidation and restriction; it could not turn into a Latin thing the Greek spirit or the Asiatic masses which that spirit dominated and informed; it was content to make certain of order within such an area as it could certainly administer.

For indeed conservation was the conscious but vigorous instinct running through all this sudden spreading out of the system called Roman. It was not occupied in conquest; it was occupied from the beginning in self-defence through organisation. It took in what was hostile in so far as what was hostile would admit alliance and a common spirit; it did not destroy save where the whole spirit of the opponent was mortally opposed, as with the worshippers of Moloch and their abhorrent rites, or where the betrayal of a treaty made the central government fear that if the betrayer were spared its own authority would be undermined. Thus when Mithridates appealed to the lingering individual traditions of the Greek cities, and when Athens stood a siege, Rome still revered Athens, and Athens continued to be for many hundred years the accepted spiritual light of Rome: but Corinth, which was held to have betrayed, was destroyed.

So it was now in the East; the Romans conquered the Asiatic reaction, Pompey, victorious in the war against the King of Pontus, made no effort at destruction, but only at administration. Before his occupation of Syria the tottering, disintegrated, Seleucid dynasty had disappeared. The last dynasty of the Alexandrian generals lingered on with the Ptolemies of Egypt.

Rome was in no haste to inherit from the one in Syria, though she was compelled to inherit it; still less to make an end of the other in Egypt, though that other must come to an end at any moment. It was only by leave of a system which was now coincident with the whole of the ancient world that any shadow of local independence remained; for indeed the old feeling of the City State, the local patriotisms, had worn down near to nothingness after the first universal effort of Alexander and his successors. Wherever strong emotions whether of religious or civil tradition remained, Rome respected them as a condition of government. How striking that was in the case of the Jews, where she did everything to meet half-way an irreducible opposition!

Syria then, the house of Seleucus ended and forgotten, had become a Roman thing half a lifetime before that "Century of Revolution" ended. To make Syria more particularly Roman, to make indeed those hills a frontier of Rome, there took place the loss of what lay beyond the desert.

Syria had been Eastern until the full tide of the Alexandrian conquest had impressed it with the stamp of the West. Even after that conquest the march of the Greek Armies far into Asia, to the Indus, left it possible for Syria to fall back into Asia and to be lost to us, as it was indeed lost to us at last when the Mohammedan came. But for the moment the communion between Europe and Syria was saved by a disaster falling on the Roman Armies which ventured farther.

It was more than ten years after Pompey had appeared in Damascus as a master, forging the affairs of the Jewish State and of all the Syrian land into one, that a Roman Army adventured beyond the Euphrates, and was destroyed.

One of the leading Romans, especially prominent from his great wealth, was Crassus. He had shared the central power in a shifting fashion with rivals; for though the competition between leaders was bound to end at last in the rule of one man, that consummation had not yet been reached. Crassus then, already old, not without energy but losing judgment, attempted a campaign eastward to fix the boundary of the new universal Roman State at least so far as Mesopotamia and beyond the desert. He marched eastward with more than forty thousand men, along the habitable land lying to the south of the mountains, to the north of the desert—the belt along which the Assyrian Armies had marched, the other way, westward, throughout the old centuries. He crossed the Euphrates not far from the town of Carrhæ, on the edges of the wilderness; the swarm of Oriental light-horsemen poured out against him, and destroyed his command.

He himself did not return; perhaps a quarter of his unhappy Army got back to safety from the wild. That day of Carrhæ fixed for many hundred years the horizon of Rome to the east. The Euphrates was to be in future the main line of a fluctuating boundary; a frontier, often with difficulty defended, sometimes traversed so that territory beyond it was held, but never permanently held.

The civil troubles within the Roman State continued; the great generals allied themselves and pitted themselves one against the other; Cæsar, the most able of them, who had extended the Roman system up to the English Channel and taken over all France, was murdered in the welter; Antony, entangled in

Egypt, was challenged by the young Octavian, Cæsar's heir, and he and his Cleopatra, the last of the Ptolemies, were defeated at sea in the Adriatic. The young Octavian was now the sole commander of all that vast society and the legions upon which it stood.

Unity had come at last, and peace for men: an accepted thing—a general country of which all were members, from the Euphrates to the Atlantic and from the Sahara to the waters of the Channel. Its monarch, since it was a thing made by soldiers, was the head of the soldiers, their commander-in-chief. This young Octavian, Imperator (a word which had become the Latin title for the highest command over an Army), Cæsar's great-nephew and inheritor of Cæsar's claims, was unchallenged. The Empire had come into being: that visible body of Europe which was later to be Christendom, our common state, the consciousness of which, even after wounds which would seem mortal, has not yet failed.

Octavian ruled for many years; from this sudden glorious youth of his with its triumph for him when he was in his thirties, to far into his seventies, when he died. He exercised active power for forty-four years: from 30 B.C. to A.D. 14. He is called with justice the first of the Roman Emperors. It was his wisdom and his foresight which made the scheme permanent. It was made permanent by intelligent dealing with the exhaustion which had fallen upon the world after a century of internal violence, and civil war everywhere from Spain to the Orient.

He kept the names of things. He ruled nominally by the authority of the Senate, from whom he obtained the many offices which he gathered into his own hands; it was their decree which made him the head of the legions, the *Princeps* (or Chief Man) of the citizens; it was they who gave him the name he has borne in history, Augustus. He even maintained the now useless form of voting, which under him was still gone through by such citizens as were present. The dying symbol of popular elective power was preserved as long as it could be, and only disappeared under his successor, when no life or reality remained in it at all.

Augustus's name stands among those very few who have used power wisely; who have combined power with right; among those very few who have aimed consistently at the good of those under their obedience. But if he was thus morally eminent and great in statesmanship, he was greater still in good fortune, coming as he did at the exhaustion of a society determined upon peace. He had an unhampered field in which to work, and none could hinder his consolidation of the new Universal State.

In one thing only was he unfortunate—or of bad judgment; he could not (it is perhaps more true to say that he would not) create the best defensive frontier for that civilisation which was destined to be the Christian world. He did excellently on the east, where vassal kingdoms or direct rule lay between the Roman power and the Persians, with the Euphrates for boundary. To the south, nature had given Rome her boundaries, for the desert stretching from the Persian Gulf to the Atlantic was impassable—and none as yet imagined that it would ever breed hostile armies. To the west, and all along the coasts of the Channel and the North Sea, the boundary was of water which no aggressor as yet proposed to cross. But what of the gap between the North Sea and the Euxine?

For all the eastern part of this gap the best boundary was obvious, it was the river Danube. But some good defensive line must be drawn from the Danube to the northern coasts of the Germans. Here again the line was obvious, it was the river line running through Bohemia, the line of the Elbe. That famous general of whom Augustus was the great-nephew and the heir, Julius Cæsar, in conquering Gaul had established the provisional boundary of the Rhine; but to make civilization secure the barbaric German tribes between the Rhine and the Elbe had to be organized. The Roman power had advanced therein and had begun to establish itself, when one check made it abandon its hold—to the lasting misfortune of our world.

A confused legal man, civilian in temper, was given the command, blundered with three legions in the wastes of forest and morass—and lost himself and them. That care for the defensive which was the inspiration of all Roman policy from the beginning overmastered the political sense of Augustus. He sent north into the German wastes his step-son, Tiberius (the man who was later to succeed him as Emperor), and Tiberius, an excellent and even a great soldier, restored the Roman prestige. But he had no orders to re-occupy. The Empire abandoned the uncultured land that lay between the Rhine and that much shorter frontier of the Elbe; it remained unorganised and barbaric.

For the rest, all that Augustus ruled was, before he died, in majesty and at peace. The noise of armies had ceased, and there lay over the world a silence pregnant with something to come: it was the silence of those mornings when, after winter, there comes a waft of genial air and a sense of growth is all around. This beneficence covered also the eastern bastion of Rome, the long Syrian hills, Lebanon and the highlands of Palestine.

Syria: Let me repeat her story now that we reach its term.

For these thousands of years that ancient country had stood along its sea, between the waters and the great desert, peopled we know not how and sprung from we know not what origins; its separated small fertile bays, its lesser plains, its hill cities and ports had grown. The plough of Egypt had come in and ploughed for four centuries; there had arisen a harvest of various polities, small but full of life, and among them Israel, a newcomer from the desert. Assyria had moulded, crushed, levelled, still further prepared that ground; and in doing so would seem to have destroyed all patriotisms, and even the Jewish hope, kept alive in one small corner almost to the end, but, under the last of Babylon, extinguished. That little flame had been coaxed to life again; Israel through the act of Persia had returned. Greece had flooded in, beneficent, life-giving, and the spirit of Greece conquered and occupied all—save Judah; and even in Judah the Grecian columns arose and the power of the Greek tongue was everywhere. Then had been accomplished fulness under the name of Rome, and the world was one.

Some thirty years or a little less after the peace of Augustus began there was born to an obscure young woman from Galilee (who had come down with her older husband for the census to Bethlehem, the little town just south of Jerusalem) a man-child. The purpose of Syria was accomplished.

The Desire of the everlasting hills had come.

XI

The Climax

THERE STOOD a small, square, white, one-storeyed house
upon the north-western shore of the Sea of Galilee, where
the little fringe of gravel at the waterside meets the grass of the
field.

In a bare white-washed room thereof, towards the water, a
young man sat reading from a roll. He was short and thickset,
with black hair not worn too long but copious and curling. His
eyes also were black and very bright. His name was Yakoub and
he was a student in the Divinity of Israel. It was already dark. He
read by the light of a graceful lamp in bronze, perfect in shape
and Greek, but having no figures carved upon it.

There came a slight evening air from off the mountains to the
east beyond the lake; very small waves lapped rhythmically, and
the leaves in the old olive trees just barely rustled. Through the
large open windows, unglazed, of that low room, came another
sound also—that of music, floating up over the water from
Magdala: distant flutes and harps.

He rose and went to the window, and looked out over the
lake. All the miles of the shore up to the north, to his left, round
opposite and so on to the southern edge, six miles away, were an
almost continuous ring of buildings and gardens twinkling with
lights and gleaming in the dusk; square ancient houses, temple
façades, and the lines of new Corinthian columns. All the
landscape of that night was one of wealth and of pleasure in the
first flowers of the year—for it was very early spring. The distant
murmur from the nearer towns which the water brought so
clearly, the distant music and the lanterned gardens filled all that
rounded shore under the great hills, and the waters reflected the
lights along them, so that this oval seemed a place set apart for all
that security could give the fortunate of beauty and of joy.

There was much more than that, he knew, in the evening
over which he gazed; the villas and the colonnades, the wrought
bronzes and marbles, the gleaming steps, the gardens, were
the framework—but there was also the business of Tiberias itself
to his right, the largest group of buildings on the lake-side. And
within that framework the craftsmen were still at their last work
at their benches, the fishermen were setting out into the deep,
with oars plashing, sails hardly filled, for the night's labour.
There were the shop-keepers of every sort, a good half of
them ministering to luxury; there were the learned, all the
group of every age who in each place studied and debated
the law of Israel; and there were the pagan philosophers and
the rhetoricians, the poets and the teachers in schools—Greek
for the most part: Syrian Greek but Greeks also from the Islands
and even from Athens. There were the very poor crowded
into their alleys, where the towns stood in almost continuous
succession, the suburbs of one meeting the suburbs of its neighbour. There stood, apart, in groves or splendidly upon their
terraces, the palaces of the very wealthy men, some of them
from far overseas, from Italy itself, who thought of this place as a
Paradise.

As he stood there, looking into the night, there walked in
upon him a friend. He welcomed that friend warmly, but
poured out no wine, for the visitor was a Greek—and Torah
was Torah. Yet clearly they were friends, these two young men,
and their friendship was the stronger from the contrast between
them. For the one, so certainly a Jew, short but strong in figure,
and so dark in hair and beard, and with such piercing eyes, had
before him a man of fair skin, yellow hair (as were so many from
the Islands), with a mouth far less full, the nose leaner, straighter,
and more in line with the forehead than would have been seen
in a Syrian born. His parents (he was an only son) were from
Cyprus, his father a merchant who had retired and built a villa
for himself in Magdala, the pleasure place close at hand.

"Have you seen Him today?" said the young Rabbi.

"Yes, but a long way off; there was a crowd about Him."

The Jew turned over in his mind words which he had heard

repeated, and which had arrested him. "You did not join them?" he said. "If I had been there, I should have done so."

"No," answered the Greek, and he laughed a little, but gently, "it would have meant running after them rather far."

"I should have run after them, if I had been there; I am determined to see Him."

"Beware of manias!" said the Greek, laughing again, but not without sympathy. "Anyhow, it's more interesting for you than for me. You understand these things—if there is anything to understand!"

"I am determined to see Him", repeated the other.

"That's quite easy, He's talking nearly every day—and saying very strange things about Himself!"

"He does more than that—and I have heard things of His repeated to me . . . and, well, wonders . . ."

"Oh, yes, He does more than preach. They're all talking about Him—and it's always worth while to see anyone who counts in one's time. I'll ask people tomorrow morning what the chances are and then I'll come and tell you. I'll be with you an hour or two after sunrise if you'll wait for me. When He does get a gathering, it's usually about then."

◆

The two men, the short, dark, sturdy young Rabbi in his solemn garments, and the upstanding young Greek, stood side by side. They had come a little late and could not get beyond the edges of the crowd, where it had gathered—moving, murmuring, jostling, along the lake-side in front of the villas, about half-way between Magdala and Tiberias.

The morning was cool, even down in that hollow which holds this Sea of Galilee, or Genesareth, this lake of Tiberias. The water was dead calm. In the very midst of it, three miles out, two boats were drifting lazily, their square sails hanging loose. The morning sun shone in an unclouded sky above the great bare hills of the farther shore.

The crowd would not be silent; it still chattered, moved and jostled, the more eager and curious trying to elbow their way through to a closer view. One poor wretch, far off to the right, on the outskirts, kept clinking his little metal saucer against his staff, whimpering the ritual cry of the blind, begging for alms, but also begging that they would make room for an afflicted man to reach "The Lord". No one heeded him, each was pressing forward as best he could. Now and then one would hear, far off, what might or might not have been a voice lifted in predication; but it was overlain by the ceaseless shuffle and gabble of the straining crowd.

"We shall do nothing here", said the Greek; "let's get round to where that beggar is making such a nuisance of himself, and see if we can't get a glimpse from the shore." They walked round the couple of hundred yards to where the blind man was still begging monotonously for alms and for approach. They came beyond him to the gravelled edge of the waters, outside the limits of the throng. It was too far now to catch any words, if any words were still being said—and this also was doubtful, for the men and women were beginning to raise a louder hubbub and to move as though something had ended: they were breaking up.

The two friends in their disappointment could see no more than a large boat being rowed outward from the shore with great sweeps through the idle air; it was making directly across the lake, perhaps for Gesara, the white houses of which along the farther shore half a dozen miles away marked clearly against the rocky hillside behind them.

The young Rabbi looked eagerly after that boat, although as the distance increased forms on board were hardly to be distinguished. He was in a mixed mood, of emptiness and awe: empty of any words or message or sign, yet awe increased on him as he remembered the things he had been told.

"It's a pity we missed Him", said the Greek, as they walked towards the main road behind Magdala, where it climbed up the slope. They proposed to follow it till they should come to a path that led down on the right through the fields to his Jewish friend's house upon the shore.

"Haven't *you* heard any sayings of His repeated to you?" said the dark young man.

"Yes, but I've forgotten them—at least all except one, which I thought commonplace but vivid. And I've lost the words of that now, only I remember it called up a picture in my mind: it was about the beauty of these flowers. They say that most of His more sententious stuff is simply a rehash of all your own traditional phrases, isn't it?"

The young Rabbi shook his head. "Not what I've heard," he said; "of course, no one of our people can avoid some of our sayings. But the rest! . . ." He was silent for a moment, and then said abruptly, "They sound as though He had known the things of life and of death."

The Greek shrugged his shoulders. "It will be interesting if He has genius", he said.

"I must see Him," his companion muttered, "I must see Him."

"That's easy enough; we missed it this morning, but the same friend who told me that we should find the crowd on the lake beyond Magdala—only he missed the hour, like a fool; but I suppose there are no fixed hours for these sort of things—told me that He was going to speak in your big Synagogue up on the slope—where the tomb of your Prophet is—Capharnaum?"

"Yes, that's the place; He's going to speak there the day after tomorrow."

They had come to the door of the Jew's little house, and the Greek had already moved off when the young Rabbi called out after him, "There can be no mistake about the hour at Synagogue. That's always fixed. I'll come and fetch you, and we'll walk up together."

"Won't that be going back out of your way?" cried the Greek from his distance.

"I don't mind that. The point is not to be late; and if I come for you myself I can be certain."

"Anything you like", said the Greek, turning to take his road; but he was too far off now for the other to hear him.

◆

On the day appointed, Yakoub rose early in the morning, for he had seen how great were the crowds and this time he would not come too late. He had to go to Magdala to fetch his friend, and then get back again up to Capharnaum; and he must allow ample time. The Greek was still full of sleep, and got up from his low couch slothfully, stretching himself, and still desiring more rest, but his friend urged him, and waited for him to put on those foreign garments of his.

"Will they let me in, do you think?" he said, with that little curl that always came upon his lip whenever he spoke of Jewish things.

"Oh, dear me, yes", answered the young Jew impatiently. "We'll wait till the outsiders begin to come in and then slip in with them—besides which, I shall be with you."

Yakoub was a little proud of the way in which he was known; his elders already spoke of him as one who had disputed cleverly, on subtle points, and he had been applauded as victorious in their debates. Yes, certainly he could pass in a friend—but anyhow, no one would mind on such a day as this.

They went up the slight slope of even grass whereon the flowers were opening; the lake lay below them on their right, twinkling in the morning calm; and already boats were putting in to the shore from villages beyond, and from farther up the coast converging on Capharnaum. There was no time to lose. The numbers of those who had come, as for a great occasion, were hastening towards the great building which stood in the dignity and beauty of its Corinthian columns above them. Already the steps were thronged.

The young Greek noticed all curiously. He had known the place for years, but only from the outside; he had never remarked its detail until today, never thinking that anything would take him close by, still less inside. He now looked closely at the cornice of the frieze, the baskets sculptured in low relief one after the other which were the motive of that ornament— baskets holding manna. And once again, as he thought of those odd stories of theirs, the slight smile came upon his lip.

But he said nothing about all that, standing close to his friend and demurely enough, for one never knew what might happen if these folk suspected blasphemy or mockery. The two passed in together at the entrance, having all about them men of every kind; the very poor; proud, well-dressed, well-fed men from among the teachers and leaders; burgesses, some of them from far away, who had started by dawn. Men who had ridden were tethering the mild little donkeys to the rings in the wall; and others were laying down their burdens, to find them again when they should have seen and heard the things they had come to see and to hear.

When they got into the cool of the great hall (for the eastern sun was already hot without, but within the last cool air of the night still lingered) they stood patiently, the young Jew a little annoyed to find that in spite of all his precautions he was rather late. There were ranks upon ranks of all sorts before him, men crippled and whole, rich and poor, all mixing eagerly and ready for what was to come. Yakoub being short could not see beyond their heads, though he stood up now and then on tiptoe for a moment when some new sound above the murmuring and shuffling made him think that the new teacher had come.

It was a false alarm, and again a false alarm: only some grandee of the neighbourhood being shown in by a side door, reserved for such, and solemnly conducted to his place of eminence.

But at last there came that movement in the crowd which is unmistakable and marks an event impatiently awaited. There were one or two cries, some hostile, and one loud call of bene-diction: then demands for silence. The officials kept a gangway clear through the press from that side door to the upper part of the great hall; the young Rabbi, putting one hand upon the shoulder of his taller friend, lifted himself to his utmost, craning his head. This is what he saw. . . .

A man neither short nor tall, of an even gait, was going forward towards the place reserved for speaking. He caught the profile, strong, the head held forward in an attitude com-mon enough with those who speak much in public—the whole carriage attaining as it were a goal—marching some-where; militant.

Some pressed forward to touch His garment and were thrust back by the officers of the place; and still as He passed came those salutations and those opposing cries. And now He had gone up the steps and was turning towards the multitude from the place appointed for those who would speak and who were attended. He looked down gravely upon them, and as He did so, His eyes met those of the young man Yakoub.

In that moment it was for the student as though there were nothing all around, nothing in the great hall, or only a general confused chaos empty of men—save for that one face turned upon him fixedly for one moment of time. He saw the long features of which he had heard: the fine hair parted in the midst, falling down to the shoulders, not very thick; he saw those brows, dark and absolutely level, nearly meeting. All these things he saw at once—the whole face in its strength.

But he hardly knew that he had seen them, though he was to remember them for the rest of his life: for ever. For he had seen also in that one moment something supreme: the glance.

Those eyes were upon him. He had heard of their compelling beauty; of their compassion; of their authority. But hearing is all words, and words are shadows. This was the living thing, and there came upon him in that moment the stroke whereby men are slain or live. It was a second; and it passed. The glance left him and ranged in its power over the pressing crowd from side to side. It had been a flash, it might have been a lifetime. Something eternal had struck and shaken the central nerve of his being.

He had not noticed the strain under which he was, craning and lifting himself up; but even as the eyes were removed from him that strain came upon him and he sank back again upon the soles of his feet. Between him and the raised place the taller figures of the crowd shut him off; it was by moving now and then uneasily from side to side that he could get a glimpse between the heads of those before him.

The voice began, as level and as authoritative as the brows had been. What it was saying he could at first hardly hear, for the ceaseless movement and murmuring of the packed audience made a disturbing screen, but now he caught one phrase, and now another. They were nothing of the words that he had expected, from all he had heard; they were nothing of a kind that any man had heard—they had either no meaning, or some meaning on which a man might meditate for ever.

"*I* came down from Heaven." . . . "This is the will of the Father, who sent *Me*." . . . "All that He hath given Me I shall raise up at the last day. . . . "Every man who sees the Son and believes in Him will have never-ending life; and *I* will raise him up at the last day." . . .

Then came a hubbub; men protesting, some calling out against the extravagance, one shouting contemptuously the name of his family, another more loudly that he was a common man of Nazareth. Then these interruptions ceased for a moment, and in the pause that level voice came to Yakoub's ears again. "Murmur not." . . . "No man can come to Me unless the Father who had sent Me draw him, and I will raise him up at the last day." . . . "The man who believes on Me shall live for ever." . . . A little louder, and in a sort of astonished silence, came words still more extraordinary, as confident, pronounced, impressed, defined: "Your fathers ate manna in the desert, and they are dead. I am the living bread, which came down from Heaven; if any man eat this bread he shall live for ever; and this bread that I will give you is My flesh, for the life of the world."

The hubbub rose much more strongly than before; it threatened a tumult. "His *flesh* to eat? His *flesh* to eat?" When once more, by some gift in Him, He had imposed silence, there came the extraordinary words repeated, more strongly than before, "He that eats My flesh and drinks My blood has everlasting life."

What more was said the young Rabbi in his marvelling lost; the noise of the disputation grew greater, there was laughter mixed with it, and jeering—but also much more anger than before. Whatever further was being said could not be heard from where the young Rabbi stood, so far to the back of the crowd. A man immediately in front of him shrugged his shoulders, muttered, "That settles it!" and struggled his way back towards the doors. And after him went another and another. He heard a man say to one of those who were making off,

"Weren't you with Him the other day?" and the other reply, "Maybe—never again!"

The crowd surged, moved in whorls, began to melt away towards the great doors. The voice of the teacher had ceased. Someone else was speaking—but no one heeded. The Presence that had been among them was gone.

The young Jew came back to himself. His eyes took the focus of common things; the feet of his spirit touched earth again. He was walking unsteadily, so that the Greek at his side put a hand under his elbow, as though to support him. "Are you faint?" he said. "It's stuffy in here."

They pushed and struggled towards the great doors, and gasped when the fresh air struck them, in the shade of the south-western wall which the sun had not yet reached. For a moment the student leaned, with his hand upon a half-pillar, one of the two which flanked the porch. He was like a man grown suddenly faint. His companion waited patiently.

They made their way back, the dark one of them still unsteadily though pulling himself together, the taller, fair one quite at his ease. The Greek said, when they had gone about fifty yards down the grass, and crossed the main road towards the shore, "Well, what did you make of it?"

"I cannot tell. . . . I cannot tell. . . . I cannot tell. . . . I can tell nothing."

Yakoub was breathing shortly, and his eyes were fixed upon the distant water; he balanced himself with his left hand clenched and thrust outwards to one side. Then he walked more disposedly, but now and then stumbling.

"You had better lie down", said his friend. "That crowd was too much for you—and no wonder!"

"I cannot tell", said the other again, twice.

"Shall I come in with you?" said the Greek. "Can I do anything for you? It was unearthly, wasn't it?"

"No," said the other, "don't come in—I shall lie down—I shall lie down alone."

"I don't like to leave you."

"I am better alone—I shall lie down."

"Well, I'll come back"—and he was off towards Magdala, but not without looking back once or twice, and halting a moment to see whether he should be called.

But the other, feeling utterly apart in all the world, and at the same time in the presence of all things, lay down upon the mattress in the corner of his white empty room. He lay upon his back and covered his face with his cloak. He did not sleep or dream. He saw before him still, and could not lose them, those eyes.

◆

Half a dozen of reverend and elderly men sat on a semicircular bench that stood in a little annexe to the great Synagogue of Capharnaum, with a passage between it and the main building. It was a bare place, lit by a skylight, used for executive meetings. In one corner workmen had stored part of the furniture of the Synagogue. There was a large desk, where one appointed for the purpose would stand and make notes upon great occasions. Today there was no need for such. Still, they had something to discuss worthy of a certain pomp. They sat in ritual order with their Chief in Authority in the centre, a little mallet before him, wherewith he would tap the desk to open the proceedings or call a speaker to order.

One of that half-dozen, among the oldest of those present, was nervous and could not conceal it. The matter they had been discussing concerned him too closely.

The last speaker was still on his feet, still speaking with vehemence: "If it is necessary, there must be a public rebuke", he said. "From his father's position the young man compromises us all."

"It was no doing of mine", muttered the poor old bearded father, from the other end of the half-circle. "God knows I have spoken to him about it over and over again." "I say", went on the speaker, more violently, "that it is a public scandal and has become intolerable that your son—who is also one of us and for whom we have done so much—should wander about, appearing among the rabble that follows this charlatan."

The Chairman briefly interposed, and the speaker sat down.

"After all, we ourselves asked this Nazarene to speak here not so long ago—I believe that was the occasion when our young friend first heard Him. Of course a great deal has happened since then, but still, as we are in part responsible, we ought to see him in private before anything is done."

"You would not disgrace him publicly? You will not thrust him out of the Synagogue!" quavered the father. The vehement speaker was on his feet again at once. "It lies with him, Rabbi—it lies with Yakoub! We will admonish him, and if he will not abandon this Disturber, then we must take action."

The father rose to answer, and it was with difficulty that the protesting zealot could be got to sit down. "I have done all I could—it is very difficult for me at the present moment—he is already on his way—he is already with them, I mean with the crowd that is following this man. And they are said to be soon on their way south, to keep the Passover in Jerusalem."

The vehement man rose again. "It is an insult to all of us—to each of us personally—to all his father's colleagues. It is an insult to myself; I don't mind saying so openly, here before you. It may be that this mountebank whose ranting has turned the young fellow's head is half-mad; it's more likely that He is a mixture of cunning and vanity like most of His sort—but that is no reason why we should overlook these abominable insults. And they are being repeated, mind you! There are villages where a child in the street will cry, 'Pharisee!'—and you will hear the others laugh. The numbers are growing. There was something like a mob when He had the luck to soothe that wretched epileptic."

The Chairman struck twice with his mallet upon the desk, closing the discussion.

"The Rabbi is right", he said, and bowed towards the unfortunate father, who fiddled with his fingers in his grey beard; "we cannot do anything for the moment. When the Feast is passed Yakoub will return, and like enough he will have got over his revolutionary fever. Young men do get these fits." He paused for a moment, and then added with a benignant smile, "For my part I am not at all sure that if this leader-fellow goes up to the Temple He will ever return from Jerusalem. He has sailed very close to the wind already. We nearly got Him the other day, on that Abraham blasphemy. . . ."

The vehement one interrupted without rising, "You *could* have got Him! Him, and all His gang!"

There came a look of terror into the father's eyes, and the Chairman imposed silence with his hand. "There is nothing practical to be done now; it draws near to the Feast, and we will wait on the event. It will be time enough to act then—if indeed—" and here the smile appeared again upon his grave face—"if indeed there should be still necessity. I have heard privately—it is not to be repeated—that they are already thinking of taking measures against Him."

The meeting broke up. The reverend gentlemen stood for a few minutes in an irregular group, asking and answering questions of Church affairs, mentioning small points of Synagogue business; and then they trooped out slowly towards the door which led by the covered way to the great hall.

◆

It was true. The student, the young Rabbi, had left his home. He had left his half-hermitage, the little house his father had given him for his studies by the lake-side. He had sent his servant up to tell his family that he had gone—but with no word of whither. They knew well enough. There had fallen upon him the spell which had fallen also upon so many others in the last few months: he was with the enemy.

All the night before his departure he had lain awake entranced—rapt out of himself in an exaltation: a man possessed by a vision. He knew not whether he were there, on that familiar fringe of the Lake of Genesareth, breathing the common air, or in some borderland between earth and heaven. This mighty thing which had fallen upon him did not vanish with the morning, it endured throughout the day, it had taken root in his heart. All the hills around right up to high Hermon in the north were filled with a Presence. Therein was he absorbed. What he had been, that he was no more.

In the evening he sent the message to his father's house, and went out through the night northward, still fasting, to where people said the Teacher and His followers had wandered.

By the morning, a little below the Bridge of Jacob, above Bethsaida, whence the waters of the lake could still be seen to the south below, he came on a sort of rough encampment. It was that of the Followers. With them were mixed a lot of the curious, the expectant; not a few men and women stricken with diseases, blind, deaf, maimed, craving for relief—but most of them serving for some small hire, or hoping for a share in the common food.

The young Rabbi had with him his purse; he gave alms, and then broke his fast. "In a day or two," said one who appeared to have some sort of leadership among them, "the Lord will return. We are bidden wait here. He has gone up into Mount Hermon with the Twelve."

◆

There is a valley, nearly enclosed, and thick with over-hanging greenery, as though it were of the north in that southern land where most of the limestone hills are burnt and bare. Through this ravine the living water runs noisily, cool from the depths of the earth where it has been fed from far above, by the snows of Hermon. For indeed this combe is at the roots of Hermon, and its foundation, which is so pleasant, breaking from the rock, and its dancing torrent, are among the sources of Jordan.

That land is high, cool even in the summer heats, refreshed; and in these early days, with the harvest not yet ripe, there was breathing over it a vernal air. So it was especially in the morning, when the sun, though risen, had not yet shown above the great body of the mountain, and the dews were still upon the fields. This place the Greeks had dedicated to Pan and the Nymphs, and on the mountainside above it where the spring gushed forth, they had raised a shining colonnade, in honour of whatever gracious spirits inhabited these green shades, and the fields by the torrent's brim.

Upon those fields, in that early morning, in that solitude, the Master stood for a moment among the Twelve. His time was very nearly come, but here He was in peace, and with His own.

When He had looked at them a little while, searching them with His eyes, He asked them what they had heard of Him—not of the disputes or quarrels, not of the insults—these He knew well enough—but of what men called Him who had seen the signs, who had heard His commandments, and who had approached the Kingdom of God.

They answered Him and told Him how some said He was Elias, come back to the uprising of men, and some that He was another of the great dead of Israel returned to earth.

"And who say you that I am?"

To that difficult question, which silenced them, one at last stood forward to reply. It was a man no longer young, square-headed, bearded, the fisherman who had been chosen so early and who felt himself, from the manner in which he had been used, their spokesman. Under that fixed gaze, the authority of those eyes, and the voice of the Questioner still haunting his ears, this man fell to his knees upon the grass, and said loudly, "Thou art the Christ, the Son of the Living God."

Simon, whom they called Cephas, the fisherman and leader, had spoken the decisive word. It was not followed by any silence or parable, not by anything needing interpretation—but by an answering affirmation as direct and as vast in meaning and as big with destiny.

"Blessed are you, Simon son of Jonah! It was not flesh and blood that revealed this to you, but My Father Who is in Heaven. You are the Rock, and on this Rock I will build My Church—and the gates of Hell shall not prevail against it. And to you I will give the keys of the Kingdom of Heaven."

There was no more said, until later their questioning turned upon lesser things. The wandering was over and the ordeal had begun.

The place on which they stood, halted at last, looked southward down the valley towards the lake, and beyond the lake to that deep trench wherein Jordan runs, far below the level of the world, to the Dead Sea, a week's long journey on. To the right, above Jordan, ran the road through the hills, the road which ended in Jerusalem. The Passover was at hand. Knowing full well what would attend Him there, and speaking of it to those whom He had chosen, Jesus Christ set forward to the south from His own country, towards the hills of Judæa and the Holy City. The numbers that would accompany Him as He went still grew, and that encampment, which He reached on His return from the uplands of Hermon and the lovely glade, joined Him—and with it now marched the young Rabbi, lost in the increasing throng.

◆

The night passed. With the morning the followers, now swelled by further contingents from the town, took the road. Yakoub went on from day to day, feeling as though he were in some fashion one of an army; and watching from far off, day after day, the Figure whom they followed to Jerusalem.

Midway from Galilee to the Holy City the road, after Samaria, passed between two great hills, bare mountains rather, to the right and to the left, famous in the religion and the ancient story of Israel: the mountains of the Curses and of the Blessings. Through the cleft between, through the pass, went the road, and above it to the right stood a great city. It was all new; save where amidst its marble and its carvings and its facades of native stone, its statues and its temples, the old houses of what had been from the time of his father's fathers—from the very days of Israel's first coming—Sichem, were imbedded in the new thing.

The great crowd, ill-considered by the city guards, camped outside, on the farther side of the road. It was evening.

There passed near the place where Yakoub sat upon the grass, waiting with the others for provision to make the evening meal, a group of three men—and his neighbours whispered, "They are of the Twelve." With them was a lad, accompanying as one accompanies a superior the leader of the little group which was making for the town. "That", came the whisper again, "is Cephas", and a finger pointed him out. Yakoub had heard of him, and saw him now quite plain, close at hand as he hurried by with his solid but eager step; a man mature, with a square, rugged face, simple, anxious, bearded. The three men and the lad with them passed on into the town, and somewhat after, just before it grew dark, the group came back again, and men made way for them to pass up to the head of the column. There followed porters from the market, bearing food.

And the next day and the next they still went forward. Yakoub still at the end of the advance too far, day after day, to hear the voice, but the fever in his soul, the flame within him, and the vision which had changed all the aspect of the land, diminished not at all. He went on south with them all, under such a captain, transfigured and in a transfigured world.

♦

When they had come near Jerusalem, the crowds about them grew still larger. The fame of that approach still spread, the myriads who inhabited Zion and the thousands who had thronged in for the coming of the Feast swelled the concourse of those who had attended the Announcer of the Kingdom.

It was so very great a press that this young man, Yakoub, this last disciple, was thrust still further from the centre thereof, and could follow only on the fringes of the swelling multitude. But from a roll of land just above the gate of the town he could see the Lord, mounted upon an ass, which two privileged men led on either side by the bridle; and he saw the tall palm-leaves from the south waving in the air, and the hubbub rising into songs, loud hosannahs of triumph.

What was this? Was the triumph indeed at hand? He from the north had not awaited any such great movement of the populace. He had seen the thing grow, he had made himself part of it, but it had been a thing in opposition—was it succeeding now? Was there to be a new world? No: for mobs are unstable, and rival crowds also will gather.

The shouting and singing was suddenly blanketed, as that flowing tide of men was constrained into a funnel, through the narrows of the gate. The city wall shut off the sound. Yakoub passed into the city through the gate, lonely enough, at the tail of that day's excitement. He found himself a lodging on the left,

not far from the Citadel, close to David's Tower. He knew not
what was toward, but an influence was all round.

◆

The town had swallowed up Yakoub; and for a day and yet
another day he was alone in the midst of its turmoil and packed
thousands. For Jerusalem was overflowing with men from every
quarter of the Empire and from beyond the Empire; from
wherever the scattering of Israel had formed communities and
synagogues, in Asia, throughout the Mediterranean, and even
among the barbarians.

He heard about him tongues, uncouth and uncultured, which
he could not understand; his soul was lost in the perpetual hurry
of feet over the steep narrow streets, the cries of the vendors, the
crowds.

He worshipped in the Temple, he returned in his loneliness.
But all the more from his loneliness was his mind filled. Never
before had he left the hills and the little towns of Galilee, the
pleasant luxury places round the lake and the mountains above
his home. He seemed here like a man thrown into a rout,
obsessed by numbers—and throughout it all there went, as the
great day of the Passover approached, that increasing sense of a
Presence, of all the airs occupied by a Presence. But now there
was mixed with this Presence something more awful even than
the majesty of the Word had been, even than the ubiquitous
sense of power which had inhabited that journey southward
amid the growing company of the Lord. It was not only the
things he had heard upon the way, nor even only the fragments
of discussion, of enthusiasm, of hatred and contempt which he
had got from passers-by and in the eating-places of the city.
Certainly there was something toward, in this matter of the
Master; some great threat, and also, as it would seem, a passionate defence.

Jerusalem was occupied with many things, but this new
interest ran through it all, and for the young Rabbi it had
become the whole of every thought and every exaltation, now
of terror, now of adoration. Had he dared he would have thrust
in somehow, through inquiry and search, into the company of

the Twelve—or at any rate among their immediates, those who saw them daily—and have got some light upon the expectations which tortured and yet quickened him.

Something was toward: that was certain. It was in every word which had been worth listening to for him, every chance echo and rumour upon the only matter whereon the depths of his soul were concerned.

But he remained alone with the enormity of the moment overshadowing him, as a violent dream overshadows the day after the dreamer has wakened—more real than any of the daily things around.

The sun was low upon the eve of the Passover; he had gone out to the high ground westward of the city, to breathe the cool of the evening. A very slight breeze did come for his refreshment from the distant sea, and the night promised to be chill in that highland town. He watched the sun as it sank in an utterly clear heaven, behind the rim of the hills that hid the plain; he went back towards the city, wherein with the coming of the dusk much more movement had arisen. All Jerusalem was awake, for the great national feast had begun, the very centre of Jehovah's year, and the first stars were already in the sky.

That evening he ate the Pasch with the pious folk who lodged him, and who treated his learned cloth with simple reverence. For the first time in his life the solemn words and their ritual, the high tradition of Israel's redemption out of the Land of Egypt, were not unmixed and clear in his brain—they were all woven in, almost as though they were lesser things, with a main pattern of his thought: an obsession: what some enemy might have called a madness. "What was toward?" "What was toward?"

Every cry in the street, every sound of voices rising from some passing group, made him wonder where *They* might be on such a night—He and His Twelve.

He could not sleep; it was as though sleep had left him for ever. What was toward?

He went out into the streets, in the full darkness; his feet took him he knew not whither, down into the vale between the Palace and the Temple, through a mass of lanes—until he heard the confusion of many voices and the echo of many feet. He turned a corner into a wider way, and found himself swept along in a multitude who were hurrying, declaiming, urging on. There must have been hundreds of them, thousands perhaps. Why were they pressing up at that very late hour, when surely all official business was at an end? He could hardly keep up, they were breasting the hill, on the height of which was the House of Caiaphas, the father of the High Priest. Yakoub fell behind, and asked of a straggler what was happening.

"They've got Him!" said the other. "They got Him in the valley outside the wall, in the olive plot. They say He was trying to get away. . . ."

"Who?" asked the Jew. "They've got *who*?"

"The Nazarene!"

♦

Yakoub halted; it was cold. Up on the hill the distant hubbub went on, there were lights in all the windows, and now and then the opening of a door shed a strong beam through the darkness. He went up, hesitating, towards the courtyard; he dared not go further. What was happening to his Lord? Upon whom was now fixed that glance which had transformed him, or what enemies had struck at last?

In a dark corner of the courtyard, remote where none could mark him, he waited for some chance of news. The main door opened again, he saw a number of servants gathered round a brazier in the hall, and at that sight he himself shivered— whether from the outward cold or from something freezing the soul. There came out through the door a bent figure; the head was bowed down, covered with the hands, and the man was sobbing. Beside the figure moved respectfully that same serving-lad whom he had seen on the journey down the hills near Neapolis. The lad was speaking in a low tone which Yakoub, hidden against the wall, could just hear.

"Come back to the warmth, master! You will do yourself a hurt in this night cold." But the bent figure gave no sound, save those continued sobs, shaking. The lad persuaded his master at last; the violence of grief was over, though he still wept. He turned him towards the doors, and as the light fell upon him Yakoub saw that same anxious, rugged, simple, bearded face which he had seen in the valley between the great hills. It was Cephas.

♦

The night was passing, and with it the cold. In the place of that cold, even before the dawn of this Passover Day, a new oppressive heat had suddenly come. The oven-blast of the desert was upon Jerusalem, and was growing fiercer, though there was now no wind at all. It is sometimes so in Judæa, during those days before summer which became intolerable for their sudden heat, the more intolerable for the violent change. Then the curse passes, and men breathe again. But in that morning, after the sun had risen, the abominable oppression increased.

There had been no sleep for Yakoub or for many others through such a night of tragedy. Doom hung enormous over the veiled skies, and the powers of evil were abroad. A brazen day dawned. He faced it with stricken eyes.

He had heard what had befallen. He had followed, afar off, the movement of the torches through the moonless dark. He had drifted with the tide of servants, witnesses, guards, clerics and excited populace, to and from the Palace and back. Then after a long wait he took a wrong turning and was cut off, but at last, by mid-morning, he heard that they had taken their prisoner to the Governor, to the Roman master of the town and its garrison. To that centre he found his way in the midst of a hurrying people. Now, as ever, upon the fringes of the crowd, attending he knew not what, but certainly some dreadful thing, he was swept on to where at last the press halted—its front ranks thrust back by the short spears of the Roman soldiers of the Guard, held level to make a barrier before the Tribunal of Pilate.

The Judgment Seat, flanked with the ensigns of authority, rose well above the ground; the platform on which it was raised stood so high that all men could see what was passing—even those who stood as the young Rabbi stood, staring, pierced with affliction, in the last ranks of the gathering.

There was upon the Western face of that Italian who was set

up in authority over them an expression of command; and yet there was hesitation in it also, though his eyes looked upon this Eastern rabble with something of contempt.

Then Yakoub saw, led up the steps on to the platform, weak but erect, the Figure whom in all those days of inward worship he had not fully perceived since that moment in the Synagogue of Capharnaum.

The sight was pitiful and disastrous: a forerunner of death and shame. The Figure stood there unmoved, not broken; there was blood upon the face dripping from a mass of thorns plaited and pressed down upon His hair, and blood had soaked also through a tawdry and torn purple garment which had been thrown over His shoulders.

There was a silence; and the Governor spoke, standing up to do so.

Yakoub could not hear his words. "What did he say?" he asked eagerly of a man who was forcing his way back to get about his business in the town—one who had come from curiosity but had tarried too long and must now be off to his shop.

"He was saying there was no harm in the fellow."

"Will they let Him go? Will they not let Him go?" But the man had gone.

The Governor by a gesture of his right hand indicated that silent victim. He spoke again words which Yakoub could not hear, but which were followed by a universal shout from the crowd—the shout of a name, which he missed. The confused angry cry of hundreds, demanding vengeance for blasphemy.

Then came, like the cry of some beast from the wild, a woman's voice, shrill, piercing everything: "His blood be upon us and upon our children!"

It was taken up by all around, the mob shouted with a volume of increasing violence, "Upon us and upon our children! Upon us and upon our children!" Yakoub shuddered; was he also of these?

He saw the prisoner led away by a guard who held the cord which bound his hands; and the Governor, seated again, held his fingers forth over a fine silver bowl into which a young servant respectfully poured water upon them from a silver ewer.

"It's one of their damned Roman customs", snarled a porter near at hand in the crowd, and he spat.

The affair was over, and the excited hundreds turned away to disperse; talking and shouting eagerly, some repeating the curse, others laughing in triumph, others repeating like a refrain, "Crucify Him! Crucify Him!" A few sneaking away as though in shame, but silent, not protesting lest evil should befall them also.

The heat grew greater; the sky took on a sort of dull bronze. It was the invasion of the desert.

The crowd, certain leaders seeming to know what direction should be followed, thickened again and turned northward across the depression below the Governor's house. The press grew so thick that movement was very slow. It was an hour—and yet another hour—before step by step, crowded and wedged in that stifling mob under the intolerable close heat, Yakoub came at last to a small gate in the northern wall, almost up against the eastern corner of the city. Through this gate he followed. It was now not very far from noon.

Beyond the gate there was a waste open space; certain tombs were there, and scattered refuse from the city. It was the place of public execution. The end was at hand.

From where he stood faltering, nothing could be seen beyond but the seething multitude. It suddenly became still. Then there came a sound of hammering, dreadful in the silence. There was a pause. It came again, and continued, with interruptions. Then another pause; and for a third time the sound of hammering. Slowly, hauled up by ropes, three Crosses rose unsteadily against the sullen sky; and as they rose shouts greeted them. He heard the shock of each Cross, as it jerked into the socket hewn for it in the rocky ground, which had in the past received so many such things. And now the three figures showed high above them. The Crosses to the right and the left were somewhat shorter, that in the middle over-topped them; and on it hung, the thorns still round the drooping head, THAT which he had followed and would follow till he should die—but vainly, for the end had come.

The young man stood there, hour after hour, not noting time, not noting that he was weak with fasting and a sleepless night—transfixed and mixing with that agony. Of what was passing so far from him he heard nothing clearly. The Figure hung immovable, though one of the criminals, he upon the right, writhed at one moment, and seemed to turn his head upwards towards the middle Cross. It was as though the tortured man had spoken. But the central figure still hung immovable, high above them all.

The heat still grew; the sky darkened yet further; the fierce little sun, shorn of its rays as by a sandstorm (though no wind blew) cast now no shadow from the wall. All was of one dull yellow; and it darkened still. It must have been mid-afternoon; but Yakoub now knew nothing of time; he was hardly of this world.

The Figure which he so watched moved at last a very little— the head lifted, as though in a supreme spasm, and a loud cry followed. Then the head sank. For some seconds there was a complete silence upon them all. What closed it was a mass of rising cries as of cursing and of triumph combined.

Still Yakoub stood on that same spot, while the mob melted, dispersed, and went back into the city, save for some few who shambled off to the fields.

The ground was now clear for him to move and to see through the murk. There was a little group about the Cross; a young man was supporting an elderly woman, who had fainted. Another younger woman helped compassionately. Friends had put up a ladder, the nails had been unclinched from the dead hands and then from the dead feet; the body was lowered by a cloth and laid reverently upon the ground with the dead face fallen sideways, reclining upon the knees of the Mother.

Yakoub saw in that group a man of a certain presence, wealthy it would seem by his garments and having some authority, who gave orders. A mounted officer (of the Tenth Legion) kept guard by the now empty Cross, not interfering. Those friends bore the body away, and it was laid in one of the rock tombs. All was over.

♦

The next day was the Sabbath, but Yakoub did not know it. He knew not indeed whether he were alive or dead. He moved slowly in a maze, after a night which he had passed, a nightmare night, huddled beneath the wall. It was the Sabbath, I say, but he did not know it. His host found him and brought him bread, and begged him to come home, but he answered nothing save a mutter of thanks, his eyes half-closed. He ate as he was bidden, still remaining there crouched until the evening.

The heat seemed to have passed, the sun set in a quiet air and all in Jerusalem was still, for the Sabbath endures until the first star. Whether he slept again before the dawn he could not have told you; but when he knew himself, though he was very weak, he found some strength to rise, and it was again broad day. He leaned against the wall, pressing it with his hand, found further strength, and returned to himself—but also to a world which could now mean nothing to him any more. He came to the market place, where there were booths selling meat and drink. He further renewed his strength with food; he was a man once more—but broken.

That day, that first day of the week, as he wandered aimlessly, neglected, through the streets, not knowing whither to go, he heard rumours. They were very strange. He heard them repeated, now here and now there. As evening fell he came upon a group who were eagerly speaking, some affirming, some denying; one very young man in the midst of it repeated excitedly, "I tell you it is true! My master saw Him. It is true. My master knew Him better than did any other." "What next!" jeered a market woman coming by. "What more nonsense!" "I tell you it is true", said the boy once more, his face so turned that Yakoub could not see it, though he seemed to recognise the figure. He went up closer to hear more. One exalted voice, from some outer member of the group, lifted high—"He is Risen!"

"The tomb is empty", repeated the boy emphatically. "My

master has seen it. The Lord has been among them; He has returned."

Then Yakoub remembered: it was that same servant who had passed him with Cephas near Neapolis.

"Take me to your master", he gasped.

"Who are you?" asked the boy, turning round; and Yakoub, catching his breath, answered, so that only the other could hear, "*I believe.*"

"Follow me", said the lad and hurried away; the young Rabbi, feeling himself oddly strong, filled with life, hurried by his side.

It was growing dark as they hastened through the narrow twisting streets, then up certain steps, till they came to a little empty square with a narrow alley running out of it; in that alley was the wooden door of a low house, within which some light was shining through the chinks. The boy knocked with his fingers.

A young serving-maid half opened the door, timidly. When she saw the boy she was reassured, but she feared who might be with him, for the terror of those last days was still upon her. She was holding a little lantern in her hand, and even as Yakoub stood there by the open door he saw, by the light of that lantern, close before him that same bearded head but the face was changed and the eyes were full of vision.

"You are Cephas?" said the Rabbi.

"Yes, I am Cephas."

In a much lower tone, just loud enough to be heard, and leaning forward, Yakoub implored, "Is it true?" The other looked at him fully in the face and nodded. Then the young Rabbi turned, and went out into a new world.

XII

The First Fruits

AFTER THE Crucifixion, Death and Resurrection of Our Lord two things happened at once: each destined to dominate the whole of future history.

The first is the immediate appearance of the Church; the Church was founded at a stroke, in the first days after the Ascension. The second is a violent antagonism between the Jews and the people among whom they are destined or condemned to live—the Roman and Greek worlds and their descendants.

First, as to the Church.

The immediate appearance of the Church was a Syrian thing; the whole of that early story, the Apostolic foundation, the missionary journeys, stands in Syria, radiates from Syria, returns to Syria. It is held in the quadrilateral of Syrian places, Antioch and Jerusalem from north to south, Damascus and the sea-coast from east to west. In Syria the thing was rooted, from Syria its influence goes out, to Syria the report of its continued advance returns.

The Church even in its embryonic form appeared as an organised thing. Just as a living being, even in its earliest and most rudimentary form, shows what it is to be in maturity, so did the Church. It appears as a mystery religion armed with instruments of authority, of definition, and of social action, linking its members together, providing for them and overlooking their activity. Its government is conciliar at the very outset: that is, appointed chiefs meet and discuss. There is a chief among them whose leadership had been marked out by the Lord Himself: Peter, he who had first proclaimed the Divinity of the Founder in that Grove in the midst of Panean beauty, in the combes of Hermon.

The central rite of this new body was the Eucharist, which was also the central mystery thereof. This mystery consisted in the giving of thanks over the elements of Bread and Wine in the presence of the initiated alone; with the intention that those elements should thus become the Body of the Lord for the communicants thereof and so perpetuate the memorial of Calvary. This new organisation, the Church, had also a form of appointment for its officering; the laying on of hands, whereby the original Apostolic authority of the Twelve who had followed Jesus and had received His instruction to Evangelise the world was conveyed by co-option to others of their choice, and so established as a tradition without end.

The term "a mystery religion" may shock many who have had no occasion to examine the character of the time. The Church certainly did arise as a mystery religion; its very name in Greek, *Ecclesia*, stamps it as such; but since that word has various meanings, it is better to rely upon the facts.

This new thing, the Church, was built round an accepted marvel, the Resurrection: and, behind that marvel, the marvel to which the Resurrection was witness, the Incarnation—the Divinity of a poor man who had just been put to death by public execution. To accept these marvels as true was to believe, and such belief was the condition of membership.

The central act of worship in this new body, the Eucharist, was yet another marvel. The rite which commemorated the last actions of this Man and His shameful death, also called down His presence among the band of worshippers, and in eating the Bread and drinking the Wine they ate and drank of their Lord. This mystery was kept jealously to its members, not to be profaned by common exhibition to the vulgar: reserved for the special community of believers. There was also Initiation, another necessary adjunct of a mystery religion; it was a rite of Baptism with water in the name of the Father and the Son and the Holy Ghost.

For and to the initiated alone were the mysteries performed, and there was appeal to further marvels; the miracles of those who would spread the new organisation and who presented such miracles—which they claimed to accomplish by the favour and power of God—as the signs of their commission.

But indeed a new religion could not have begun in that first century save as a mystery religion. Everything must be conditioned by the spirit of its time; the early Church appearing as anything less than a mystery religion would hardly have been thought a religion at all by the men of those generations.

The Church had from its very origins this further mark of mystery religions; that initiation into it was initiation into Immortality and Beatitude, the expulsion of death and of evil—that is, the Initiated were offered Salvation. Finally, there was in its first central mystery, the Eucharist, a gesture which may be compared to a password: there was a particular manner of breaking bread which manner was introduced by the Founder Himself while He was upon earth; and men so breaking bread were thus secretly recognised by their fellow members.

The predication and planting of the Church began from the Day of Pentecost, seven weeks after the Passover, the day upon which fell the Jewish Festival of Weeks; for which Festival Jews from without, from the Diaspora, were gathered in the Holy City.

The disciples met together on that day in secret, within one room apart, and having with them the Mother of the Lord. They there professed to have received (to the accompaniment of yet another marvel) direct inspiration from Heaven; the Holy Ghost, sent them according to the promise of the Leader now no longer on earth, descended upon them.

At once, to the assembled multitudes in the Capital, the predication began, and it was claimed that by a gift of tongues the men of the Diaspora who listened to that predication on this first day in Jerusalem, men brought up in the speech of the various provinces which were their permanent habitation, could each and all understand things spoken to them by the man Peter, the chief of the Apostles, though his own native speech could only have been the Aramaic and Greek of Galilee.

There was claimed as the harvest of that first day some thousands, perhaps three, perhaps five: a general movement had begun. There was in these first origins so considerable a body accepting the doctrines announced and therefore prepared for initiation: the doctrine that this Jesus who had been crucified had risen from the dead, that He was a Divine Being, the Son of God; that He had certified His claim by so rising from the dead; that He would come again later to judge all men, not only those alive at the moment of His second Coming but also those who had died before it—"the Judgment of the Living and the Dead".

So much for the immediate predication by a Galilean and His companions to their fellow Jews, with whom they continued the common worship and law of their race.

But very soon another mark appeared, which was to be characteristic of the new thing; what is called "Catholicity"— that is, this new organisation was to be universal. Again it is Peter who affirms this and claims his right to affirm it from a double vision; a vision granted to himself and a vision granted to one of the Gentiles, a subaltern officer of the Roman Army of occupation, a centurion—that is the commander of a Roman Company unit (some sixty men). The centurion, awed by his own vision, was for treating Peter as Divine, casting himself down before him. But Peter bade him rise and said, "I also am a man"—whereupon he baptised that soldier, though he was not a Jew, and the receiving of this alien from outside the fold of Israel began the universality of the *Ecclesia*.

Now this new body, though its members continued to worship with their fellow Jews, and to observe the details of the Law in eating and drinking and association, was nevertheless destined to a conflict between itself and the original Jewish body within which it had sprung up. The conflict was inevitable because the *Ecclesia* proposed for divine worship not only Jehovah but a Man. It affirmed as its chief doctrine that which Judaism had been inspired for all those centuries to deny at the risk of every torture and of death: a Man as an object of adoration. This new *Ecclesia*, this New Mystery Society, affirmed as true that which, being in the ears of the Jews an intolerable blasphemy, had led the Jewish authorities to demand the death of Jesus—He in making His claim to a Divine origin had blasphemed with a blasphemy most horrible to them.

The New Church was destined also—and as inevitably—to engage in a still wider conflict: a conflict with the general body of the Græco-Roman civilisation in which it was to develop; but in these first days the initial friction was between themselves and those whom outsiders still looked upon as their fellows, the mass of the Jewish people.

Contact between the opposing forces was taken, and the battle joined, at the very origin, through the incident of Stephen.

The occasion was this: The Church, as we have seen, was not only a mystery religion, it was also a social organism concerned with the life of its members. It worked for the relief of all those members in material things, arranging a pooling of goods with that object. In order that this relief should be distributed officers must be appointed, and the leaders of the new body named seven, one of whom was a Jew from North Africa, another a Jew from Antioch, and another this same man with the Greek name of Stephen. Stephen, having come into collision with the Jewish authorities in Jerusalem, displayed at once another mark of the new body—its aggressiveness. He not only defended his doctrines to the men before whom he was arraigned, he carried the war into their own territory; because *they* had put Christ to death *they* were, said he, traitors and murderers. "*You* put Him to death" are his words to the Jews. He was but repeating what his chief, St. Peter, was energetically to affirm—that God had made Lord and Christ that Jesus whom *you* crucified. "For it was *you*," said Peter, "*you* and *your* High Priest and the rest, who delivered Him up to Pilate, though Pilate wanted to let Him go."

Stephen thus acting was found intolerable; they dragged him out from the city by the north-eastern gate and stoned him to death.

There was for a witness to all this, and an approver, and in some sense presiding over those who killed Stephen, a young man of distinction and of some social position. He was a Jew from the great University city of Tarsus in Cilicia, who was for the moment in Jerusalem. His Jewish name was Saul, but by some adoption in connection with his Roman citizenship (for his family was of that standing) he also used the Roman name of Paulus; perhaps his people had been protected by, or affiliated with, the great Roman family of that name.

In this first clash and this first tragedy of a martyrdom there was a scattering of the Church in Jerusalem. Its members were dispersed to Cyprus, to the cities of the Phœnician coast, to Damascus and especially to the capital of Syria, Antioch, where was a very large Jewish body, enjoying especial privileges ever since the foundation of that Greek city over three hundred years before.

The energetic offensive to which the Church was now bound drove it on to missionarise. Its influence began to be found on all sides outside the Syrian boundaries, and the man whose activity in this we know from tradition to have been most conspicuous, and on whose labours we have details from fortunately surviving documents, was that very Saul or Paul who had distinguished himself by his most Israelite zeal against the new dissident faction.

There is a danger of exaggerating and so distorting the effect of St. Paul on the early Church. In a sense one may say that the effect of St. Paul cannot be exaggerated, for he was certainly the character through whom most was done in the immediate spread of the new organisation through the world outside Syria—not only among the Jews of the Diaspora, but among the Gentiles, and the Greek and Gallic cities of Asia Minor and in Greece itself, and at last even in Italy and Rome. Nevertheless there is a sense in which one can say that the effect of Paul can be and is exaggerated through the disproportionate place given to documents today in history and the corresponding modern neglect of tradition.

We know that there was much missionarising separate from that of Paul; and though the traditions of this are, like many very ancient traditions, confused and warped and vague, there is sufficient to show that the effect was a general one.

Thus one of the Apostles, Thomas, certainly did work far to the East, reaching India. We have, in the midst of wild legend, a piece of solid evidence in the name of one of the rulers of

North-eastern India who is certainly historical. There is also a tradition of another Apostle, Bartholomew, who also went eastward and was also according to tradition martyred—perhaps in Armenia. Again, the companions of Paul were missionaries of their own initiative. Barnabas, his early companion; Luke, a Greek and Gentile physician; Mark, who was, especially later, attached to St. Peter; all these names, and both the records and the much vaguer traditions attached to them, are evidence of what was in the very nature of the new effort—its spreading upon every side through the intense zeal of those who had come to believe.

Paul, however, not only through the writings of his companion Luke, but through his own letters, is the outstanding apparent figure in the story of the first expansion. He claimed to have received a blinding vision on his way up from Jerusalem to Damascus, whither he was going with letters of introduction to the authorities of the Jewish body in that town. These letters were to authorise him to speak for the further suppression of that new sect, the Church: in this blinding vision on the Damascus road he claimed to have seen and heard the Lord; to have obeyed the Divine command, witnessed to by yet another miracle—for he went blind and was cured.

He reappears as a most ardent member of the new Church, coming in among them at Antioch from his home at Tarsus to which he had returned; and, from Antioch, he set out with Barnabas on their first missionary journey.

It is characteristic of this new-born *Ecclesia* that its members could not preach until they had been duly appointed by its authority. These two thus appointed went to the port of Antioch, Seleucia at the mouth of the Orontes, and sailed thence to Cyprus, where they were received by the Roman Governor, who seems to have thought St. Paul a man of consequence. In prolonged journeys repeated throughout the Gaulish population on the high plateau of Asia Minor, the Greek cities of the Ægean, and beyond the Ægean in Attica and in Corinth St. Paul laboured with the energy of a character extraordinary and vividly marked, converting Gentiles in great numbers as well as the

Jews of the Diaspora in the various cities. He was strenuous for the policy of universality, which Peter, as the head of the *Ecclesia*, had first declared.

Peter himself, though he had, as leader, been the first to proclaim the admission of non-Jews to the Church, still kept apart among the Jewish members. Fearing to offend the strict Jews of the original body in Jerusalem and their President (who was a relative of Jesus), he strictly observed the Jewish custom and would not eat with Gentiles: it was due to the energy of St. Paul that the accepted doctrine was everywhere acted upon. The Gentile converts were not required to be Jewish even in social life, still less were they required to submit to circumcision.

By the end of St. Paul's effort, twenty or thirty years after the Great Passover and the Resurrection, the Church was of every speech, of every race and city with which it had come into contact. There were congregations deriving from it and attached to it everywhere; among the Celtic-speaking Gauls of the Asia Minor plateau, the Greek-speaking cities, and at last at Rome itself, whither St. Paul was sent on his appealing as a Roman citizen to Cæsar against his condemnation by the magistrates, and where he was put to death.

Of St. Peter's travels we have no such record; we know that he went missionarising along the sea-coast, that he is soon in that city of Antioch which was becoming a second place of origin whence the new religion was to spread—and you may still see the Grotto in Antioch to which tradition attaches his celebration of the Eucharist: it is still there celebrated now. Like St. Paul, St. Peter also wrote letters to the new congregations; and he also ends at Rome.

But we have no fixed and certain dates for him, save an approximate date for his martyrdom. That date is the great persecution under Nero, who had laid to the new body the crime of insurrection and of the great fire of Rome. We are fixed within a short limit of time as to the year in which the two leaders were put to death—Paul by decapitation outside the walls, being a Roman citizen, Peter by crucifixion in the Vatican Gardens, where there was a horrible holocaust of Christians—many burnt alive as living torches to illuminate the dreadful night. It is, within a short margin of error, thirty years or so after the Crucifixion of Our Lord, probably a little more, that the two great missionary chiefs of the Apostles were martyred in the capital of the world: *Felix Roma*.

Within those thirty years the members of the *Ecclesia* had acquired the name of "Christianoi": "the Christ-men": "Christians". It is said that this was first given as a sort of nickname to the community in Antioch—a city quick at nicknames—and by the time the work was accomplished and sealed by the twin martyrdom at Rome the universal *Ecclesia* was everywhere; in the main no longer Jewish of membership, but Italian, Greek, Gallic, Syrian, Egyptian.

It is an example of the innumerable anomalies of history—but among the very greatest—that the one man in the new movement whose writings have come down to us in an almost violently Jewish form, alive with the Jewish clench and twisted (to our ears) by the Jewish trick of following the word rather than the idea in the development of his thoughts, should have been the chief instrument for divorcing the Church from Jewry.

For St. Paul's manner is almost wholly Jewish, and in this at violent contrast with the Greek air of the Gospels. There is nothing of Galilee or the fresh pastures about him. One would say that this flame of his was a breath from the desert, as though his supreme energy had about it something of that which the first examples of his race had shown when they came in from the sands on to the fields of the Palestinian highlands, and there established Israel.

St. Paul's work was done, its aim reached, by that Jewish tenacity at which we still marvel today. He was, in his small, indefatigable body, a gnarled man, it would seem, as well as certainly in his burning soul; his strength was the strength that you will find in the texture of a contorted oak. As for Peter, the leadership of the congregations of the *Ecclesia* had passed with him to the capital of the world. As Luke was the recorder of Paul, so much more was that young companion Mark, whom Peter calls his son, the recorder of Peter. These two also were the authors of two among the very few documents transmitted to us from the origins of the Church.

It is a great misfortune to history (not to religion) that these same origins of the Church are supported by so little documentary evidence. What no one can deny to be the most important institution of the last two thousand years, the thing that made Europe as we know it, the Catholic Church, rose in obscurity. That is all to the good, for it thus rose freely and sincerely. But though we have its spirit, its character, its soul, amply exemplified by tradition—and by what is all-important, its fruits—though we know well enough what the Christian Church is, yet the lack of documentary evidence upon its origins gives opportunity for fantastic misrepresentation.

There arose in connection with the predication of Jesus Christ and His profound effect upon a restricted but ultimately triumphant group, what were evidently a large number of records direct and indirect: records accompanied by conjecture and legend. Among such documents purporting to convey the evidence on Jesus Christ and the teaching of His life, fragments of over fifty years can be traced, and we have a right to presume that there were many more. But we must remember that very few of the documents of antiquity survive. They have come to us (after the breakdown of material civilisation in the Dark Ages) through Mss. copied and re-copied in such a fashion that for many of the most important we have only very late examples.

In the case of contemporary or nearly contemporary narratives upon the origins of the Church, there is not only the agency of time at work to lose documents in oblivion, but the acute motive of orthodoxy. It was essential for the Church itself to stamp as authentic some few records and to denounce as untrustworthy the great mass of others, lest the unity of doctrine should fail. Those declared false by authority tended to be forgotten; those accepted as true and read in the Churches remained.

As to what documents and records should be officially recognised as inspired and pronounced part of the Divine message, a fixed rule (or "Canon", as they call a rule in the Greek language) was slow to become established. The accepted records of the sayings of Our Lord, His Life and Passion became fixed, more or less in their present form, early enough—within seventy years, and universally accepted in the century following. But the whole of the New Testament (as we call it) did not take its present form until much later. Documents such as the letter of St. Clement were read in the Churches and have since been dropped, and on others, such as the Apocalypse, there were debates which took long to settle. One may say that the "Canon" was fixed in the West by the fourth century—in the East long after, and more doubtfully.

But the essential thing to remember about all this is that *the basis of belief was not documentary*: it was traditional.

It was tradition which judged the document, not the document which established tradition. The Church had only as documentary evidence this very small book, three fragmentary accounts of Our Lord's sayings, miracles and passion; written one of them by a man who knew Him and two by men who had not known Him but had known His Apostles, and who were virtually contemporary. These three, Matthew, Mark and Luke, went over much the same material of note, record and remembered sayings and deeds, though their accounts are clearly separate and individual. Endless guesswork has been printed upon what the sources of their information were.

Towards the very end of the first century the last surviving Apostle *and eyewitness*, St. John, added to this collection a fourth account.*

To these four "Gospels" (as they were called—that is "The Good News") were added a number of letters written by St. Paul and other leading figures to various congregations of the *Ecclesia*. On these also modern guesswork has run to every kind of extravagance.

---

* I cannot resist the temptation to add the immortal comment of a famous modern sceptic, who, it is true, had more common sense than the rest. He admits of the Gospel of St. John that some large part of it came directly from the Apostle, and that the rest "undoubtedly contained much Johannine material".

As time went on these documents were appealed to in disputed cases of morals and doctrine; and as the Church had declared them to be divinely inspired, their authority was very high, especially where they purported to quote the actual remembered words of Jesus Christ. But the idea that documents lay behind the Church, or were the origin of the Church, or could be appealed to against the Church, is a grossly unhistorical error bred by the violent passions of a religious quarrel only four hundred years old.

Of documents in the lifetime after the last personal witness to Our Lord was dead there are very few indeed, but such as there are confirm (as might be expected) the traditions of the Church. The martyr Ignatius presided over the Church of Antioch less than a complete lifetime after the Crucifixion, and as he has borne witness to the strength of the Church's organisation, especially the authority of the Bishops, the reader can imagine how continually and violently his evidence has been attacked.

We have on the Eucharist one very remarkable passage in the writings of a Jewish convert to the new religion about forty or fifty years later: in this there is detailed description of the main doctrines which have run through the Church on this matter from the beginning. "It is not ordinary Bread" (after the Eucharistic prayer has been said over it), "but the body of Jesus Christ."

So far, then, documents are few and there is room for the widest speculation, although, few as they are, they always confirm tradition. But by the end of the second century there comes in a stream of material which goes on increasing throughout the third and becomes a flood by the fourth and fifth centuries. There is a whole body of Christian literature by which we know, even in details, what the Church then was.

We find it organised from of old under Bishops—that is taken for granted; each Bishop an individual at the head of one local Church. We have lists of previous Bishops in certain places taking us back to the time of the Apostles—notably for the Church of Rome and its origin with St. Peter. Those who desire to believe that Episcopacy was not an original institution have brought out another mass of guesswork contradictory in all save this, that they agree in belittling tradition. Now (as is always the case in this sort of negative phantasy), one argument against them is conclusive. Episcopal Government is everywhere clear and strong when the lists are drawn up, and there is no trace of a protest against such government having arisen in earlier times. If it had been an innovation there would certainly have been some such protest.

All the enemies of the Christian name have noted the coincidence between the rise to power of the Church and the decline of the old civilisation. It was precisely in this late second century and during the third century (A.D. 200–300) that our ancestors went through the worst crisis in their culture, and that the glory of Greece and Rome came near to perishing. By the time ancient pagan society had pulled itself together and maintained a united rule for another two hundred years it had become a thing changed materially for the worse. The great poetry had disappeared, and the great prose; the sculpture had become degraded; the details of ornament coarsened. What was perhaps worse, continuity with the great art and thought of the past had grown enfeebled and in danger of breaking.

Now was this decline on the material side of our civilisation due to the spread of the Faith, or was the exact contrary true— that the Faith saved (in so far as it could be saved) the treasure of the antique world?

Some would say, "Yes. The Church was to blame. The Church was Syrian in origin, and Syria, being Oriental, corrupted the West; softened and disintegrated our noble stock."

Others, with a better sense of history, say rather, "The Church had long ceased to be Syrian, and though it is true that Syria in its softness, its Oriental mood, did weaken the texture of the Roman Empire, the Church was a stiffening against all that, a discipline and the main factor of strength and permanence."

To judge between these contradictory estimates we have two criteria: (1) the dates, and (2) the nature of the Christian institution, the Church.

As to the arguments from dates: The breakdown begins when that weak man, Marcus Aurelius, for the first time abandoned the old tradition in government by which the Roman Empire had lived: Adoption. Ever since Octavian had united the world under the title of Augustus, each Roman Emperor was supposed to name his successor. It was a solemn political duty which he owed to society to choose one capable of just and vigorous rule. At first, of course, the successorship went on by choosing members of the original Julian family, the connections of Julius Cæsar, who was the true originator of a united command. When that Julian House failed there were military revolutions, and the nomination by troops of successive generals; but the principle of adoption continued, and it saved the authority and value of Imperial power for two hundred years—until Marcus Aurelius, in his folly, nominated his worthless son. It was what one might expect from the complacent and blindfold husband of Faustina.

The reign of that son Commodus begins the debacle. A soldier of intelligence and character, but not of the rank and education required for the post, Septimius Severus somewhat restored things after the welter; but he was not only lacking in the social tradition which the master of the Roman Army should have maintained, he was also jealous of those who possessed it; therefore the officering of the forces began to decline in his time.

Then came, a little after the year 200, a very shameful episode of Syrian origin; Severus as a soldier not yet Emperor had married a Syrian pagan woman, and her descendants disgraced the Empire. The worst moment was that in which a lad from Homs, on the Orontes, Heliogabalus, was made through the influence of this woman's family (Syrian priests of the Sun) Emperor and Commander of the Armies. The episode covered half a lifetime, and it was yet another Oriental who ridiculously presided over the grand ceremonies which celebrated the thousandth birthday of Rome.

The third century, then, saw a violent and prolonged crisis, with authority divided among great numbers of generals, and all our culture in peril of death. There was another restoration under Aurelian, and a last one under that soldier of genius, risen from the ranks, Diocletian; he, with his colleagues, ends the story of the old pagan empire.

Now this long story of breakdowns and confusions and rallies depended of course upon much more than the mere personality of the Emperors: there were economic troubles, and there was the general trouble of old age coming upon a civilisation; but the point to remember is that the trouble was *not* coincident with the triumph or even the last rapid expansion of the Church; it began before that expansion. The numbers of the Church in proportion to the pagan population in which it lived continued to increase especially in the eastern, Greek-speaking part of the Roman Empire.

But that increase in strength and numbers came date for date and point for point *later* than the corresponding moments of decline on the civilian side of things.

So much for dates as a test: but that other most vital test, the nature of the institution, confirms the verdict.

Whatever else the Church was, it was disciplined. Whatever else it was, it was eager for exact thought, perpetual definition and what may be called "the muscles of the mind". No one can deny that the Church stood for man's control over his passions in a time of debauch, for moderation (that is temperance) in conduct, and in a certain sense—new though the Church was— for continuity in tradition. The Church was the most solid thing in a dissolving world.

In this matter two sentences have come down to us in the voluminous writings of Christian apologists. One of these sentences appeared at the beginning of the cultural decline, another towards the end of it. In the first the defender of the Christian religion calls the Roman Empire and the Church "twins"; and to emphasise the truth that the Church might yet save society, he says, "So also the Cæsars should be Christian—if indeed the Cæsars could be Christian." The second is the famous judgment of St. Jerome, wherein he says that if only the Church had triumphed somewhat earlier she might have saved all the material side of civilisation as well as giving it, as she did, a spiritual life strong enough to carry it on through the Dark Ages.

But there is this much true in the position of our enemies, such as those noble pagans of the mid-fourth century who cried with Ammianus that all the disasters were due to the spread of "the odious superstition". This element of truth in their complaint is the fact that the Church was a body *within* the Empire, but not wholly *of* the Empire. It was a State within a State, and therefore at issue with the authority and general spirit of the medium within which it grew. It had spread its influence beyond the boundaries of the Empire, even among the barbarians; it did not identify itself with Rome, it was at issue with the underlying doctrine by which the Empire had lived—the doctrine that the Empire itself (and, for that matter, the Emperor at its head) was Divine. Hence the persecution of the Christians, breaking out from time to time, and especially violent towards the end of the third century (A.D. 300); by which time men could clearly see that either the new religion must be given a free hand, or crushed once and for all. Men who were not of the Faith (certainly a very large majority in the West even at the end of the business, and probably a majority in the East); men whose family, traditions, and the whole inheritance of whose culture was rooted in the pagan thing, hated the Church as an irritant, foreign body—indigestible, and therefore poisonous to the State.

Now the Church *was* all that. The Church and *her* claims could not co-exist with the traditional pagan Empire and *its* claims. There were two spirits at war. No man can serve two gods; and that of which Imperial Rome had made its god was other than the Crucified. Nevertheless it is true that if the central authority of the Empire had accepted the Faith in time, or even given the Faith its freedom, the fulness of the old civilisation might have been saved.

The Church was not only the strongest, the best defined, the most universal institution for the saving of our culture in peril, it was also by far the most *living* thing. Men who followed Jesus Christ did intensely believe, while men who opposed Him opposed Him only by routine and inheritance, with no one, fixed philosophy to pit against the Nazarene. The old gods had become jests, or shadows; varying rites, conflicting philosophies stood, already weak and failing, in the presence of a vital force, united and determined. It was not possible but that the second should master the first.

The last persecution was breaking down, though still virulent in patches of the Western world, when, somewhat less than 300 years after the Crucifixion, some 250 after the first expansion of missionary effort and the founding of the congregations among the Gentiles, the policy of the Empire in the matter of recognising the Church went through a revolution.

Those who for very different reasons desired to end the violent quarrel between the Church and society—the strong Christian believers, the wearied, the indifferent, the vested interests demanding peace—combined to recognise as legitimate and to establish in full freedom what had been up to now a quasi-usurping power in society, a State within the State.

Of the four official generals (two head ones, each with a coadjutor), who, by Diocletian's plan, were ruling the Greek-speaking East and the Latin-speaking West, one—Constantine—marching from Britain where he was born, became the champion of the new order: not yet declaring himself Christian, but the man through whom the Church was to take over power. He defeated his rivals and opponents; he conquered, if not in the name of Christ, at least in the name of the Cross, for the very shape of which he had a curious personal reverence that might almost be called superstition. He became, by the year 325, the sole head of the vast Imperial State, from the Scottish highlands to the Mesopotamian desert, and from the Danube and the Rhine to the African wilderness; and the new era, a Christian Empire, had begun.

So much for the first thing which had appeared immediately upon the Crucifixion and Resurrection of Jesus Christ: the growth of the Church, within the Roman Empire. It has been dealt with in some detail in these pages because the development was gradual over the long space of some eight generations, and was by far the greatest episode in the story of our race.

The contemporary event, the second sequel to the Resurrection, the sudden antagonism between Israel and our civilisation, can be told more briefly. For it was not a gradual development, it was the immediate product of a single shock, which covered but very few years—though the effect of that shock has continued for centuries.

◆

I have said that this second sequel to the Crucifixion was the quarrel between the Jews and the European society in which they found themselves.

Hitherto that singularly preserved race, with its conviction of a Divine mission and of an invincible power protecting it, though it had astonished and often irritated the Græco-Latin world, had been, upon the whole, on good terms with this last of the Empires. Judah had almost perished under Assyria, had re-arisen under the Persian rule, had begun to flourish greatly, and spread throughout the Eastern world under the Greek successors of Alexander. It had, in a fashion so strange as to read miraculous, maintained itself as a Maccabean State in the midst of Grecian Syria in spite of the Seleucid power. It had re-established its capital and its King.

When Rome took over all that and made Syria a department of her universal rule, when Pompey took over the Syrian thing, the Jews were still privileged and still favoured. Rome was careful to consider the (to her) astonishing and exceptional religion. She would not offend by putting pagan symbols upon the coinage that circulated in Palestine. She was ready to restore the national dynasty as a subordinate kingdom; there were Royal Jews intimate with the Court of Rome itself; the Jewish rulers were the friends of Cæsar, and there was to be a moment when a woman of the great Maccabean family had been loved by Cæsar himself and was close to becoming Empress. Jewish Customs were studied in Rome with curiosity, the antiquities of the Jews fascinated the intellectuals, the Jews had made proselytes on every side, especially in the wealthier ranks. Even their special practices—the sacred Seventh Day, for instance, the Sabbath—were being imitated or adopted as a fashion. But all this was suddenly to change.

The process of Jewish expansion did not, of course, continue without friction; there would be riots here and there against them, and Tiberius had, during the lifetime of Our Lord Himself, shown a dislike for the Jews and attempted to get rid of them from the capital, Rome (wherein, of course, he failed): but taking the situation as a whole the Jews had not only spread throughout Græco-Roman society, numbering millions, everywhere privileged with some form of self-government, such as Julius Cæsar had given them in town after town (Sardis, Ephesus, Laodicea and plenty of others), but their leaders were close friends with the greatest men among the Romans. With all of this went their money-power, everywhere felt, through the action of their great bankers, who had a sort of financial centre in Alexandria.

When, in the year A.D. 26, a little before Our Lord began His teaching in Galilee, the Roman official Pontius Pilate was appointed Procurator of Judæa under the Governor of Syria, he lived (in spite of an obvious reluctance to do so) in some fear of the Jewish power at the centre of things, in Rome; he feared also their power, political and financial, in the cities, not of his own little district only, but all around him. Reluctantly, but frightened into it at last by the threats of the Jewish authorities and the last Jerusalem mob, who clamoured for the shameful death of Our Lord, he had permitted that execution upon the Cross.

Following on that considerable event, the tide turned, and with it turned backwards the whole current of Jewish activity in the Græco-Roman world. It had hitherto been with the stream. It was henceforward to become, as though by a sort of fate or design, and in spite of those in authority who would have had it otherwise, hostile to, at issue with, the general society of the Orient and Europe in which it was now so widely dispersed and so powerful.

The quarrel now arose and was beginning to take on a

permanent virulence, to become, as it were, a *cosmic* quarrel, affecting the whole world; and it followed immediately upon the predication and sacrifice of Our Lord.

There was no direct connection between the Passion and the national catastrophe that followed. The catastrophe had been prophesied by Jesus Christ, whose disciples vividly remembered those words and handed them on to posterity; but nothing done by the new and very young Christian body led to the official Roman resentment against Jews in Palestine. The mortal quarrel that was on the point of breaking out on the soil of Palestine was a quarrel between the Roman Empire and the Jews, not between the Roman Empire and this new small body, the *Ecclesia*, of which the Empire as yet knew little, even in the East, and which it rather protected against the main Jewish body for the sake of order.

Shortly after the Crucifixion came the "Incident of the Standards". The Standards of the Legions bore an effigy of Cæsar —a thing odious to Jewish religious feeling. The Imperial authorities in Palestine reluctantly gave way on the matter. Next came the tumult about the confiscatory taxing of the Temple funds for the building of an aqueduct. Then came the brief but dangerous and significant incident of the Emperor's statue to be set up in Jerusalem. Half a dozen years after the Crucifixion, the Emperor of the day having ordered his statue to be put up in the precincts of the Temple, the excitement was such that the Commander of the Forces in Syria had to mobilise the Army. He marched from Antioch with three legions (all the soldiers he could spare from the garrisons) and a mass of Syrian auxiliaries as well.

It was clear that the temper of both sides was leading to war. To the Jews, idolatrous worship was intolerable, and that it should impinge upon their holy centre of national life was a thing to be fought to the death. To the Roman Government (and indeed all the civilisation which that Government represented) this claim to special historical immunity from the general life of mankind was equally intolerable. The Emperor who had insisted upon his statue defiling the Holy Places was a madman and soon got rid of—but the crisis was bound to reappear.

Roman soldiers offended the Jews even in the midst of their worship; there was a case where one of them burnt a Book of the Law; another where one of the garrison grossly insulted a religious ceremony. The last Procurators sent by the worried Imperial power to deal with this local problem inevitably became the enemies of the people they had to administrate.

Florus, who was Procurator in the next decade, was remembered for having lit the final fire. The Jews of the Holy City confidently appealed to the Governor of Syria (Gallus) against the local government of Florus. In the Passover of A.D. 65, Gallus came down to Jerusalem from Antioch as head of the Government, but the quarrel was not appeased. There were troubles in Cæsarea, Florus took a present of money to save the Jews from the hatred of the townspeople, and the Jews complained that though he had taken the money he did not act. At last Florus was determined to make an end, and marched on the city. Vast crowds met him, invoking Cæsar with loud cries. He allowed his soldiers to sack Jewish houses. He massacred nearly four thousand of the recalcitrants. He crucified not a few, and exasperated the rebellion by scourging Jews who were Equites —that is, men of important social position who had acquired (usually by payment) a title of honour.

Florus did not succeed. He withdrew his troops, and with this sign of weakness the zealots clamoured for war. In the north of Palestine the great-grandson of Herod the Great, a man who bore the official title and traditional name of Agrippa (for that great Roman general had been an intimate friend of Herod's) exercised a petty authority, and was called King. He saw (as did the mass of educated men) the impossibility of Jerusalem standing out against the organised might of the Roman world. He came down and harangued his fellow Jews, begging them to compromise their quarrel, but he was turned out, and in the summer of A.D. 66 the war party was so much in the ascendant that they captured a Roman garrison on the shores of the Dead Sea and forbade the usual sacrifices offered in the Temple for the welfare of the Emperor to continue. What history calls "The Jewish War" had begun.

The fort Antonia, which dominated Jerusalem, was taken by the rebels; the small Roman garrison in Herod's palace was surrounded—it surrendered on promise of safety, and was *then* dreadfully butchered, to a man. After that treachery, there could be no compromise or treaty. Rome proceeded to act as a state; bad Jewish riots in Alexandria had already warned the Imperial power that they could not delay.

The great mass of the Syrian population heartily approved of the Imperial severity. In Antioch, the capital, there was a very large Jewish population with special privileges and power of self-government which was sufficient to prevent popular vengeance against it; in Sidon also there was a truce; but everywhere else the Syrians rose against the Jews as a prelude to the coming campaign. That campaign was conducted by the Roman generals on the largest scale. It was in full progress when Nero committed suicide, and the Empire fell, after a brief interval, into the hands of one of those very generals at work in Syria. It was Vespasian. He went to Rome to accept the throne which his soldiers had given him, leaving the conduct of the war to his son Titus, who prosecuted it with all the military force available, and was determined to bring it to a complete victory.

Siege lines were thrown round Jerusalem, within the walls of which were crowded an enormous body of Jews, not all of them in sympathy with the rebellion but all now under the power of the rebels; and those rebels, cooped up now in the Holy City, the last refuge of their effort, refused to consider any compromise.

At the end of May, in the year 70, the fourth year from the beginning of active hostilities, the Roman Army captured the first wall; but the main inner defences still stood, and throughout the heat of that summer the attack went on. By the early autumn it succeeded. On the 26th of September Titus had entered the city, and all was over. In the siege, and the massacre that followed, it would seem certain that over a million were killed. The number sounds incredible but it is vouched for by contemporary evidence and by the detailed, boastful, time-serving, but careful Jewish historian, Josephus, from whom we have a full account of the catastrophe. He appeals, as evidence for the truth of his figures, to a census which had shown those figures to be credible.

Apart from the numbers of the slain there was wholesale deportation; Jewish men and women were sold by thousands into slavery. The Romans sent batches of the conquered hither and thither throughout the Mediterranean; one very important group being exiled to the furthest west, to Spain, where they formed the origins of that powerful Spanish Jewry which was to work for more than a thousand years, now with, now against—but generally against—European civilisation in the Peninsula.

There is a saying, current in Europe today and for long past, often repeated on the Continent, and very true: "No one attacks Israel with impunity." The overwhelming victory of Titus, the destruction of the Holy City, the later building of a new Roman and pagan capital upon the site, splendid with Temples, was not the end. It was not even the end of Jewry in Palestine, let alone of the power of Israel throughout the world—and Israel always takes its revenge.

On what a scale that revenge could be, and to what white heat all these horrors had inflamed the mortal quarrel, we know from the epitome that was made of Dion Cassius's lost historical books. There was a Jewish rising in Cyrene (on the shores of North Africa, west of Egypt), in which over two hundred thousand of the Gentiles perished, amid inhuman scenes which disgust the reader. The avengers of Israel fell into a frenzy, making garlands of their victims' entrails, sawing those victims asunder, flaying them and using their skins as garments. The Romans and Greeks might then understand that what today we gently call "The Jewish Problem" had not been solved with the fall of the Holy City a lifetime before.

There was another still more awful massacre of Romans and Greeks by Jews in Cyprus, where nearly a quarter of a million Gentiles were butchered. The Empire took its revenge, also, in turn, of course, in proof of how strong such passions could be.

But we shall see later how enduring those passions were, and how they reappear throughout the centuries. Indeed, indeed, what Rome had called "the Jewish War" was not ended by the material destruction of Zion: Rome had discovered, in Syria, an enemy that cannot die.

The triumph of Titus, which concluded the first campaign, and filled the streets of Rome after the downfall of Jerusalem, was not an end, it was a beginning. Decaying in the Forum you may see today the triumphal Arch of the Roman General who had conquered forever the Holy Place, the Temple of Jehovah, and levelled the habitations of His people to the ground. You may see there the seven-branched candle-stick, symbol of what had happened. The triumphal Arch of Titus, still splendid and intact, is a permanent monument standing as proof of that unending "Jewish War" which the Roman conqueror centuries ago thought to have ended. So far from ending, the struggle continued side by side with the growth, the triumph, and, in these, our last days, the decline of the Christian Church.

Thus had these two things, the Church and the Jewish quarrel, arisen side by side. They sprang side by side into existence, on the morrow of Calvary. Nor after twenty centuries is the fate of either resolved.

XIII

The Christian Victory

THE FOURTH CENTURY after the Incarnation—A.D. 300 to 400—was a transformation of our world. It was the remoulding of the Roman Empire which we were and are. Henceforward we were Christendom.

The centre of government was officially Christian early after the turning point in the first years of the century. All society gradually became Christian, absorbing its still vigorous pagan remnants in the course of the next hundred years. After three centuries—that is, in the seventh century after the Incarnation, from a little after A.D. 600—that small first strict group, the Church, had converted the whole Empire. By an organisation at its origins partly secret, a body intense, determined, the prophesy was accomplished: "Fear not, I have overcome the world."

The doctrine, the morals, the ritual of the *Ecclesia* were becoming those of all men, even in the ultimate and distant province of Britain. Jesus Christ was worshipped everywhere as GOD—as very God—and His now admittedly divine Revelation was the light illuminating all. His Eucharist was becoming the universal sacrifice wherein all communicated, His affirmation of our Immortality and attainable beatitude, the universal hope.

Syria, after what Tertullian thought impossible had come to pass; Syria, after the Cæsars had become Christian and with them the official world of the Mediterranean, was the scene of two things: politically a frontier against the Orient, religiously the revered seed plot of the Faith.

First: Syria continues to be more than ever the bastion of our civilisation against the Oriental. This is a paradox, for the Syrian is himself an Oriental by his climate, traditions and blood. Yet does Syria stand as our bastion against the Oriental for so many hundred years because the Euphrates had become not only the average eastern boundary of the Roman Empire but the frontier of that Empire against the only great civilised power which could seriously be regarded as an enemy: Persia.

Second: though Syria is but a part of the vast Imperial State—a small frontier part at that—yet, during the violent religious conflicts which are the very essence of our history in the first Christian centuries of the Roman Empire, Syria, the original source of the Christian religion, is a Syria which held Jerusalem of the Resurrection, Nazareth and Bethlehem and Antioch: the Nursery of the Church.

◆

As to the military position of Syria in the first century after the official conversion of the Roman Empire, that is, between a little after A.D. 300 to rather after 600, we can best understand it thus:

With the unity of the Roman world under one head—the system which we call the Empire, which with its beginnings under the first Emperors was called the *Principatus*, "the rule of one head man", Syria had acquired capital political importance.

The new world-state, the foundation of all our modern civilisation and the summing up of all the ancient one, was vulnerable politically in only two ways, through the infiltration of the barbarians and by defeat at the hands of the civilised Asiatic—the Persian.

There was no danger of Roman arms being defeated by the unorganised Germans, Moors and Picts, Slavs and the rest. They had no desire to defeat the Empire, only to enter and take part in its advantages; and when they urged too much they could be mastered. They could always be cut to pieces whenever they raided across the frontiers, and they always were; but there was a danger that the continual filtering in of these outer people, the fringe of the Empire, as slaves and hired soldiers and colonists, would coarsen and weaken the stuff of our Western civilisation—and so it did at last: they did not and could not overcome but they could and did percolate.

But on the east there was a military frontier zone; for there an

organised power existed, and wherever there has been an organised power or one sufficiently strong in arms upon the Asiatic
side of us there has been peril of death. Centuries later, as we
know, that peril took the form of a new Arabian religion and
its armies sweeping over half the territory which Rome and
Greece had established. But in the end of the dead pagan world,
just before the Incarnation, the only Asiatic peril our civilisation
knew was the menace from Persia—the Persian (or Parthian*)
peril.

The frontier that was watched with acute anxiety was the
frontier of the Euphrates. On that frontier Rome had suffered
defeat and was to suffer defeat again. From that side was to come
serious invasion, and it became the principal task of the Empire
to secure its citizens from that armed menace.

Thus does Syria become the essential frontier thing it is from
the days of Augustus. It is no longer only a highway nor even
only a battleground. It is a principal outpost, a garrison, a fortress
against Asia, against conceptions other than our own and a
culture which might destroy our own.

This idea of establishing river frontiers is essentially Roman
and has been inherited by Romanised Gaul. It was never taken
to kindly by the outer Germans after the Christian armies had
civilised them: nor by the Slavs. At the root of a river frontier is
the double idea that such a frontier is definite and calculable as
well as being an obstacle; and that is where it differs from
mountain frontiers which look but are not more formidable
obstacles than a mere belt of water. The Roman, and the Gaul
after him, being possessed of hills cannot rest upon them. He
tries to push forward to a river that shall be his boundary. When
the Roman Army was disturbed rather than imperilled by barbarians to the north of the Alps it could not rest until it had
reached the Danube, although between Italy and the Danube
there lies the most formidable labyrinth of mountains in all
Europe.

Many things show how important Syria had now become in

* Parthia was a corner province of the general Persian world, a province for
some generations in ascendency over the rest.

the military organisation of a united world. Of these the most obvious is the size of the garrison, the most morally striking is the new prestige of a Syrian governor.

Of all the local administrators of the Empire, the provincial superiors, the man who held Syria was chosen for the highest rank. He was the Viceroy, socially superior to other provincial governors; his office was the "plum of the profession". Not that the governorship of provinces was a profession under Rome, but that in so far as man entered public life with a view to distinction, to be given the administration of Syria was as high a post as he could attain.

It was perhaps not only the frontier character of the province which did this, but also its great wealth concentrated upon so small an area. The words used continually throughout this book, "belt", "ribbon", "strip", "highway", "band", will indicate what I mean. From the northern Gulf of Alexandretta to the southern desert is a length comparable to the length of Roman Britain, but the breadth of the partly habitable land is nowhere half that of Roman Britain, and within that partly habitable land the greater part is not fully habitable at all. But men can sow and reap from the fields along the Orontes to beyond Aleppo. The Bekaa—the central valley—though a marsh under bad government, can become useful pasture under a good one. The little plains along the sea-coast to the north and the larger ones to the south, each with its city or cities, are fertile enough, if restricted. The oasis of Damascus and its neighbourhood are wealthy amid inhospitable, stony land, and treeless waste. In places where men can take root in Syria and where the cities arise, wealth, under strong and good government, is packed. It was never more so packed than in the days of Hellas and Rome, in that great thousand years between the excellent arrival of the Greeks and the evil arrival of Islam.

Another symptom or example of what Syria had now become in the full development of Roman power is the garrisoning there of *one-seventh* of the whole Roman Army, *one-seventh* of all the legions and auxiliary forces from the Sahara to the Grampians and from the Atlantic to the Euphrates. Syria is in area not a fiftieth of the Empire, yet of all the regiments under the Imperator—the Commander-in-Chief in Rome—one-seventh stood to arms on that little frontier line between the Gulf of Alexandretta and the Egyptian desert beyond Gaza.

There were three legions at least—later four—that is, three compact organised army corps of six thousand men, each with their due proportion of auxiliaries, probably as much again as the regulars. Counting together the legions and the auxiliaries fifty thousand men were permanently organised as a military force in that narrow frontier edge of the Syrian hills.

The legions—the regular armed men of long service—had been in the pagan days before Christ mainly Italian; and even after were still all legally Roman citizens. The auxiliary forces which had grown up side by side with the legions, beginning as an experiment, ending as an accepted part of the Army, were local bodies serving under their local chiefs or little kings. It was the way in which Rome recruited extra strength without breaking what had been so long a sort of sacred rule that the legionary must be a Roman citizen.

The Greek civil and military capital of all that area was the very great and wealthy town of Antioch in the north. The legions were planted out either as garrisons in the Syrian cities or encamped in barracks and huts immediately outside them: an arrangement in favour on the other boundaries of Rome, and one which was to have great effect upon the future of the Near East.

The north-eastern part of the Persian Empire, which had come to be known as *Parthia*, had been during the first centuries when the Church was expanding but before the Emperors had become Christian, the chief menace to Rome on her eastern frontiers. There had arisen under that menace a constantly renewed struggle in which the occupation of territory by Roman officials was pushed sometimes much farther eastward than the Euphrates, and at other times had to fall back upon the Euphrates line. During that struggle there were also armed Roman invasions right into Persian territory, not permanently occupying it; and corresponding Parthian raids right into

Roman territory, not permanently occupying it. The mountain kingdom of Armenia, a sort of buffer state, becoming Christian, had been the thing at issue. A long lifetime before the appearance of Constantine, in the first generation of the third century, just when the dangerous confusion of Roman affairs was getting to its worst, between A.D. 180 and A.D. 260, the central Persian power recovered control over its Parthian province, and right on until the coming of Islam, four hundred years later, the Persian dynasty of the Sassanides was the main enemy of Rome on the east.

At the beginning of the welter Rome still held posts beyond the Euphrates, but in the middle of it the powerful Persian King Sapor I conquered Roman armies, took the Roman Emperor prisoner, carried him away captive, raided into Syria itself and even into Cappadocia, and overran Cicilia. The Persians occupied Antioch for a brief space: then with the restoration of Roman power which began with Aurelian and was clinched by the reorganisation under Diocletian in the last years before A.D. 300, the whole of the State had pulled itself together, in spite of the last violent quarrel between the Empire and the Christian body within it which had grown so powerful, and which Diocletian's persecution failed to end.

When Constantine became universal monarch the military position changed; and it changed in a way which showed how effort had had to be concentrated against the Persian menace in the East, and on the defence of that Euphrates border which was essential to our civilisation. Constantine moved the capital of the Empire from Rome to Byzantium, which took the name of Constantinople. Henceforward the Army no longer looked to Rome but to Constantinople for orders, and later on, as the old structure of Roman and Greek society changed, the defence of Constantinople against barbarian pressure of all kinds was the principal business of the Army.

That Roman Army was now everywhere more and more barbaric in recruitment: and it is at this point of the first importance to understand what was meant by the word "barbarian".

The modern English word "barbarian" misleads the reader of history. The modern word gives the idea of something savage, in violent contrast with the world of civilised men. Now there was a contrast and a strong one, which everybody felt, between the highly civilised Greek and Roman governing classes and the outer tribes who were filtering in. Their dress and their language (though they very soon learnt to speak like their neighbours) and their manners *did* shock the writers of the old world, but in varying degrees. The Mongols, when they appeared later, seemed impossible—and so they were. But the Germans and Slavs, soon fully acclimatised Roman citizens and later Christians, were accepted; so were Arabs and Moors. There was between the leaders of German, Slav and Arabian troops on the one side and the upper class of the Empire on the other nothing like the contrast which we now express by the word "barbarian". The word meant, rather, "originally of exterior extraction". The important German and Slav officers in the Army, the important Orientals from the desert frontiers, not only held command but enjoyed high social status. They could and did rise to be Emperors. But there was felt to be a novelty and a somewhat degrading novelty in their growing position and influence. They could be as capable for administration and even as refined in culture as any of their colleagues from the older social strata, but the difference of origin was felt. The older noble families of Gaul, Spain and the Greek world felt it, yet were they all of one world with the Gothic and Vandal and African and Asiatic army officers. That is the essential fact which explains what followed.

In the great change that was coming, a social change as well as a religious one, Germans, Slavs, Arabians, were mixing more and more with the stuff of the Græco-Roman civilisation. They came in to enjoy it and to settle in it; they pressed upon it more and more—not as enemies, but as men claiming a part of the advantages which civilisation could give and which they so lacked when they remained in their outer world. There were hordes of them present within the Empire as small free cultivators, as slaves, but particularly as soldiers. It was difficult to get a fully civilised man in this new state of affairs to take up the burden of long-service military life, so not only the rank and file but the bulk of the officers became increasingly barbaric in blood. And all the while society as a whole, the original Græco-Roman elements and infiltrated barbaric elements also, was gradually becoming Christian.

The way in which the Army grew barbaric in recruitment and later in officering, until the whole texture of it was of that kind, can be seen by the names and careers of those who led it.

Take three very high examples: Alaric, Stilicho, Theodoric.

Alaric was probably a German,* one of the Princes of the German troops called Goths. He became a Roman officer, and all his advancement was that of a Roman officer in the Roman Army. His career filled the years following—a long lifetime after—the appearance of Constantine. His big quarrel with the authorities had nothing to do with the contrast between barbarian and original Rome—it was a quarrel about what position he ought to have in the higher command. He wanted to be Commander-in-Chief, and though he was already nearly at the top, there was a social feeling against his being granted so very high an honour. That was why Alaric started a civil war, in the course of which he took and sacked the city of Rome itself. The Army that followed him to the last was made up of all sorts, though originally based upon a presumably German (Gothic) recruitment, but to the end it was a Roman Army Corps and nothing else.

Stilicho, the man who commanded the official forces against Alaric in that civil war, and who represented the central Imperial power, was just as much a "barbarian" as Alaric. He was a Slav (so far as we can judge the meaning of the tribal names of the day): presumably a Wend.

Theodoric, the great Roman general who became ruler over Italy, was a Goth by blood; but he was the son of a regular Roman official and he himself was brought up at the Imperial Court. The Emperor made him a Patrician and a Consul, and he

---

* It is arguable that the Goths were not Germans but Lithuanians. It is not an important point.

only went to Italy under the direct commission of the Emperor, who sent him with a mission to replace another man of his own kind.

These important generals who appear as the heads of the Roman forces from the fourth century onwards are "barbarians", but they are *not* invaders. They are part and parcel of the Roman structure, brought up within it and incorporated in it.

The Roman Army, now grown barbaric in recruitment and largely in officering as well, tended of course (each part of it) to obey its commanders as separate authorities; and the Emperors at Constantinople could not resist this tendency in the distant West. Theodoric, though he was an Imperial Envoy, became virtually independent in Italy. Other generals took over the command of Spain and Southern Gaul, and an incorporated band of barbaric soldiers, probably Slav in origin and leadership, was called in by a Roman official to North Africa and started an independent Vandal Government there.

In the East it was possible to keep up a stricter discipline; partly because an anti-Christian enemy was evident close at hand in the shape of Persia—strongly armed, civilised, and a clear menace to the whole of society. In the West only one such serious menace occurred—the Mongol invasion of the middle fifth century under Attila, which the Western generals combined to beat off. But the Army in the East was also kept more in hand because Constantinople, the capital, was close by and could deal with the Greek-speaking world as one body. The Army of the "Eastern Empire", as it was now called (though the whole Empire still felt itself to be one) was subject to the Emperor directly, and its generals did not establish independent governments. It came to form a united body which is usually spoken of today as the "Byzantine Forces", and it was these that kept up the fight against anti-Christian invasion from the East, until the novel and disastrous appearance, three hundred years after Constantine, of the invaders from the Arabian deserts.

There is another point of importance to be noted in this new Byzantine Army. Its strength lay in heavy cavalry, not in infantry. That was part of the great social change that was going on, part of the general dislocation of society.

Infantry strong enough to stand up to cavalry presupposes a high organisation. As social coherence weakens, and the professional soldiers cannot be so strictly disciplined, the production of an infantry that can stand up to cavalry gets more difficult. A degraded infantry will collapse before a heavy cavalry charge. Cavalry became the essential arm not only of the Byzantine forces, that is, the forces directly controlled by Constantinople, but over all the old Græco-Roman world. Infantry did not take its old place again on the battlefield until the end of the Middle Ages, a thousand years after the great religious change. Not that there were not great masses of foot-soldiers (sometimes myriads of them) recruited for main struggles between one power and another within the Christian world, or even for action beyond its frontiers, but that these agglomerations were not the permanent military strength. Battles were henceforward decided by the horse; and when the horse of one side overthrew that of the other, the masses of foot-men present on the other—when there happened to be such masses present—dissolved and went to pieces.

This preponderance of cavalry was in favour of those who were menacing our civilisation and at the end, when Islam conquered us in the East, it was Islam on horseback that conquered; the Mongol Huns who attempted the destruction of our civilisation under Attila more than a century after Constantine depended upon horse, though they were followed by hosts of men on foot as well; especially by such Germans as they had subjugated. But particularly was this new rôle of cavalry valuable to the Persian power. When a Persian Army defeated a Byzantine Army, it was a mounted force that did the work.

Such defeats at the hands of the Persians were suffered again and again throughout the three hundred years, though they did not succeed in permanently breaking the frontier of the Euphrates. They came nearest to it towards the end of the sixth century, and at the beginning of the seventh. Even in Constantine's century, during the pagan reaction under the Emperor Julian

(Constantine's nephew, the Apostate), the Persians beat back the Byzantine Army which had reached Mesopotamia and Julian himself was killed.

In A.D. 573 the anti-Christian Persian Army, advantaged by quarrels in the Christian camp, again captured Antioch and when they ebbed away took with them one-third of a million Syrians. This late Persian victory was not the last; Syria was overrun again in 607; and half a dozen years later there is a Persian garrison established in Antioch once more. That invading Army seized Damascus as well; and the next year, A.D. 614, they took Jerusalem.

It looked, for a moment, like the end of Syria. The True Cross was taken, and another great herd of Christian prisoners from Jerusalem, the numbers of which are differently handed down to us (some say ninety thousand, none less than thirty thousand, but at any rate a very great number), were taken captive to be sold into slavery.*

There was in command at Byzantium at that moment a very remarkable man, the Emperor Heraclius, the last of those who kept up the fight for Syria and the Oriental frontiers of Rome. Not ten years after the catastrophe of Jerusalem he organised a great rally, based upon the religious enthusiasm of his subjects. He dedicated his efforts to Our Lady and Our Lord, whose images he had borne before him. He destroyed the Persian Army opposed to him in Asia Minor, and although barbarian swarms were menacing Constantinople itself, he established himself at the very end of his effort in Mesopotamia gaining a great victory near the ruins of Nineveh.

Chosroes, the Persian King who had triumphed at Jerusalem, was dead, his son would not keep up the struggle, and the symbolic act which marked what was apparently a final and decisive Christian victory over the Orient was the restoration of the True Cross.

---

* It was recorded that this was the occasion of another Jewish revenge, the last before the coming of Islam. The Jews had been forbidden to inhabit Jerusalem by the Christian Empire. The Jews bought up, it is said, the Christian prisoners from the heathen Persians and massacred them.

The power of our civilisation seemed, by a sudden reverse of fortune, restored in Syria for good, and the Christian name would now attach to all that land for ever. The name of Heraclius might stand as that of Constantine stands; he might have been the pacificator and rebuilder of everything, to whom we should look back as the second founder of Christian peace throughout at least the eastern, Greek, part of the Mediterranean world. But the event was enormously otherwise.

Even at the moment when the Holy Cross was being restored and our power over the Orient triumphantly affirmed, with the re-establishment of Christian Syria once more as a permanent bastion, there was rising unsuspected a force which was to undo everything. The desert was about to return. Islam was born and was upon the march to conquer—but of this Heraclius amid his Christian triumph knew nothing.

◆

This military effort to save our civilisation, its frontier of the Euphrates, its bastion of the Syrian hills, its centre and capital in Constantinople, was going on side by side during these three centuries with what was essentially, though not superficially, an even more important struggle for religious unity against heresies. That struggle began with full violence in the very midst of Constantine's glory and his re-establishment of authority. It continued not only to the coming of Islam, but throughout the generations uninterruptedly. What we have to follow in these last three hundred years of Christian domination over the East and over Christian Syria is a spiritual war which has indeed no end, but which, in this field of the Orient, and for that space of time, A.D. 300–600, is the key to all our comprehension of it.

It is a great misfortune to history that just at the moment when detailed historical study began, some two and a half centuries ago, there also began that gradual but increasingly rapid decay in religion which made it more and more difficult for those who would write history to understand the vital importance of doctrine.

Almost every force has been called in to explain this and that in the past—except the force of doctrine: dogma. Race has been appealed to; economic circumstance; military circumstance (certainly more important than the other two) has been appealed to, and the chief rôle has been given (by those who understand and value a decisive victory) to the fact that men were what they were because of this and that battle.

All these forces have their place in the story of change, but until quite lately the supreme factor of religious conflict has not been understood. It has puzzled and it has irritated, so that commonly it has been dismissed. Yet supreme it is.

The central thing in the business of Europe is the Doctrine of the Incarnation: the affirmation that God had appeared among men, and the denial thereof. From the first public announcement of that affirmation about A.D. 29–33, it has been the main issue dividing all men of the Græco-Roman world, moulding and unmoulding our society.

Constantine had established his peace, he had founded his new city, he was prepared (from A.D. 325) to administer vigorously and with justice a united, orderly, permanently established society, when he found himself at the outset confronted by a storm within that world which took him by surprise, puzzled, and exasperated him. The magnitude of it he at last perceived, though he could not understand why it should be so great—and by the time he died it was the main issue in the world over which his successors were called to rule.

This storm had arisen on the fundamental question of Our Lord's Divinity.

Let there be no error; the question is fundamental not only to that time but to our own. It remains the root question for those who ridicule the doctrine, for those who are indifferent to it, and for those who would defend it. With Jesus Christ as God incarnate there is one view of the world. With Jesus Christ as a Prophet, a model, or a myth, there is another: and the one view is mortal enemy to the other. The meat of the one is poison to the other.

The point in that early day was this:

There had been presented before the world by this new thing, the Christian Church—this *Ecclesia*, this new society

226

which had permeated and at last transmuted our civilisation—a compact set of doctrine and morals and a whole way of living dependent on those doctrines and morals.

There had arisen in Syria and spread throughout the civilised world, even into the East (where it was being persecuted and would ultimately be crushed), all over the West from the Euphrates to the Atlantic (where it had triumphed), a Christian society into which men became compact. It took some time to amalgamate the millions of the Græco-Roman world into that body. For two lifetimes at least after Constantine there remained recalcitrant exceptions; but anyhow, the New Thing had, by 325, won.

It had changed the values of human action, and the nature of social life. Despair, which the old pagan civilisation universally admitted, from which it turned away its eyes by following pleasure on the one hand, however shameful, or honour on the other, however sterile; despair, Epicurean or Stoic, was, by the Christian hope, denied its empire. Not only was man immortal, as the wisest of men had long known, not only was he possessed of human dignity, as all the pagan world well knew, not only were slave or freeman, millionaire or pauper, equal in essence; but men (said this new authority, the Church) are destined to Beatitude.

Then, again, there had been a setting right of balance between vice and virtue; the old virtues were re-established by the new authority; decent living, and the family, and all that the simpler, traditional heathens well knew to be right. The sexual perversions into which the heathen world had fallen were denounced by the *Ecclesia* as horrible and insufferable; so also were denounced the excesses of cruel revenge. All these evils continued to be indulged, no doubt, but not accepted. This new authority denounced them and the conscience of mankind responded to it.

With this revolution went the new conception of holiness. Holiness there had always been, of shrines and of great souls; but now by this new authority holiness was a direct personal attachment to the Divine, which all might attain in communion with the Divine Man. Attached to Him as examples, great influences, and models, were His famous proclaimers, the Apostles, and that Holy Mother by whose consent He had been brought into the world, and whereby His Humanity was attached to His Divine Origin.

His Divine Origin? That was the crux. All this new message, this good news, the Evangel, was not of value nor could rootedly endure save as a supernatural revelation. Its impact upon the world had come through One walking and teaching in Syria, Who had said that He spoke with the authority of the Supreme God, by Whom He was sent, Whom He knew, Who knew Him, to Whom He would return and with Whom He was bound up in some mysterious relationship, as of a Father to a Son; and what was more by a unity of relationship which made each inseparable from the other.

This affirmation was of the essence of the new authority. The Christian ethic is a burden to man's common reason and appetite. It cannot hold unless it is accepted as proclaimed by God, man's Creator and Judge. It did not repose upon the charm or sweetness or what not of the things said by its Founder—for all that charm, sweetness and the rest might be self-delusion—but upon the claim of the source whence those things proceeded. Jesus Christ had called Himself Divine: His followers repeated insistently and triumphantly that enormous claim.

Divine. But in what manner Divine? Not as a prophet conveying a message: Israel also had proclaimed God through prophets, and those prophets had conveyed their message—but this was something new. This was the Divine apparent on earth. God had in some way appeared among men—at least, so this Man said—and *said it of Himself.* If that affirmation were the illusion of megalomania or the exaggeration of His followers, the message lost its value: for that message depended upon His credibility: He, who laid claim to Divinity. If that claim to Divinity were abandoned by posterity He was a liar or a madman and the message was lost: also it was too hard to bear. The hope was lost, the new triumphant but most difficult morals, the restoration—that is, the Salvation—of the world was lost. All that.

But God was One, or God could not be God. Now, the new highly organised triumphant society proclaimed that this Divine Teacher was Himself also God. He was Man, He was what our modern jargon calls "an historical personality", as common sense will say, a Being like ourselves with a body and the frailties and limitations of a body. He had been born as men are born, He had suffered as men suffer, He had even died in great agony, still claiming that He did so for the Redemption of the world.

To so extraordinary a claim the Church maintained that He had given substance and proof by His Resurrection from the dead, and that this Resurrection had been followed by His own solemn command to announce His claim to all nations. But if He was indeed God, were there then two gods? The Divine Unity was essential to the conception of Divinity; Israel had known that by Revelation and the pagan world had come to know it too by sheer reason. How could this mere man be God? Yet if He were not *in some way* God the whole message failed. It was not sufficient in itself, without supreme authority, to change, to revivify, to re-establish mankind. The Sacrifice of Calvary would be no full sacrifice, the new link proclaimed, the Incarnation, by which alone there was now full fellowship between the Creator and the creature, was snapped—and yet how could that link, the full Divinity of the Founder, be reasonably maintained?

That was the essential issue; the reconciliation between the two apparently irreconcilable propositions—that Our Lord was God, and yet that God was One.

It was successively attempted in many ways: by saying that Our Lord was indeed God Himself, but only apparently Man— as though a phantasm; by saying that the Godhead came into Him during His predication and used a human body for its purpose—and so on. The solution which became suddenly fashionable just before Constantine achieved full power took the name of Arianism.

The origin of names is capricious; the French are called the French because the Roman general at the head of the Frankish auxiliaries, a small Flemish army-group, took over the government of Gaul. England is called England because a few sea-raiders from the Angle, the "Angulus" of the Romans, the "Bight", the corner between Denmark and North Germany, raided a narrow strip of land and established themselves on the north-east coast of this island. Asia is called Asia from the name of one small town on the Greek seas.

So with "Arianism". It took its name from a second-rate man called Arius, an Egyptian priest, who happened to provide a head-line.

He had begun making (or accepting) popular verses and songs against the Godhead of Christ, a little before this year 300. His name accidentally stuck to the movement; no doubt he was glad to find that name so unexpectedly important. But the movement was not important through Arius; it was important through the violent desire of millions to be certain upon a mystery which was vital to them—and to be rid of the bother of it. The attempt to be *certain* upon a mystery. The attempt to rationalise it.

The "Arians" invented a subtle complicated way out of the dilemma: Our Lord was Divine all right; Divine in origin because the Divinity produced Him, as a Divine Being, before the beginning of time; and that Divine Being had been the agency whereby all things were made. Christ was not fully God, but had come forth from God before the ages. That explanation fell in with the popular philosophy of the moment, in which crowds of thinkers had been steeped for two lifetimes—the feeling that the Godhead worked by emanation, sending out as it were waves of influence, and thus creating the world. They could accept Our Lord, if not as God, yet as a Divine Being at the very origin of these waves of influence. He was at the very source of all created things, Begotten of the Father, and all the rest of it. *But not fully God*: not identically God. That was what they were after: to get rid of that stumbling-block, the God Man; to revert to ordinary, comprehensible things.

To this the instinct of the Christian Church replied, "No; He was fully God. . . . Not after this or that fashion, somewhat derogating from His complete Godhead, but God from all eternity."

When I say here "instinct" I mean that unconquerable tendency in any organism to fulfil itself; to be itself, and to preserve itself against destruction. The Catholic Church could not continue to live if it denied its founder's Godhead. This instinct was universal in the masses of Christian men, it was strong among their intellectual leaders, and among their official leaders, the Bishops. Still, there ran side by side with it that other human instinct, the necessity for the use of reason. The mystery of the Incarnation had to be reconciled with reason; and how could it be so reconciled without some compromise?

The battle joined in men's minds was a battle between the humble acceptation of the Faith, with all its Mysteries, and those rationalist tendencies by which the Faith, and all its social consequences, and all its effect upon the individual, are ultimately destroyed. Had the Arians won, the Faith would have quickly died.

To the Emperor Constantine, now master of the newly consolidated world, the newly re-established and strongly confirmed Roman order, this discussion, raging everywhere among his subjects, was merely tiresome.

He had slipped into sympathy with the Faith through the atmosphere of his time. His emotions had been strongly moved in favour of it, not without the influence of curious personal superstitions. As a politician he saw how the tide was running, but his emotions counted more.

He had never been baptised—but that meant little. Many men postponed baptism to the end of their lives, so as to secure remission of sins with certitude. What did count was that he had never conceived of differences in doctrine as important. They seemed to him unessential, as they must seem to anyone who has not thought these matters out: and he, a soldier, had had no occasion to think such things out. What he did, as supreme authority in the State, was to ask the Christian Bishops from all over the Empire to come and settle things at a General Council, which was to be held at Nicea, not far

from Constantinople, on the mainland of Asia, in this year
A.D. 325.

From the West very few came, but among them delegates
from the See of old Rome, the Primacy of which was generally
admitted, and without whose adhesion no conclusion could
have held. The vast majority of those who came, came from the
Greek-speaking East. The Emperor commissioned them to discuss the affair and to come to a conclusion.

Now how did Syria stand in this all-important debate?

The question was of the first moment, for this reason, that
Syria was the native ground of the Church: all her historical
authority came from Syria. The Bishop of Jerusalem was the
custodian of the Holy Places, of the site of the Resurrection.
The Bishop of Antioch was in the succession of those who had
nourished the infant Church in her cradle—St. Peter himself
and the great St. Ignatius had presided there. There was not a
congregation in Syria but could speak from knowledge, handed
down from father to son, of things that had happened among
them not so very long ago. In Syria, men who had talked with
the Apostles survived to speak to men whose sons had known
the elders of the Nicean Council. The oldest Syrian delegates at
Nicea stood to the last of the Apostles as old men today may
stand to the early eighteenth century.

An old man today can testify to what people whom he knew
in youth had to say about America when men who had
signed the Declaration of Independence were still alive; and
the oldest of the generation which saw the Declaration of
Independence could well remember the first generation of the
eighteenth century. I who write this am not yet old, but I
remember one who talked to me in childhood of the French
Revolution which he had seen, and the old men of the French
Revolution had seen Louis XIV. The Syria of 325 was still in
real and living touch with the whole story which had transformed the world.

Now Syria, orthodox as all the Church was orthodox, nevertheless provided arguments for Arianism. Arius himself was the
disciple of a great teacher in Antioch, who had not indeed

taught his doctrine, but had spoken in those undefined terms which now required definition.

Cæsarea, the great Imperial town on the coast of Palestine, had for its Bishop one of the most famous men of the day, Eusebius, the capital historian of the Christian Church; and Eusebius, after his fashion, sympathised with Arius. He could not wholly accept the full Godhead of the Christ.

That other Eusebius who had so much influence over Constantine, the Bishop of Nicomedia, had also been taught in Antioch by the same teacher as Arius; that same teacher who had not denied the full Godhead of Our Lord, but who had presumably used indeterminate language upon Him—and this Bishop of Nicomedia was Arian in sympathy.

In the Council, Arianism was swamped. The numerical vote was overwhelming—but counting noses is never a final operation in human affairs. Men are divided within themselves as well as by parties; and there remained in favour of compromise upon this doubt on the full Godhead of Jesus all manner of forces at work within the minds of men.

To begin with there was the very large remaining pagan body, with whom we must count of course that which is present in all great controversies, the huge majority of indifferent men who await the issue or anyhow care very little about it. Among those outstanding pagan conservatives, especially in the West, but also largely represented in the East, were the swarms of philosophers, and the proud, wealthy, traditional families.

Then there was the inevitable smouldering conflict between the civilian and ecclesiastical authorities. The Emperor had come to call himself Christian, and his successors were to call themselves Christians save for one exception; but the power of the organised Church was a rival to the power of the Emperor and his officials; and among those officials very many were indifferent to the Church, and many in different degrees hostile.

Then there was the latent rationalism present in all men, because men are reasonable beings, and, as reasonable beings, are irritated by mystery and inclined to attempt short cuts out of it.

There were also uncounted thousands who troubled very little about the subtleties of explanation, but who said to themselves, "Well, after all, there can't be One God and Two Gods! A person can't be finite and infinite at the same time—he can't be at the same time creature and Creator. And what is more, these controversies tire me. I am content to worship my Lord."

More important than any other factor in the affair is that which is so much overlooked in our modern histories of the time—the Army.

The Army, the thing which held the Roman State together from the Atlantic to the Euphrates, from Scotland to the Sahara, was largely Arian; its commanders who gave the tone were Arian. The barbarian rank and file who composed it were either still pagan, or, by influence, Arian. This was partly because a zealous missionary who had introduced the Christian religion in the Gothic recruiting field, had been an Arian; but much more because the Army naturally felt itself opposed to that other rival body in the management of Roman affairs—the Church.

The Church represented to the soldier the despised civilian— and the soldier would take the opposite side to the Church in a direct quarrel.

On the top of all this was the feeling of fashion. The soldiers would not trouble themselves very much about the subtleties of theological controversy, but they knew that Constantine had Arian sympathies, they knew that his sons, who inherited his Empire, were divided and that the Court was full of Arianism. The officers of the Army felt it was "the thing" to be Arian.

Many modern historians, especially of the last generation, like to pretend that the Army of the fourth and fifth centuries, and onwards, was Arian because they were noble Northerners, filled with simplicity. That is nonsense. There was nothing simple about the Arian business. Its theology was as complicated as could be. What was certainly present was this political antagonism between the generals and the Church; between the officers and the Church socially; and all this was mixed up with the latent antagonism between the Court and the Church. There was a feeling among the generals that they should stand up to the

234

Church; among their subordinates a feeling that to be Arian was to be with the Court and all that was socially most important in the Roman world.

We all know that those who are not quite sure of themselves in society naturally drift towards what they believe at heart to be fashionable. The generals of the West, over whom Constantinople in the next generation lost all direct control, men ruling in Gaul, Spain, Italy and North Africa, went intensely Arian, and were proud to remain Arian even when Arianism was dying in every other part of the Empire. They had established themselves as rulers, and at their Courts Arianism was the official religion, separating them from the rest of their subjects. They were proud of the label which distinguished them from the popular leaders, the Bishops, in Gaul and Spain and Italy. It made them feel superior—just as minorities in control of the official machine within our own memory have liked to feel themselves superior to the popular religion, in Ireland, for instance, or in Poland.

After Arianism was played out, new heresies with new names followed, the discussion on which filled (and also vitalised) our society throughout the fifth and sixth centuries. But though these heresies took on new names they were really at heart all the same thing: the continued desire to be rid in one way or another of that incredible thing: the Godhead of a Man.

What is called the Monophysite heresy (that is, the heresy of "The One Nature") was rooted in the conception that Our Lord, if He were God, could not have the nature of a man; and if He were a man could not have the nature of God. Its successor, the Monothelite heresy (which means the heresy of "The One Will") ran thus: "Well; we have been beaten by the Church on the single nature of Christ, but we will at least insist upon this, that He had not two wills, a human and a Divine; only one will." The logical consequence of that theory must be that Our Lord's will accepting the Passion was not accepting it in agony as would the human will: there was no true sacrifice.

All these successive heresies were not a ringing of the changes upon mere verbal distinctions; they were inflamed by one burning issue—whether God had truly been seen here on earth and had truly been also as we are. The whole thing was a battle upon the Incarnation. If the enemies of the Faith had won the battle we should have been as Islam is today. The very character of our civilisation would have been other than it now is.

In all these things Syria played its part. It was at Tyre and then at Antioch that St. Athanasius, the champion of orthodoxy, was condemned. Syria furiously debated the subsequent consequences of Arianism. In the great Monophysite quarrel, for instance, which had swept the East (Egypt in particular, that most important province, had made the heresy an excuse for a nationalist quarrel with the distant Government of Constantinople), Syria produced leaders like John of Ephesus (who was Syrian by birth) and the Bishop of Baalbec. To this day the Monophysite tradition is strong and separatist in the remaining shrunken Christian bodies of the Orient.

While these questions were still debating; while Christendom was thus divided because the very central principle of Christian civilisation was fighting for its life, against the Army, against local separatism, against a hostile philosophy; while the Empire itself, on the material side, after fighting for its life against the anti-Christian forces of Persia—a revolutionary thing, a new enemy, arose.

Roman civilisation and the Church had apparently triumphed through the Christian zeal of Heraclius when there suddenly arose that major heresy which was indeed to do what neither Arianism nor any other of its derivatives and successors had been able to accomplish. The most powerful denial of the Incarnation, the denial which came armed and victorious, was gathering in the desert and coming upon us without our dreaming of the danger: Islam.

XIV

The Return of the Desert

THERE HAD not been and was not to be again in all the business of Syria and of the world such an affair as that which followed upon the apparently final triumph of Heraclius and his establishment of the Christian name, of the Mass and all our civilisation, triumphant over the Eastern heathen.

All our culture was again one, and though the last three centuries had soon so thorough a rearrangement of that unity, yet a unity it was.

The Arian garrisons with their petty kings upon the West were failing; Gaul was governed in the Roman tradition of orthodoxy and was Catholic again, even at Court; Italy and Africa had been recovered from rebel Arian generals; even the Court of Spain could not long maintain its outdated heresy: all that was directly under Constantinople—Greece, Asia Minor, Egypt, North Africa and Syria itself—though the religious quarrel had profoundly disturbed it and though the infiltration of the barbarians had transformed the texture of it in the Balkans and all the neighbourhood of the Imperial City on the Bosphorus, was Roman again and Roman for good.

Then there came, more suddenly than we can conceive and as unexpectedly as an earthquake, a cataclysm—a tidal wave.

None had foreseen it. There were no preliminary symptoms. It broke at once, and submerged everything. The triumph of Heraclius was not half a dozen years old when there came riding rapidly out of the desert from the south that light cavalry of whom no man had heard anything save, vaguely, that there were such fellows, wandering about on horseback over the sands for centuries past, and that they were of no effect—chance nomads and marauders. These swept up between a night and a morning, as one may say, out of the wilderness into the stable land, riding in from the places where there was no settled thing, nor verse nor column nor majestic court of law, nor throne nor official—and overthrew all these things.

What was their strength?

Numerically it was very small at first, and never grew in itself to be very great in mere numbers; some four thousand of the lean Arabian spearmen, crouched on their short stirrups, were the vanguard of the thing. Many followed, and as they conquered they recruited; but it was never by numbers that they achieved their new, astonishing, and complete domination.

It will never be explained; we can only say that it happened; but we know that there was behind them and filling them with fire, a religion—"Islam"—"the submission", "the acceptation"; almost the same idea as that which lies behind our Roman term, "The Faith". A chance enthusiast had preached, far off down the caravan road, half-way down the Arabian littoral to the east of the Red Sea, something which was not a new religion but yet another heresy, and which proved of greater power than any of the heresies as yet lit by the stirring of the Christian thing.

Mohammed was the man who started the flame, but Mohammed did not make a new religion—remember that. He did not preach one. He preached a *Reformation*. He based his movement on certain fundamental doctrines of that Christian thing which had apparently conquered the Roman world, but he proposed a settlement of difficulties by denying the Incarnation.

No one proclaimed more exaltedly the splendour of the Christ—yes, and of His Mother, to whom the devotion of Christendom arose and whose image had led the armies of Heraclius to victory against the hosts of the Persian pagans. Jesus, said Mohammed, was the last of the great prophets. *But He was not God.* He was a man. He would judge mankind, as He had said, in that Resurrection of the Flesh which His followers had announced—the great Last Day. Our Lady, the Lady Miriam, had borne Jesus to the salvation of mankind. That Christian vision of beatitude as the end of man—immortality, yes; *individual* immortality—which had inspired the world with hope; the resurrection of the flesh to immortal life; the awful and equally immortal penalty of evil—all these things were included in the fierce predication which Mohammed had imposed upon his little group, the little fighting nomad bodies far off there, along the Red Sea borders. But that difficult matter, the Godhead of a man, he denied, to the comfort of all who had so long doubted that impossible thing.

There was this strange thing about the new heresy, which was to master and to swallow up all the rest, that it did not arise *within* the body of the Church; it came from the very fringes and from without.

Yet a heresy it was, I say; not a new religion. It drew its substance from the Christian Faith; it founded all its strength on certain main Christian doctrines; it maintained that strength (as heresy always does) by making a special appeal through a selection of those doctrines. It presented those which the men of the time could savour; it rejected those which the men of the time had forgotten or misunderstood, or come to ridicule, or abandoned. So, today, men will accept the mercy of God, but not His justice.

Mohammed's burning appeal was an appeal to simplicity and the relaxation of the intelligence; and to relaxation also of restraint over the appetites of man.

The Christian world of the East was filled with monks. The monastic institution had spread to the West and was becoming the strength of society therein. Celibacy was the discipline which gave it power. That rebuke to human passion the new Mohammedan heresy resented and threw down.

It even, through the spirit of the place in which it arose, rejected the age-long Western ideal of monogamy; it permitted—as the older Orient had permitted—a plurality of wives. The strain upon the mind of thinking deeply upon absolute truth, all that we call theology and its divisions, which had so profoundly disturbed the Greek world and—politically—the West as well, Mohammed threw aside; and he threw aside priesthood too, because there was therein too much of complexity; and he threw aside the Sacraments, because there was therein too much mystery. Further—most tremendous of innovations!—with the Sacraments Islam threw aside the Mass, round which all our Christian society had centred.

So equipped, the new heresy, with none to fight for it at first but these few thousands of the desert, brought the desert back upon Syria and upon all the Eastern world, of which Syria was the centre and the symbol. The desert returned.

According to whether Syria be with the West or the East, according to that fluctuate the fortunes of our blood. It had been with the East; it had been the western bastion of the eastern and southern desert through all the Assyrian and the Persian time. The glory of the Grecian advance, the splendour of Alexander's armies and their achieved purpose, had given it back to the West. When the West was united under the Roman name, Syria so remained a test of our recovery; and from having been, for innumerable centuries, the western edge of the eastern desert thing, Syria became, for a thousand years, the eastern rampart of the western European thing. In that character it had set forth the Gospel of Christ, so that we of the West became the heirs thereof.

But now the unseen powers had reversed the tide, and Syria was to fall to the men of the desert again; it was to be of the East once more; and with the loss of Syria, with the loss of that symbol, went the loss of very much more. We lost (alas!) not only Syria, but all the African side of the Mediterranean, everything up to the Ægean, and later much more. For generations we lost Spain itself, the best fighting blood of the West. There was a moment when Islam reached the middle Danube, and yet a later moment, not much more than two hundred years ago, when it surged up thither again, and came very near to the destruction of our civilisation.

It is a thing forgotten—yet pre-eminently to be remembered—that in the days when William of Orange had been set up by the rich as their puppet on the throne of England, in the days when Louis XIV of France was already growing old, when the great French poets of his reign had already become classic, when Dryden was at his full, the Mohammedan was grasping

Vienna; with one more victory he would have reached the Rhine.

All that. And the beginnings of the affair were in this upward sweep of some few thousands, crouching on their short stirrups, on their light little mounts of the desert, with their rocking-horse tails, nervous neighing nostrils and pawing hooves.

They came up, I say, in their few thousands, and they did all they willed. Others followed them, but they were always far less than the hosts they had to meet; yet those hosts they everywhere overthrew. Recruiting as they went, but never superior in mere mass, always superior in something we cannot now explain, a driving power, an enthusiasm, they swept right over what had been all the military organisation of Persia to the east. As for us upon the West, though they did not fully flood us as they flooded the East, they did, even in the first shock, go very far indeed.

That first shock began by their riding up the road the use of which goes beyond all human memory, up by the east of the Dead Sea, up by the east of Jordan and so towards Damascus.

There, on the banks of the Yarmuk, the gorge running down into Jordan from the east, just opposite the central highlands of Palestine below the Lake of Galilee, they won their victory—complete and crushing—against the very much larger ordered Byzantine ranks: the Regulars of the Roman Empire.

They took Damascus, the strategic key of Syria, forcing it after a long siege; they took Jerusalem, the Holy City; and between the time when the young lads, filled with glory at the first charge, had grown into their latter twenties and were becoming solid men, captains of troops, they had been wel-comed in Alexandria, they had ridden up the Nile, they had begun their advance towards Carthage. Especially here in Syria, the central point where East and West are joined, they had fixed themselves—as it proved, immovably.

Heraclius, who had so nearly saved the East, gave, on aban-doning it, a prophetic cry: "Farewell, Syria."

I have said that so sharp a miracle and one upon so vast a scale was driven by some force we cannot explain. But we can at any rate appreciate certain characters in that force which half account for its astonishing fortunes.

It was manifestly religion. Those who (true to the old traditions of the nineteenth century) still attempt to give a material explanation of history, are driven to their wits' end in the effort to find here a sufficient material cause.

They have pretended that the power which inflamed these amazing conquerors was the drying up of Arabia. Swarm after swarm of Arabs (so they tell us) had come out in successive waves during the past three thousand years and more—always because they found their pastures getting less; and it was this physical phenomenon which accounted for all. They could point to the parallel of the Mongolian hosts that from time to time came sweeping out of Asia upon the west: movements undoubtedly connected with change of climate.

But in the case of the great Arab conquest the parallel does not hold. There were no vast hordes. The essence of the miracle was the inferiority in numbers of the conquerors over what they conquered. The Mongols of Asia had no mission; they came with no message; the Arabs were wholly taken up with their mission and message—that of their Prophet.

The thing was essentially religion from beginning to end, it was from within man, not from without; and it was because the organisation of Christian society had grown brittle with age and lack of renewal, because it was already divided by heresies, that this new heresy from the desert found such strength, came against an insufficient opposition and was, even at first, widely accepted.

Those who seek for a lesser explanation than religion would do better to concentrate upon loot than upon climate. The society both of the Persian Empire and of the Roman to the right and left of the Arab advance was a splendid prey for marauders; it lay open with its accumulated wealth for any successful invader to pillage; and without doubt the conquerors enriched themselves out of all knowledge in those few years. But the motive of loot will not do either; the loot was very great, but it was not sufficient as a spur to action. It cannot explain either the rapidity or the exaltation of that cavalcade. And after all, what were the words continually on their lips? What was their own explanation? It was always the same, their Arabian word for God—"Allah"—cousin to all the Divine names in all the Semitic languages, "that which is", "the sole Being", *EL*.

There is the negative side to be considered. Even did we understand the nature of the driving power on the victorious side (which we cannot perfectly do) it would not explain the sudden collapse of the defeated. The Battle of the Yarmuk, the slaughter in that gorge of Syria, was decisive; it was perhaps the most decisive battle in the history of the world. But why were the fruits of it garnered so rapidly? Why did not only the East, which had always been subject to sweeps of this kind, but the West, solid organised Christian Roman society, the Byzantine lands, including Syria itself, where the Roman framework had been established for over a thousand years—why did all this collapse also?

Whatever be the causes of that disastrous defeat, the grand sequel was not the true result of the battle. Very often in history it has been so; one decisive action has changed in a day the political future of a whole country, even of a whole civilisation—or conversely, prevented such a change. It was so with the day of Hastings, it was so with the defeat of Attila in Champagne. But what followed on the first clash between the new bewildering Arabian flame and the long-settled Christian world was not a military consequence of military things, it was a social revolution. Islam poured over like a flood, not because it beat down opposition by force, but because opposition was lacking, and because those over whom the startling transformation came were ready to receive it. The process was not like one whereby fire destroys some old but solid structure: it was rather like an explosion; the disintegration of a mixture which is already in highly unstable equilibrium. For what happened was that the Greek and Roman world, over more than half the ancient Empire, fell almost automatically under new masters. One could almost say that it accepted them rather than yielded to Islam.

Now why was this?

Here you have the most startling change in all our records, both for its extent, for its rapidity and for its success. A shepherd boy tending his flock above the heights of the Yarmuk valley and looking down on that massacre of the packed victims along the river bank in the gorge far below might have lived to hear news (in his extreme old age, it is true) of the conquest of Spain. He would, while still in his young manhood, have heard how nearly all the Roman land south of the Great Sea had fallen to Islam, and all the famous wealth of the Nile. Already in his middle age he would know that the armies of the new religion had reached the Bosphorus, and the same group of years which saw the passage of the Straits of Gibraltar saw the eruption of the cavalcade into the arid lands beyond Persia. One long lifetime sufficed to cover that enormous business, but in a mere twenty years the great bulk of it was already accomplished: the subjugation of Persia, of all Syria, of Egypt, and far into North Africa. Not only had half (and almost the best half) of the Græco-Roman inheritance of Christendom passed into the control of this alien thing, but it had overwhelmed the rival and most ancient culture of the Persians, it had even set foot in the East beyond.

How could so enormous a turnover have come?

Islam itself sets down the thing in terms of the miraculous, of a special act of the Divinity; Islam points to its early lightning stroke over all those thousands of miles and its triumphant foundation therein (destined to such permanence!) as a proof of its divine mission. There is a more sober explanation—at least for the capture of the Christian land. That explanation lies in the complexity of the Christian culture.

Islam presented to a society entangled and fatigued the obvious and fatal lure of simplicity. To men burdened not only by the weight but by the intricacy of debt and usury, it promised a new economic peace, the apparent end of anxiety; and to very many of the slaves in a world where slavery was ubiquitous it promised freedom! The slave who accepted Islam was free. In place of the exhausting subtleties of the lawyers and the heavy

burden they had laid upon mankind with their perpetual demand for tribute, Islam promised justice free as air; and in place
of codes incomprehensible to the multitude Islam promised the
plain guidance of simple and universal maxims.

In place of a complicated theology which the millions could
not follow and which had neglected to instruct those millions, it
promised few and clear statements of a sort to which they were
already accustomed: these, but no more.

There was an end to Priesthood, to Mystery and to Sacraments: the plain Fatherhood of God, the plain brotherhood of
men—and their equality—were enough. Nor was there any
Christian enthusiasm among the indebted peasants, and the
mass of the slaves, to counter the vivid violence of those who
now so suddenly overrode the old order. Africa had been dis-
affected for generations; Syria, with Palestine, had been a
battlefield, full only recently of murderous antagonisms; those
whom Islam now conquered had long ceased to rally with
affection to the new Rome; even the awe of the Emperor's
capital had faded.

We have had in this, our day, some parallel to all this, though
on a lesser scale and lacking the wide sweep and the complete
success: I mean the Communist experiment which a handful of
aliens has imposed upon the millions of the old Russian Empire.
To make a true parallel with Islam we might imagine what is
called the Bolshevist Movement sweeping over Poland, trans-
forming the Germanies and occupying the Southern Slav countries as well. We are told that the Bolshevists were upon the
point of such a triumph when they were checked by the decisive Battle of Warsaw.

There came no Battle of Warsaw to arrest the tidal wave of
Islam. What forces made the irruption of Communism into
Europe possible or probable, we know: our industrial system
with its mass of wage-slaves was in unstable equilibrium; even
our peasants were in many districts so burdened with usury that
they might have welcomed the change. The society of the Near
East, and of Roman Africa from Palestine to the Atlantic thirteen hundred years ago, had similar burdens of anxiety and of

disaffection against unworthy authority. To the slaves, debtors, and spiritually neglected men, Islam came as an emancipation.

◆

It was an emancipation indeed for the moment, and that accounts for the revolution on its negative side; that is why opposition broke down in spite of vigorous fighting—as in the great battle for Carthage and in the long resistance behind the walls of Damascus. But that emancipation and immediate release was none the less destructive. Here again you have a close parallel between the Arab conquest and the effort called "Bolshevist" in our own time. Communism also promises relief from a strain—from the intolerable strain of industrial capitalism. It professes *immediate* relief. But it also entails a general debasement and ruin of civilisation.

The ruin that followed upon the Mohammedan advance was gradual. It is masked by the glories of certain centres, whether of learning or of art, which shone in the Mohammedan world for centuries; in Mesopotamia, on the Nile, in Spain. But ruin it was none the less, and that ruin is apparent to the eye today. All the majesty of the ancient world was drowned. Islam destroyed the forests and dried up the water-courses; it could do great things only where it retained a large surviving body of the old Roman Christian citizenship subject, but keeping its own traditions in all the crafts. The Græco-Roman baths, the Græco-Roman cupola and dome, mosaic, glass, ship-building—everything—was that upon which the new governing power reposed. Islam of itself did nothing save slowly to destroy.

It may be urged that this destruction was more the work of the later invaders from Asia, the Turks, than of the original Arabian wave, and this is true. The original invasion did not destroy the elaborate irrigation system of Mesopotamia, nor leave it the waste it is today. But the letting of all civilisation down on to a lower level was in the very nature of the new simplified creed. What had been Roman provinces could not but retain some great part of our inheritance; but that inheritance began to fail.

It failed also in the West, when the West was beleaguered by heathendom and all its energies devoted to a difficult maintenance against the threat of northern pirates, Asiatic hordes, and Islam itself working from the islands of the Mediterranean and from Spain. But the West maintained its central principle, its superior religion; it preserved the seed and recovered itself after the strain: it restored civilisation at last.

Islam could not do these things. Yet Islam held. That is perhaps the most striking thing of all. Islam was of its nature fluid in government, one leader succeeding another, each master jealous of all around him; each in succession murdering right and left to make his throne secure. Islam had no fixed boundaries. We are alternatively astonished by the thousands of miles over which the orders of one centre are carried out, and at the ease with which a local leader will establish his independence and maintain it. Islam seems to have no political principle of unity by which it should survive; yet survive it does, and expand. It is never uprooted, nor even threatened with uprooting, during the more than a millennium through which it has carried on. The simplicity of the religion and the fierce conviction of it keep the stream flowing without a check.

You may today hear, in the squalor that once was Tiberias, in the ruins that were once Cæsarea, in the emptiness that was once the lovely templed vale of Paneas, in the shrunken little relic that is still called Antioch, the repeated formula of Islam. And the men you meet in that Syria of today, the peasant in Palestine whom it is proposed to dispossess by an alien and hated invasion, the street peddler in Damascus who, like the wealthiest of his fellow citizens, is at one in maintaining Islam against the new unbelieving master, are all crying the same invocations, reciting the same prayers with the same vigour and the same adherence to their faith as those first horsemen who rode into the land thirteen hundred years ago. Alone of the heresies Islam possessed and possesses this secret of endurance.

In its first conquest the new heresy which was soon to appear a new religion, did not dispossess the old. It did not even attempt at first to dispossess the old. In Syria at least—the nucleus of the whole business, the citadel now recovered by the men of the desert—the Christian Church survived and even survived vigorously.

This attitude on the part of the conquerors has been called "toleration". That is quite the wrong word. The conquerors exacted tribute from those who would not accept the Prophet and his message; the revenue of the Mohammedan rulers depended upon the very large Christian population which, for generations after their appearance, was the great majority of the population. Damascus and Jerusalem and Antioch were at first Christian cities with only rulers and a garrison that was of Islam. The process of change was gradual, and there have survived as a matter of course Christian communities who worship today as their fathers were worshipping when the desert cavalry rode in.

Those who first joined Islam were naturally enough the Arabs on the eastern fringe of Syria, then, more slowly, the farmers of the fertile land; lastly, the bulk of those in the towns. The cities that are the ports of the desert, Aleppo, Homs, Hama, Damascus, after a very long process ended by being spiritually absorbed. The cities of the sea-coast maintained and maintain a Christian minority; Syria as a whole was only dyed with the Mohammedan colour in gradual fashion; and though that colour is now the background of all, it is still not universal.

To understand the way in which the Christian community survived, an early and very vivid example is enough; the example of St. John of Damascus, "St. John Damascene".

His father, a Christian of course, had been given a great official post about the Court, the administrator of the finances, and the new masters called him by an Arab name, Mansur. The son, John, was born between forty and fifty years after the invasion. He was a man already middle-aged when the influence of Mohammedanism on the world had begun to affect the Imperial Court at Constantinople and the Emperor made war against the use of images in the churches.

In sermons and in a mass of writing St. John of Damascus defended vigorously the use of the holy images, and though all that he said and wrote was blasphemy to the new conquerors, he was allowed his full effect. He relied openly upon the populace, among whom the tradition of images was strongest; he was at the root of the resistance to iconoclasm and the victory of the use of images among the Christians of the East, as the Popes contemporary with him were the centres of resistance in the West. For in the West also this reforming zeal against images had spread; and Charlemagne, who was to claim Empire in the West as against the Emperors of Byzantium in the East, had been tempted to follow the fashion of that other Imperial Court.

St. John Damascene was more than the restorer of images; he was also the hander on of philosophy; he was one of the first of those possessing a Christian and civilised tradition who passed on our inheritance from Aristotle, of which the Mohammedan universities of Spain were later to make such use.

The new religion, then, did not spread universally. What did spread universally through the Mohammedan conquest was the Arabic language. The official Latin, already disappearing in the East, the apparently eternal Greek, were lost: and in their place came everywhere, even among the poorest in the cities, even among the most remote villages in the hills, the language in which the Koran had been written and in which Islam proclaimed itself. As much or more than Latin in the West was Arabic the common medium throughout the whole half-world throughout which Islam had spread. In Syria the similarity of the popular Aramaic helped that change, but it was not peculiar to Syria. Arabic was to be found supplanting the immemorial tongue of the Nile; the Punic and the Latin of North Africa; and there, though groups of the old mountain languages survive in the Atlas, Arabic also is the general tongue.

As for Syria, the revolution in speech has long been accomplished there; and the native Christian today, telling you his aversion from Islam, expresses that hatred in the tongue which Islam itself has made universal. He even prays at Mass in a liturgy that is Arabic.

◆

To grasp the magnitude of Islam's unity, the quality in it which, in spite of all vicissitude, maintained it substantially one and still conquering, still expanding, one has but to mark the stages of its apparent instability in government.

The very early Caliphs, those of the first dozen years of the conquest, are murdered one after the other. Abou Bekr, first general at the head of that cavalry, who died in the second year of his triumph, named Omar to succeed him in the year 634—the same who took Jerusalem. In ten years Omar was stabbed. There followed in the next ten years (644–655) killing upon killing: Omar, before dying of his wound, named a sort of committee to choose a Caliph, but in that committee was Ali, the son-in-law and cousin of the Prophet, and an elderly noble from among the Arabs called Othman. Othman was chosen, he was murdered: Ali, his rival, succeeded. But Othman's great-nephew, Maouia (to spell him in one of the various ways), was all-powerful in Syria; and Syria was still the centre of the whole business. It is an example of the way in which the Arab cannot hold together politically (and yet how his religion has held together throughout all this time!) that Mohammed's own widow took sides in fighting Ali, because in the old days, when Mohammed was alive, Ali had desired her to be repudiated.

Maouia, master of Syria, continued to excite men to civil war among the True Believers; the bloody shirt of the murdered Othman was shown daily in the mosque at Damascus to urge his avenging. Then comes a course of personal hatreds and killings, the attempted murder of Maouia fails but Ali is killed, so is his son! The Syrians march down to take Medina itself, stable their horses in Mohammed's own shrine, seize and sack Mecca. Then the descendants of Mohammed's uncle (any sort of blood-relationship would do!) grasp at power; that uncle was called Abbas, and his descendants ruled as the dynasty of the Abbas-sides. They won, and in their winning they killed, among others, one said to be Mohammed's own son.

The dynasty of Maouia, whom we call the Omeiyades, was at an end, and Syria ceased to be the centre of Islam. The new dynasty abandoned Damascus as a capital and built Baghdad, in Mesopotamia; Baghdad, descendant and representative of the ancient Mesopotamian capitals, the successor to Babylon and a

neighbour to the ruins thereof. The last of the Omeiyades fled
westward, and restored the strength of his name in Spain.

The Abbassides, ruling from Baghdad (for a century with real
power, later less powerful, but still ruling), were the chiefs of
Islam: but once again a dynasty could not hold—though Islam
held. Baghdad at its height and the dynasty at its height, not long
after its foundation, was represented in history and still more in
legend and tradition by the great Aaron—"Haroun"—whom
the great Charlemagne of the West saluted as from the setting to
the rising sun. Haroun in his splendour had one sharp Arabian
quality—his cruelty was remarkable. Among other things we
know that he delighted in having a rebel cut in pieces before
him, joint by joint; it is no wonder that he was called "Ar
Rashid"—"The Just".*

But in another hundred years the power of the Abbassides
was dissolving into a number of almost independent local governments. As for the Caliphate, it broke up; instead of there
being for the future one central Caliphate at Baghdad, there
were three: one in Baghdad, one in North Africa (first in the
west and then in Cairo) and one in Spain. The Roman tradition
which had still inspired Islam and given it some political unity,
the Caliphate, receiving, and master of, a vast revenue, was,
as an Empire, no more.

Yet Islam stood. That is, I repeat, the central fact; to us of the
West almost inexplicable. But those, even Westerns, who have
steeped themselves in the spirit of the East, assure us that once
the spirit is understood, the permanent survival and unity of
Islam (unity as against the Christian thing) is a matter of course.

Anyhow, Islam stood. But it was about to run a risk of
destruction, and in this fashion:

There had come in from the steppes of the north from Asia
north of the mountains, a Mongol barbarism, nomad soldiers
hiring themselves out and also imposing themselves. Their various bands and successive groups are known to us as "The
Turks".

* More properly "ar-Rashid"—"the rightly directing". It is one of the names
for the Divine Power also.

There is something about this Mongolian impact upon civilised man (meaning by Mongolian not the high civilisation of China, but the Mongols of the deserts and half-deserts outside the boundaries of China) which is all for destruction. It does nothing but evil. It comes with its ruinous influence upon us of the West, the Romans, and even upon our enemies who succeeded to part of the Roman name—Islam; and it comes without any power of creation, merely destroying.

It had come thus under Attila at the end of the old united Empire; it had then been beaten back and had ebbed off like a tide; but it returned to menace the capital of the world at Byzantium. It swarmed over the great plains of Europe north of the Black Sea. It was checked again with difficulty, centuries after Attila, by the Germans on the Bavarian rivers; it subjugated the Slavs of Greek religion; it occupied the Hungarian plain, and the language of the finely European and noble Magyars of today is a Mongol language—proof, if any were needed, that language is no test of culture or of blood.

Now of these Mongol adventurers and nomads, one group, whom we know by the name of Seljuk, their original leader— the Seljukian Turks—became a bodyguard to, and masters of, the last Abbassides.

They adopted Islam, of course; they continued to reverence its religious ruler; the Caliph at Baghdad was still in a fashion the head of Islam or of that branch of Islam which he ruled—but the power to give orders and to act was in the hands of the Turks during this, their first wave of advance.

The effect of this innovation was such that by a certain reaction Islam was threatened as it had not been threatened since it had launched that first thunderbolt now more than three hundred years before, and sent the Arab horsemen careering over the Syrian hills—since the days when Heraclius had said, as he left the battleground, "Farewell, Syria!"

The new Turkish power was not seated in Syria, but in Syria its harshness was fully felt, and among other things in the approach of Christians to the Holy Sepulchre. The great mass of Christian subjects dwindling in numbers but always accepted, losing their culture but still the basis of all the culture eastern Islam knew, was treated by this new Mongol power as an enemy.

Now this was the very moment when a certain resurrection of life was stirring in the West of Christendom; the abominable pirate invasions from Scandinavia had been defeated; the reconquest of Spain from the Mohammedan had strongly increased, the Gaul, which sent its chivalry down to help the reestablishment of the Faith beyond the Pyrenees, was full of the enthusiasm thereof. The Papacy had undertaken to revivify religion, everything was stirring; and it was at this very moment that the Turkish control of Syrian Islam challenged our pilgrim devotion to the Holy Places.

Though we had lost Syria politically, yet the Faith was still strong there; the Mass was said in Antioch, in Jerusalem; and Western pilgrims had come in a constant stream to worship at that hollow stone whence Jesus Christ had risen from the dead: the stone we are still privileged to know—for it is certain, and has never been forgotten.

With that custom of pilgrimage to the Sepulchre the new and barbaric Turkish rule interfered, hence the breach with the now restored West of Europe; our Occident, growing into a new life, began to plan some great expedition for the recovery of the Holy Sepulchre.

There have come down to us certain words of that time recited in French and illuminative of the hour: "God is enthroned in His Holy Heritage; now shall we see whether they will not come to His succour whom He redeemed from slavery by His Blood when He died upon the True Cross which Turks now hold! Know well that those who will not march are base indeed, unless they are too old or in weakness or in poverty. But they that are young and full of life and have the means, none such can hold back without shame."

That was the lyric preaching which stirred the new French chivalry, of that same sort which had followed William of Falaise into England, which had joined the Princes of the Pyrenees to recover the Iberian highlands and thrust back the

Moslem masters of a Christian people there. This is the spirit which suddenly inspired the northerners of the Belgic lands and the southerners of Toulouse and those adventurers from the Cotentin on the Channel shores who had fought their way into Sicily and South Italy, the sons of Tancred of Hauteville, near where one overlooks the sea towards St. Michael's Hill, the rock in the middle of the waters. We shall see the Pope himself coming into Auvergne and preaching, concluding the message which lesser enthusiasts had preached before him: we shall hear mobs shouting that God willed the uprising. First in a confused way, then in order and by companies under their chieftains the French-speaking nobles of the West, myriads of men streamed out eastward to the recovery of the Holy Sepulchre. It was the Crusade.

Before we deal with this last effort—and failure—to recover our Syrian bastion; the last rally and failure of the West against the men of the desert—let us ask what would have happened if (what was impossible) they had succeeded? With the French chivalry permanently established in Syria, Islam would have been cut in two. Its eastern half might have survived, its western would have been doomed. The Mediterranean and its islands, which had fallen into the power of Islam, would have been Roman and Christian again; there would have been done in a fruitful Christian time what is now being attempted in our own sterile time of Apostasy. Roman land would have been recovered in its entirety—and Christendom would have become Christendom again.

For Syria is the keystone. To hold Syria permanently, with sufficient recruitment and armament, is to cut the bridge between Asia, including the men of the desert, and North Africa. Syria strongly held makes the enemy hold over Egypt impossible, for Syria strongly held is the holding also of the neck between North Africa and the Levant. Syria strongly held cuts all advance from Asia towards the Bosphorus, for it flanks the highlands of Anatolia. Syria strongly held is the recovery of the Roman East. Had the Roman West been able to conquer Syria and hold it strongly now after this first enthusiasm of the

Crusades, Islam would have been thrown back to where those other enemies had been before the defeat of the Byzantines on the Yarmuk. But that splendid effort—the last effort—was to fail.

XV

The Last Rally

O UR PEOPLE, then, the West, Christendom, made a last rally of our race for the recovery of Syria from the men of the desert. It is called the "Crusades".

That forlorn hope stands vividly in the European mind as a glorious episode of its past: half legendary. All men see the chivalric story on a scale larger than reality, and suffer the illusion that the victory might have been won.

In truth under the conditions of that day the victory was impossible. Syria could not be recovered.

It could be half-grasped by a sudden onrush from the West; but there was not then among us the organisation which would have made so distant a conquest permanent; even had the first strategy been as well ordered as it was, in fact, imperfect. Even had Damascus, the key of Syria, been taken at once, we could not have maintained ourselves there. Our numbers, recruitment and communications were all three insufficient to the task.

The original ephemeral triumph of the Crusaders was due to one of those divisions in the Mohammedan world which are perpetually appearing, but as perpetually disappearing again under a united command. When that united command of Islam was achieved it was inevitable that the chivalry of the West should be driven back into the sea. For the weapons of Islam were then as good as ours. Its science equal or superior. It was on the spot, while we worked from thousands of miles away. And it had ten men to our one.

The first strong blow was delivered just before the year 1100, by men who were filled with the recent victories of the Cross over the Mohammedans in Spain. Two hundred years later, in 1291, the last of the Crusading garrisons was driven out of St. John of Acre. For over six hundred years onwards save for the momentary flash of Buonaparte, the men and the religion of the desert remained in full power. They remained in full power over the soil of that Syria which had been so mightily prepared for the Divine Event, and for the foundation of the Church; they remained in power over Antioch, where the Christian name was first heard, over the Christian colonies upon the sea-coast, over the Holy Places themselves: Nazareth, Bethlehem, and the Sepulchre of the Resurrection. After the surrender of St. John of Acre in 1291 we were exiled, as it would seem forever, from the place whence the inspiration of Christendom arose and the living principle of our civilisation: from the fields and the cities of the Lord. With the Crusades the story of the battle-ground ends.

What started this marching out of Christendom eastward was in the first place that coming of the Mongol just spoken of, with his desecration and ruin and drying up of things, into the very body of Islam. It was the story of barbaric attack on pilgrimage that inflamed the new Christian West to its attack for the recovery of the Sepulchre.

This indignation came just when all Western Europe was astir with new life. It was the beginning of the compact Norman order in the North as in the Mediterranean, of the new great architecture, of Parliaments arising in the Pyrenees, and of the new spring of philosophy.

These were the prime conditions. But there was more. This new Mongol thing, mastering the eastern Mohammedan world, already soaked in Islam but barbarising it, was threatening what was still the chief political capital of all Christendom, Con-stantinople; the Emperor's throne, twin to Rome. The old Arabian Empire with its centre in Baghdad, had not passed eastward of the Taurus. It had made forays up to the Bosphorus itself for centuries, but had not held Asia Minor. But when the Turks came in from the north-east through Armenia, they swamped the mass of Asia Minor and the peril of the Emperor in his capital was extreme. His appeal for succour to his fellow Christians of the West was the second force which launched the adventure.

That adventure was French. There marched out among the first confused hordes many from the German-speaking belt of the Rhine; there were contingents of Flemings; there were even here and there to be found, later in the business, a handful of princes and nobles from north of the Channel. But the French language was the main language of the host, and particularly of its mounted leaders, drawn from the chivalry of Gaul itself and from the Norman adventurers who had planted themselves in Sicily and South Italy.

The first swarming was shapeless: uncounted masses of excited populace marching eastward by the Danube road, so confused that they could reach no goal. But behind this effervescence advanced in regular organisation the great feudal forces under their high rulers and these converged upon the Imperial City, whence, beyond the Bosphorus, the main Roman road to Tarsus was still in full use, and the avenue for advance towards the Holy Land.

All the effort was by horse and foot; the sea played but an insignificant part, and the advance was to be one endless advance of dwindling cavalry and marching men, armed and unarmed, facing two thousand miles of road until they should reach Jerusalem—not a tenth of what they had been at starting.

The Pope, who was a Frenchman from Champagne (under the title of Urban II), a type of that invigorated Papacy to which the monk Hildebrand had given so much life, and which, as Gregory VII he had set up in renewed greatness, launched the rallying cry in the mountains of Auvergne, at Clermont. There great crowds answered with the drawing of swords and "God wills it!" That was in November, 1095. No Kings could leave their governments, whether strong and but newly established like the Norman Crown in England, or more ancient but weak and jealous of powerful feudatories like the Capetian in Paris; but the higher Barons marched—men who were indeed local Kings in power—from Normandy, from Flanders and from Toulouse, from South Italy. They converged before Constantinople in the end of 1096, and the first weeks of 1097. In the March of that year the last arrivals had camped before the city, and some two hundred thousand were eager for the task—but unfitted.

They were not an army; they were a feudal levy. The fighting unit was a noble and his followers—it might be a great noble with a very large number of followers, or a small independent man with very few, but of united command there was none, save when one such was improvised for a crisis—and thus dissolved again.

Leaders looked for personal gain, making themselves Lords of territory on the way, garrisoning a town or district and remaining there. Also, there could be no more than the most elementary tactical formations among units of all shapes and sizes, divided according to no plan, with no combined manœuvres. The only tactic was a straightforward charge of heavily armed knights against the opposing line. If the charge knocked the enemy over the battle was won; no other kind of victory was attempted, save by siege. The Western knights, stronger in build and character, overset at first large bodies of Orientals. They won battle after battle against greatly superior numbers. But these very advantages were a disadvantage when the effort was spread over a long space of time, and had to be undertaken in a hot climate with successive burning summers, murderous to Western men.

On the main Roman road across Asia Minor the first obstacle was the city of Nicea, garrisoned by the Turks. It was within a few days' marching of Constantinople and blocked the way. The Crusaders besieged it in the first week of May, 1097, and took it by the end of the next month; but the garrison surrendered to the Emperor, not to them. This was the difficulty which beset the Crusaders, the conflict between their interests and Constantinople's. The Emperor and his subjects, at any rate in the capital, thought themselves civilised men superior to the half-barbaric Westerners. The Emperor demanded that what had been, within recent memory, his own land, should be handed back to him; and a feudal society, with chiefs independent of the central power, was not tolerable to the Byzantine mind.

From Nicea the Crusaders met their first opposition in the field about a week's march on, at Dorylæum, where the railway junction is today. It was the main shock between the two opponents, and the heavily armed Christian chivalry won a complete victory. After this dispersion of the Turks the Roman road lay open before them; they suffered fearful losses in the dried up, empty lands, which are the high tablelands of Asia Minor, but they carried through to Antioch, before whose walls the camp was pitched towards the end of October, 1097. It was nearly two years since the Crusade had been preached at Clermont, and nearly eighteen months since it had begun its first advance from Constantinople. They had covered some thousand, some nearly two thousand miles from their starting places, and their homes and their ultimate base of recruitment lay all that way behind them.

There were diversions of effort, the principal one of which was the adventure of Baldwin of Flanders, who took off his men eastward, after a quarrel with Tancred, the South Italian Norman, about the possession of Tarsus. Edessa, the Christian city lying right off beyond the Euphrates, threatened by the Turks, welcomed Baldwin, and the Senators of the place chose him for their Sovereign. The large indeterminate area of which Edessa was the centre counted as one of the Crusading divisions so long as it held (it was the first to go) and Edessa was the northernmost of the feudal principalities to be attached to the kingdom of Jerusalem.

It was only for a few years past that Antioch had had a Turkish garrison, and the vast Christian city—for it was still of great size and remarkable for its wealth and architecture—was not only a prize of the first class, but an obstacle of the first class also. The general body of Crusaders were not only diminished by Baldwin's adventure off to the north-east, but still more by their very heavy losses in crossing the ill-watered plateau of Asia Minor.

During the winter, famine fell upon the besiegers of Antioch, and it was not till the summer, 1098, that the Turkish garrison was reduced. Immediately afterwards a very large Turkish army, just too late to save their fellows, but not too late to destroy the diminished Crusading bodies, came upon them from the east. Bohemond, the Norman from South Italy, to whom the city of Antioch had fallen and who became its first Lord under the new feudal arrangement, won his battle against this greatly superior relieving force. It was a remarkable proof of the vitality of the Western blood, that after such months of wasting and famine and the moral effect of delay, an overwhelmingly larger Oriental army, well equipped and well fed, should have been thus broken in front of the city.

A further delay came from the dread of a summer campaign. It was already the end of June (the 28th) when the main Turkish Army marching to the relief of Antioch had been broken. The Crusaders should have marched south when the cold weather came, but quarrels between the feudal leaders and the necessity for supply halted them. At first they went on south by the Orontes valley, and had there been any definite strategical plan *this was their opportunity for deciding the campaign.*

They ought obviously to have marched along the fertile strip between the desert and the hills and taken Damascus; for when Damascus should have received a Crusading garrison all Syria would have been organised as a Christian thing. Damascus—still partly Christian—would have cut the communications between the northern Mohammedan garrisons and the southern; supposing the barely sufficient numbers of the Crusaders had been concentrated for the effort.

But the prime error was made, Damascus was left aside, and those who still were willing to go forward—a small fraction of what had gathered at Constantinople two years before—crossed Lebanon and made for the sea-coast. There was another delay for the capture of Arkah just north of Tripoli, then hesitation as to whether they should wait for reinforcements from the Greeks, or take advantage of the early harvest (which ripens in Syria before May) and after provisioning themselves set out. They did at last turn out in the middle of May, 1099, following the coast-road with fairly regular marches, until they had come by Whitsuntide almost west of Jerusalem.

Here again there was hesitation, as to whether to strike at

once for the Holy City, or to march across the Egyptian desert for the delta, and the strongest centre of the Mohammedan power, Cairo.

It was a second opportunity, not so good as Damascus, but one that would have been strategically sound if there had been men for it—but there were not. All through the Crusading business this penury of numbers upon the Christian side decides the final issue. There were barely thirty thousand left all told, and of these perhaps half were fighting men. Of that half, say fifteen thousand armed soldiers, only one-tenth were mounted and fully armed knights. Such was the little army now: the remnant of a thing more than ten times its size, which had begun the march across Asia Minor. It took the eastern road from the coast up the hills, towards Jerusalem and the Holy Sepulchre.

Jerusalem was not in Turkish hands; the dissident Mohammedan power of the Nile had got hold of it and garrisoned it. But it was strongly held, and the difficulties of the siege might prove too much for the remaining Christian forces. Certain of the main leaders were still there, Godfrey of Bouillon from Northern France, Raymond, the Lord of Southern France, Robert of Normandy, son of the conqueror, and Tancred, the Southern Norman. The day was famous on which the vanguard of that small column—what we should call today a division or less—first saw Jerusalem with their eyes.

It was the first dawn of Tuesday, the 7th of June, 1099; the Army had assembled round Emmaus and was ordered for the march. The column breasted the lift beyond the depression, the vanguard had come to the height above, when suddenly (where the Sheik's tomb is today) they caught sight of domes and pinnacles against the morning light, the nearest not two miles away. Skirting these buildings was a dark line of city walls. It was Jerusalem.

All pressed forward, deploying to right and left, as they came up, and forming line to greet the goal and shrine of their array, and pressed to hear the name passed round the ranks: Jerusalem.

"When they had heard that name, Jerusalem, they began to

cry aloud and to fall upon their knees, all, and to give thanks to Our Lord who had so loved them that He had granted them to see the crown of their long pilgrimage, the Holy City, where He had chosen to save the world. They lifted their hands to Heaven, and those on horseback dismounted and kissed the ground."

Behind those walls the Vizir of the Governor of Egypt had mustered a great garrison; it was a force of Arabian and of trained Saracen soldiers. Every Christian had been thrust out of the town. From the walls the sentinels saw the column of the Crusade, the newly risen sun catching the slung lances, and whatever was bright in the link-work of the mail: not much was bright after such an advance in the dust of a Syrian June.

It was after six weeks of effort under the intolerable heat that the end came. The Crusaders stormed Jerusalem on Friday, the 15th of July, 1099; after two days' violent assault the walls were carried, and a general massacre followed throughout the crowded streets, until the last keep, the enclosure of the Mosque upon the Temple Hill, was stormed.

No peace followed, of course, but some organisation of that narrow ribbon which could call itself now "The Kingdom of Jerusalem." There was in the north a certain extent of territory from beyond the Euphrates to the Gulf of Alexandretta, extending occasionally into the Cilician plain. This northern patch was broad enough to give, while it lasted, a solid basis for further effort. But south of Antioch the Crusaders held only a thin chain of fortified posts, which they rapidly increased in strength, but never wholly joined up into one solid territory.

The whole thing was arranged upon the feudal model, with semi-independent Lords having vassals under them. There was the Count of Edessa in the north, next to him the Prince of Antioch, claiming the strip of coast down to below the castle at Markab, which stands out so grandly upon its spur of hills overlooking the waters of the sea. Next came the Count of Tripoli, claiming about a hundred miles of the narrow coastal plains, to the river north of Beyrout; and south of that point the kingdom of Jerusalem proper. Within each such limit stood behind their walls the lesser Barons, such as the Lord of Sidon and the rest, holding under tenure from their overlords.

But the whole thing was a broken hotch-potch; the Saracen could and did raid continually to the sea-coast itself, and on that coast he could hold some places permanently. The French south of Antioch held no castle more than fifty miles from the sea; in many places they went far less. The castle of Banias in Cæsarea Philippi, where St. Peter had confessed the Divinity of Our Lord, was but an outpost—and yet it was not thirty miles from the direct road on the coast.

In the Lebanon, the strip was far narrower; behind Beyrout, into the mountains, there was no effective occupation beyond twenty miles. In the south, the last castle south of the Dead Sea was much further inland, but here desert not subject to effective occupation.

The nearest thing to a real occupation of territory was on the hills of Palestine themselves, in Galilee and over the plain of Esdraelon. Northward all the way along the coast from Carmel to Latakia the Crusaders stood behind castle walls, gathering their tribute and exercising their rule over restricted districts between the spurs of the hills.

However, a constitution was formed, and a moral unity maintained: a first King was elected, though from humility he would not take the title—Godfrey of Bouillon, in the Ardennes below Sedan; and his successor was that same Baldwin of Flanders who had occupied Edessa.

So long as the Mohammedan world (surrounding them upon every side like a sea, interpenetrating their very narrow strip of intermittent occupation) was divided among many local rulers, the experiment might appear successful. The military Orders, Templars and Hospitallers, helped the defence, and there was now established a fairly constant communication with Europe, ships arriving from the Mediterranean and even from northern ports, and pilgrimage and recruitment. There were craft from the North Sea at the taking of Sidon, from Genoa at the taking of Tripoli, from Venice at the taking of Tyre—and so on through fifty examples. But it was certain—doubly certain since

Damascus had been left alone—that whenever a strong and united rule should appear over the Mohammedan world without, the Crusaders, in spite of their castles, were doomed.

The aim of the prodigious thrust had been accomplished; there was a King in Jerusalem, a feudal organisation of the French-speaking Western Christian nobles under him, each in his own principality with his vassals ready to his summons: and there was a moral unity confirmed by the function which all these commanders exercised of holding the Sepulchre and its approaches against the Infidel. But what was the true strength of all that? What was its real situation?

Eighty-eight years separate the storming of Jerusalem, in 1099, and the decisive defeat of Hattin, 1187, from which the precarious hold of Western chivalry upon the hills never recovered. But it only so held even during that short space by standing continually upon the defensive.

Half-way through the business it had already lost its principal outlying post, Edessa; and the remainder, a very narrow chain of posts, was preserved at the expense of constant struggle against the much greater Mohammedan forces inland.

This perilous defence of the Westerners against the desert and its creed, against the Lords of the towns that fringed the desert, the Lords of Aleppo, Hama, Homs and Damascus, could only continue with the aid of immense defensive works—those castles which still stand as marvels to the eye today. The Crusading Lords were not unsupported by the native population; there was remaining in the twelfth century a very considerable body of native Christians even far inland; they were probably then a majority in the towns of the sea-plains and on the western slopes of Lebanon, where they are still a large factor in the population today. But the experiment remained an experiment, tied to a desperate defensive, dependent for its life upon strongholds.

Those strongholds were developed under the necessity of the struggle, the whole art of castle-building advancing rapidly in complexity and value in the first years of the occupation. We are astonished today at the magnitude of these fortresses; the labour expended in their establishment and the hardly credible results, not only in design and scale but in numbers. It is some consolation for the failure of the Crusades to see their relics still standing thus gigantic and ubiquitous over the 400-mile line from the Gulf of Alexandretta to Monréal.

The Syria of the Crusades became especially a land of castles. There are more than a score of the first rank, and any number of lesser ones, down to the smallest square keep or peel. By an historical accident they remain today the chief mark of the whole region. If a wanderer who knew nothing of the past were turned loose to range the sea-plain and the inner hollow of the Orontes and Litani, the upper Jordan and the Holy Land down to the mighty ruins above the Red Sea road, the strong image that would remain in his mind would be the image of these huge and elaborate buildings. The beauty of the old high civilisation, the temples and palaces of Greece and Rome, are in the dust. But the Crusading castles are everywhere against the sky, still standing proudly, even where their material has been quarried and they are struck by decay.

The holding of that land—even with such great works— would have been impossible from the beginning had not the Arabian fighting tradition been bad at siege-work. The Mohammedan did, later, build fine castles of his own—though simple; witness Aleppo. But it was not native to him to rely on walls or to carry on long sieges. With the Crusaders it was the other way. The military talents which are native to the Gallic blood are best seen in defence: the defensive as a preparation for counter-offensive. Most Gallic wars begin with defeats: a retreat after an initial advance. Most of those which are successful are only so through a rally. The most soldierly of qualities is endurance, and of military talents the most useful is an eye for a defensive position. That quality and those talents are demanded by and expressed in ability for fortification.

But there is another character in societies of a military sort, which also made for this Crusading castle-building—political division.

The castles were not only established as bases for resistance to the Mohammedan, and as posts built to support each other in the holding of the sea-plain and the hills immediately behind it; they were also built for the particular advantage of their particular Lords, to confirm the position of the Prince of Antioch, or the Order of the Templars, or of the Count of Tripoli, or of the King of Jerusalem himself. The men who built these castles came from that feudal society of which the French had given the model to all the West of Europe, and wherein the local magnate was, within his radius of action, a sovereign commanding a small army of his own, and always ready to fight his neighbour. That tradition of division continued in Crusading Palestine. It continually reappears throughout French history, a centrifugal force often developing so far as almost to wreck the unity of the society in which it works. That society had been saved more than once by reaction towards the strengthening of the central power, but normally "the political vice of the Gauls is civil war".

Yet another condition which favoured the creation of these huge monuments, the Crusading Castles, was the isolation of the separate territories in Syria, that same geographical condition which, from the beginning of recorded time down to our own day has split up that limited belt into so many separate units.

The spurs running down from the ranges to the sea, the small enclosed valleys between them, the more extended but still limited little plains walled in by hills, each with its landing-place, had created a multiplicity of political centres which not even Rome could unify, and which more than three thousand years of recorded action by great Empires, Egyptian, Assyrian, Macedonian and Roman, have never obliterated.

The thing goes on to this day, it is not only the rivalry of French and British, it is the very structure of the country which thus cracks it up into a mosaic. You have the railway, and a good motor road, and flying, and one modern first-rate port (Haifa), to be followed presumably by many more—and yet Beyrout remains something quite different from Tripoli, and Tripoli from Latakia. Antioch is a personality. The guardian towns on the edge of the desert, Aleppo, Homs, Hama and Damascus, are individual and apart: Palestine has been from the beginning and is now again more than ever an inter-mixture of opposing elements. The great trading ports each become (as Tyre and Sidon were in their time) capitals.

Now this division of a district by nature into isolated groups, directed and confirmed the castle-building. And beyond that there was a special demand for the castles to command the few roads and that essential thing, on which the story of all the Near Orient depends, all that is on the edge of the desert—water.

The castles then arose everywhere, but even behind such walls the effort of our forefathers could not endure.

The first symptom of what was to come was the loss of Edessa. It might have seemed the most secure of all the new possessions, there was a population almost wholly Christian, there was a city to support the keep, and ample provision. The way to it lay through difficult mountains; it had not like Syria already been held permanently by the Infidel. Therefore when it fell, the warning was grave indeed: and fall it did before the young men who had marched in with Bohemond were grown old. It was as early as 1128 that a vigorous Seljukian Turkish Governor of Mosul made himself master of Aleppo. By the next year he was on the middle Orontes, and confirming his power over the string of towns that are the ports of the desert. Zenghi was his name. As yet he had not crossed Lebanon, nor attempted to reduce the invaders who had now for forty years precariously held the sea-coast and Jerusalem. He struck at Edessa, and captured it in 1144.

It was the first great defeat with lasting consequences that the Christian adventure had suffered; it awoke Christendom, it compelled Europe to further action, and there followed the grave failure called the Second Crusade.

This time the Kings themselves were so moved to action that they ran the risk of absence, leaving regents in their place and facing eastward for this supreme attempt.

The society of Europe had far advanced in the generation between the first adventure and the fall of Edessa; armies were better organised and on the whole better equipped, governments (especially in France) were stronger. The King of France, Louis VII, and the Emperor Conrad III of Germany brought their large combined forces to bear; but meanwhile the Emperor of Byzantium had had experience of how little he could expect from the Westerners save the pushing back of the Turks. His whole action was hostile to the Crusaders, and the result thereof was that the Germans were beaten back at the beginning of their march, and the French only reached the Holy Land after losing the greater part of their Army and suffering a disastrous defeat on the coast of Asia Minor.

The remnant made its effort where the *first* blow should have been achieved fifty years before, against Damascus. It was too late. The town was not taken, and it was certain after the Easter of 1149 (after which the King of France sailed back home) the next Mohammedan coalition would make an end.

That coalition was to come through the energy of a man who was a boy in his fourteenth year when the Second Crusade before Damascus failed.

He was the son of the man who had been Zenghi's Governor of Baalbec and was later Governor of Damascus; a Kurd from the mountains beyond Mesopotamia, and one who had been a leading general in the Turkish armies, by name Ayoub—that is, Job. This man had brought up his heir in the fullest traditions of the Mohammedan culture (during the years after the failure of the Christian siege) in this same town of Damascus, which was the very centre of that culture. The boy was called Salah-ed-Din, "The glory of the Faith", of which we have made "Saladin".

He had gone as attendant upon the General, sent by the orthodox Mohammedans into Egypt to re-take it from the dissidents. Nureddin was the man who was now thus collecting the orthodox Mohammedan world into one and encircling the Crusaders. These made an effort to break the encirclement by themselves occupying the "Neck", the bridge of land between Asia and Africa, the holding of which would cut the Mohammedan world in two. But they could not hold it.

Saladin, who had succeeded to the local command when his

superior officer died, imposed orthodoxy upon Egypt. He succeeded in this not so much by force as by skill in negotiation,
which was perhaps his chief talent, though he was a great soldier
as well. Rather less than thirty years after the failure of the
Second Crusade in front of Damascus, Nureddin died, and
Saladin, now a man of forty, determined on uniting all the East
under himself. He had the capacity for the task, on the civilian as
on the military side, and his power rose steadily in the next
twelve years. By 1186 he had gathered into his own hand the
armed force of the Mohammedan world in the Orient—and
against such unity of strength under one command the Christian
defence could not but break down.

Saladin, in uniting the Mohammedan world of Egypt and
Syria under his control, had been compelled as much to continued negotiation as to scattered fighting; it was necessary for
his success to keep the Christians from attacking him while he
was concentrating; and it is characteristic of the situation that the
Crusaders were glad to accept relief in the form of a truce. This
did but put off the evil hour. Apart from inferior forces the stock
of the Crusaders, of those at least who were descended from the
original Lords of nearly a century before, had deteriorated. They
were still individually the superiors of the Orientals, but they
had no longer lived with the full vigour of the earlier invaders
from over Western Europe.

Saladin, having made himself master of all the anti-Christian
forces, took the first opportunity he could of breaking the truce.
Such opportunities in the loose conditions of the time were not
lacking, and one came ready to his hand in the capture of a
caravan by Reginald of Chatillon. The pretext was the better
because, with that caravan, was captured the sister of Saladin
himself.

Reginald of Chatillon was the bravest, the most energetic,
and at the time the greatest of the Crusaders in Palestine; he had
shown extraordinary vigour in the past, equipping a fleet in the
Red Sea and making an attempt upon the Holy Places of the
Mohammedan world, Mecca and Medina. To break the truce
with such a man would appeal to all Moslems, so the truce was

broken. But any occasion would have sufficed for Saladin, now that the time was ripe.

The Moslem was besieging the castle of Tiberias upon the Lake of Galilee. The Crusaders gathered every unit they could of their depleted and insufficient strength, leaving only skeleton garrisons in the fortified places, and concentrated upon the relief of Tiberias. This brought them into the open field where they could be overwhelmed by numbers. Against their concentration as it approached Tiberias the hosts of Saladin marched, and the shock came on the greensward that rises in one even slope, traversed by the road to Nazareth, as it winds up the hills from the lake, half a day's march above Tiberias. At the summit of the slope stand two lumps of rock, known, from the name of the village on the far side, as "The Horns of Hattin". These give their name to the action.

There, on a burning July day (Saturday, the 4th of July, 1187), the Christians had drawn up their line. They had been contained in the night by the immensely larger forces of the Moslem under their great leader. They were cut off from supplies, and during all the hours of that day they got no water. As they attempted to cut their way through to the lake, charging down the slope of the greensward, the dry grass was set on fire by the enemy so that the smoke should further confuse them. Somehow or other they managed, sinking under the heat and the torture of thirst, to carry on the struggle till the late afternoon, but long before the sun was low the end had come.

The first prisoners were brought to Saladin's tent, Reginald of Chatillon among them. He was offered his life if he would renounce his religion. He refused—and Saladin murdered the disarmed man with his own hands. That day of Hattin was the mortal stroke from which the Crusading effort could never recover.

Garrison after garrison fell; and at last, in the first days of October, 1187, Jerusalem itself was in Saladin's hands. The only town of consequence which still held out was the seaport of Tyre.

Had Saladin been able to rush Tyre there might have

been a complete collapse: as it was, a door was left open for reinforcement.

Reinforcement came, though it came to no final effect. The whole of Europe moved, shaken to its depths by the loss of the Holy Places. The French came under their young King, Philip Augustus, with the forces of Eastern France; the Plantagenet western half, under Richard, Angevin King of England and still Lord not only of his heritage, Anjou, but of Normandy, Poitiers, Touraine and all Aquitaine as well. The greatest of the German Emperors, Barbarossa, came forward also with his host —all these arose; the last of the efforts—coming too late—the Third Crusade, gathered for the recovery of the Holy City.

In such numbers something of an equal fight could be maintained—for a time at least—but even this Third Crusade was not a true offensive; it was a defence, and it broke down. For the moment most of the sea-coast was recaptured. Special attack was concentrated against the port of St. John of Acre, which was carried, and Richard, King of England, marched down south along the sea towards Jerusalem: but the situation was hopeless. The King of France had sailed home; Barbarossa was dead; Richard, a man of fierce courage but continually ill, now quite broke down in health; his small remaining command turned back within the neighbourhood of its goal—and Jerusalem was abandoned.

For a whole century isolated posts were held, but without hope of further advance. A Fourth Crusade, which should have made yet another effort, was wasted in the temporary capture of Constantinople, whither Venice had deflected its transports— for gain. Half-way through the century, Frederic II, the chief figure of Europe, in the midst of his struggle with the Church (which might well have ended in the destruction of our religion), negotiated a strange peace: it enabled him to be nominally crowned King of Jerusalem—but on condition of openly compromising with the Infidel. He went back to the coast and sailed away, having certainly betrayed what was left of the Christian cause, and denounced as its worst enemy. A few years after his death, St. Louis of France came over, re-fortified certain of the coastal towns and struck unsuccessfully at Egypt; sixteen years later he again unsuccessfully attacked the Mohammedan power for the last time in North Africa. There, upon the hill of Carthage, he died.

In another twenty years the end of the drooping business came. Acre was stormed, and the last shred of the kingdom of Jerusalem disappeared.

"Farewell, Syria."

Epilogue

With the end of the thirteenth century, 640 odd years ago, that great debate of which Syria had been the field seemed ended. The Christian effort at recovery had failed. The failure was permanent. The idea of the Crusade remained for nearly two hundred years more, and during the earlier part of those two hundred years one expedition after another was undertaken against the Mohammedan world. Spain was wholly recovered, but in the East things went otherwise; the Moslem seized Constantinople itself, pushed on into the heart of Europe, and was not beaten back until less than 250 years ago.

Syria, lost in the East, isolated by all those miles of sea and land from the West, should remain untouched by the West forever.

The inland towns became almost wholly Mohammedan; in the Holy Places there were foreign hostelries and convents and a certain influx of pilgrims at Easter, especially from Russia. The Mohammedan had become rooted in the place, apparently forever, and therefore the greatness of the past in road and building and cultivation fell to ruin.

One might take as the central example of that decay the country of the Lake of Galilee. Tiberias remained, but remained in squalor; the Greek column was overthrown; of many a famous place of habitation so little was left that men debated whether Capharnaum, Bethsaida, had stood here or there; and all the wealth had departed.

Then came the attempt at a new world, so insufficiently launched at the end of the Great War.

Syria was artificially divided. A country built up by nature in parallel bands that run from north to south, a country which was essentially *longitudinal*, was cut across latitudinally by an arbitrary line corresponding to nothing in race or physical feature. The thing was done in spite of promises of independence, or at any rate of Moslem rule, which had been made to the Arabs in order to secure their help against the Turk, and were then broken. It was a bad beginning for anything permanent.

Syria was now put under two foreign Western masters, ruling on either side of an imaginary line which is such that no man can know when he has crossed it. It cuts across the roots of Lebanon and Hermon, across the uniform Eastern Steppe, across the desert, across the sources of Jordan, across the sea road and the sea bays, without rule or meaning. And these two masters to whom Syria was thus artificially given, the French and the English, are hostile rivals—potential enemies.

Under this divided alien rule two quite different official languages are the languages of those who govern; two unconnected currencies; two of everything—and yet Syria is essentially one. Such a "settlement" contradicts the nature of things; therefore, presumably, it cannot endure.

Nothing endures forever, and this political settlement would seem of all settlements the most unnatural and fragile. But when we ask the question, "Will it last?" or to put it better, "How long will it last?" our answer must depend upon more particular and detailed considerations than the mere obvious artificiality of the unnatural arrangement.

We have to consider first of all that which is at the basis of all historical sequence, Religion.

The two Western Powers now [in 1935] nominally masters of Syria, and for the moment in possession of organised rule from the desert to the Mediterranean, have behind them no strength of religion. Their motive has been and remains in part the odd modern exaggeration of nationalism, much more greed—the opportunity for economic advantage particularly in oil, that dominating modern necessity, which frames and underlines half our policy: oil, without which men cannot fly, or maintain navies, or travel by road.

That inmost thing, Religion, whereby a community lives, is

absent from the new occupation of Syria and its governments. It is present in individuals, it is not present in policy.

Western rule, atrophied of religion, has to maintain itself in the face of hostile millions who, on their side, have not lost the religion which made them and by which they live. The French and English officials, the armed forces which obey them (and these are not numerous), stand isolated in the midst of a sea of Islam all around.

That same force which destroyed the Crusades is present in Syria today, and it is as active as ever. It is disarmed, or partly disarmed, on the material side; but spiritually it is sufficiently armed. Whether Islam throughout the Eastern world, from the Atlantic to the Ganges, will recover material equality with us of the West we cannot tell; but there is no rational basis for denying the possibility of that resurrection. The Moslems contemporary with Richelieu and Cromwell were better armed than the French or English of their day. It may be questioned whether Europe will now long maintain that modern supremacy over the Moslem which we have so long taken for granted. Moreover, in the face of the Moslem of the Near East, in Syria, the two Western Powers whom it is no longer accurate to call Christian are divided one against the other, and even so the advantages of each are enviously watched by other powers of Europe, who will not admit the lion's share to fall unchallenged to those whom they regard as equals or inferiors.

But apart from this general problem of the attempt at establishing Western Power amidst the masses of Mohammedanism, there are the particular problems facing France in Syria, and England in Palestine. The difficulties of each Power are peculiar to its situation.

The difficulties of the French are these:

They thought to lean upon the local Christian population, the Maronites. These indeed are more friendly than most to the new state of affairs, but they are only a fraction of the population, and that fraction mainly upon the sea-coast. Through an initial blunder which was only repaired after military disaster in the Druse country and a violent revolt in Damascus itself, the

French Power started ill; there remains the memory of blood-shed and a desire for vengeance.

The French Power is faced also by the complexity of what it has to deal with. The Druse community in the bare volcanic hills of the south-east is one thing: the Syrian Mohammedan population along the edges of the desert, along the string of towns from Aleppo southward, served by the single main railway, is another. The more open coastal region of Tripoli, Beyrout, Tortosa, and the rest is another; the tangled mountain land to the north of the coast beyond Latakia is another; and the frontier province, the old Sanjak, facing the Turk and containing Aleppo and Antioch and Alexandretta, is yet another.

Each of these districts demands its own form of administration, each has its own special difficulties and problems: in each the main trouble is ascertaining, and as far as possible meeting, the opinion of the governed.

This is especially difficult in the division east of Lebanon, called "The Syrian Republic", as distinguished from the Lebanese Republic on the coast. In the so-called "Syrian Republic", the effort to govern with a Parliament in Damascus would have had a better chance of success had not English policy weakened it by the sudden granting of partial autonomy to Iraq. The Mohammedans of Damascus, of Homs and of Hama, of all the middle and upper Orontes valley, and of the habitable desert fringe below the hills, can and do repeat, "If Iraq can be free, why not we?"

Iraq is not free, but it has the outer forms of autonomy, and these weigh heavily with men of the same culture and religion further west. For between Iraq and Syria there is a bond almost of identity, which runs back at least four thousand years, and was strengthened by the Arab conquest, the spread of the universal Arabic tongue, and of the nearly universal Arabian religion.

The increasing weakness under which the French suffer and will continue to suffer so long as they are burdened with a detested and detestable form of Parliamentary government, poisonous with professional politicians, adds to the problem; thus, the violent initial revolt against them was provoked by a foolish official, who owed his place to nothing but the political intrigues of the Metropolis.

But perhaps the worst handicap under which the French labour is economic.

The oil of Mosul, coming from the Tigris, across the desert in a pipe-line, is divided between the two Powers; the pipe-line bifurcates near Palmyra in the midst of the wilderness, one branch of the Y running through the notch of upper Lebanon to Tripoli, the other through territory under British control, to the harbour of Haifa, under Carmel in Palestine. But the source of that oil is in Iraq, which England controls, and with which England is in direct communication through the rivers falling into the Persian Gulf.

Further, the French have no such field for taxation under their Mandate as we have; though the population they control is somewhat larger it is impoverished.

Syria throughout the centuries has principally lived upon the commerce passing through it, from north to south and from east to west.

After the decay of the Phœnician coast, the towns on the edges of the desert were still great emporiums; Aleppo was the market for all that came along the half-fertile belt north of the desert from Mesopotamia; Damascus was the market for all that came across the desert directly by caravan. To this ancient prosperity a blow was dealt, even before the end of the Crusades, by the abominable Mongol invasion—the last to come out of Asia, which ruined the irrigation of the Tigris and Euphrates' alluvial plain and left its towns mere heaps of dust; but much commercial power still centred in Aleppo and Damascus until the Great War. The recent artificial division of Syria as it proceeds, must increasingly impoverish those emporiums on the edge of the desert; if it endures it will kill them. With Iraq a foreign country, with Southern Syria under separate rule, and masters who are also the masters of Iraq, such commerce as may remain will sooner or later take the southern route. For the moment Aleppo and Damascus are stricken, their value as centres of exchange is halved: it may sink to nothing.

Such are the burdens that weigh upon the French; what are those which may give anxiety to the English?

They are two: the task of supporting an interest not English, and the existence of a new land frontier.

The task not of English interest which has been undertaken is the support and protection of continued artificial Jewish invasion into a territory the age-long inhabitants of which regard that invasion with intense hatred. The new land frontier is that arbitrary line, corresponding to nothing in nature, which bounds the English mandate on the north.

Let us consider these two points.

The land frontier men have not much noticed: it has played no part—as yet.* The nature of the innovation is unfamiliar to the mass of Englishmen; but to those who are concerned with military realities it is a grave matter.

The whole policy of England, ever since her power became based upon an invincible navy after the 1st of June, 1794, was a policy having for a fixed rule the avoidance of a land frontier. English rule occupied and exploited areas which could only be reached with any ease by sea; they are either actually islands, or they were cut off by desert or by impassable or nearly impassable mountains. A similar policy has been by the very nature of things imposed upon all other aristocratic commercial maritime states; their power not being by land but upon the waters, the waters were their means of access and at the same time their secure defence. Of permanent land forces sufficient for the defence of a land frontier they had none.

This new land frontier, as yet no actual menace, but a potential menace, begins a revolution in the strategic position of England. Mark also how that innovation having been made, other land frontiers are beginning to threaten: one on the Sudan, one in Libya. Modern transport is such that with organised communication even the Libyan frontier, that is, the approach to Egypt from Cyrenaica, has to be considered.

The Jewish affair, the Zionist movement, may be taken last as being by far the most important.

* Words written on October 9, 1935.

The advantages to this country of acting as protector and supporter of Jewish immigration into Palestine, an immigration which is rapidly possessing itself of that land, are very great. The most obvious and the one which was the original motive of the policy is the strengthening of that alliance between England and international Jewry, especially as a force in finance, which has been as characteristic of this country in modern times as it was characteristic of Holland in the seventeenth century, and of Spain in the Middle Ages.

But there is a particular advantage, very striking when one sees it at work on the spot: it is economic. The Jewish immigration, fed as it is by wealth poured into it from the whole Jewish community throughout the world, provides the revenue of Palestine with almost more money than it can use. England might, of course, have used her position as a great banking country to subsidise the experiment at her own expense: as it is, the thing now floats and more than floats itself.

Thus the fine harbour of Haifa, the only harbour worth calling a harbour, in the modern sense, of all this coast, is built on Jewish money: the French have not yet built one. They still hesitate between Tripoli and Beyrout. They depend for their large vessels upon roadsteads. The little ports of antiquity and the Middle Ages are quite insufficient, and mostly silted up. Now Haifa would not be what it is but for the flood of wealth coming in with the Jewish immigrants. The same will be seen shortly in the development of roads, in the reafforestation of land, and is already manifest to the eye in a mass of new building. All the outskirts of Jerusalem, for instance, are already transformed. In the plain of Esdraelon, in Bethlehem, on the slopes above Tiberias, the new building goes on everywhere.

But in the midst of all this we must remember that what is being done is not being done directly for English power, but for the Jews. As the Allies of English power, the advantage of the Jews may be an English advantage, but it is not a direct advantage: and there is attached to it this very grave drawback, that of all the forms of foreign disturbance suffered by Syria in these new days of change, Zionism is the most violent and the most detested by the native population.

That hatred may be called ineffective; the Jewish advance is bound to continue so long as there is peace and so long as the English are in undisturbed possession. The Jews bring with them a much higher material civilisation, trained scientific experts, a largely increased exploitation of the land, and of all natural resources. There is an inexhaustible reservoir of population upon which they can draw. The stream would immediately flood the whole country but for the partial restriction still imposed by the authorities. As it is, one has but to look at the place to see that the Jewish effort is already triumphant. The capital in especial is transformed; Jerusalem is now a Jewish town. But all this reposes upon one foundation: the policy and the material force of a great European power. If or when that Power is occupied in other fields, or that policy changes, the Jewish effort in Palestine will be at an end.

It has behind it what none of the other forces intruding upon the Syrian world can boast—a strong moral motive, not technically religious, but having the force of a religion. The Jewish race as a whole, in spite of certain dissidents, and certainly the Jewish immigrants pouring into Palestine, are inspired by as strong a motive as can move men to action. But this strength alone would not maintain the Jews against the fierce hostility of the Moslem world which surrounds them. That hostility is another moral force with which the future cannot but be filled. We in the West do not appreciate it because we do not hear its expression, we are not witnesses of the gestures nor partners in the conversations which fill the Near East; but if we ignore it we are ignoring something which may change our fate.

INDEX

Index

Judah, 74, 77, 86, 91, 92, 93, 99, 100,
101, 102, 103, 124, 138, 162, 207
Julian the Apostate, 203, 223, 224
Julius Cæsar, 161, 203, 208

Kadesh, 58, 59
Karkar, 85, 87
kings, 30, 36, 50, 53, 54, 88, 90, 125,
127, 139, 218, 237
Kir, 90
Kishon, 71
knights, 259, 262
Koran, 249
Kouf, 48

Lake of Galilee, 241, 271, 274
languages, 28, 29, 41, 43, 62, 64, 96,
129, 156, 200, 220, 233, 249, 252,
258
Laodicea, 123, 208
Latakia, 123, 264, 267, 277
Latium, 145
Lebanon, 7, 11, 20–22, 26, 29, 36, 54,
56, 59, 62, 80, 82, 85, 87, 123, 128,
162, 261, 264, 265, 268, 275, 277,
278
Legions, Roman, 209
Leontes, 33
Libanese Republic, 277
Libya, 279
Litani, 10, 11, 21, 33, 54, 80, 128, 266
Lombardy, 146, 150
Lot, 35, 38, 41; his wife, 40
Louis IX, St., King of France, 272–
73
Louis XIV, King of France, 232, 240
Louis VII, King of France, 269
Lucretius, 128
Luke, 196, 198, 200
Luxor, 48
Lydda, 131
Lydia, 39, 97

Maccabees, 105, 124, 132–36, 138,
139, 140, 151, 207
Macedonian Empire, 55, 98, 112, 113,
116, 125, 147, 149, 267

Magdala, 53, 164–69, 174
Magnesia, 151
Manetho, 51
Mansur, 248
Maouia, 250
Marathon, 81, 99, 109
Marcus Aurelius, 203
Marius, 154, 155, 157
Mark, St., 196, 198, 200, 279
Markab, 263
Maronites, 276
Marseilles, 107
Maru, 33
Marx, Karl, 107
Mass, the 237, 240, 249, 253
Mattathias, St., 131, 132
Matthew, St., 200
Mecca, 250, 270
Medes, 97
Medina, 250, 270
Mediterranean, the, 1, 2, 8, 10, 13, 20,
22–25, 31, 33, 39, 43, 44, 62, 63,
73, 77–80, 85, 88, 108, 109, 119,
120, 125, 135, 139, 141, 145, 147,
148, 150, 152, 156, 181, 212, 214,
225, 240, 247, 254, 257, 264, 275
Megiddo, 58, 59
Melkarth, 128
Merom, 10
Mesopotamia, 8, 23–26, 30–33, 35,
37–44, 59, 78–81, 88, 95, 97, 107,
108, 121, 122, 125, 131, 133, 159,
206, 224, 246, 250, 269, 278
Messiah, the, 34, 76, 101, 124
Messina, 149
Middle Ages, 55, 60, 223, 280
Midian, 62, 89
Mithridates, 157, 158
Moab, 20, 21, 62, 64, 70, 75, 84, 128,
135
Modin (Modein), 131, 134, 136
Mohammed, 14, 238, 239, 250
Mohammedans, 17, 26, 76, 84, 105,
117, 123, 159, 239, 240, 246, 248,
249, 253, 256, 257, 261, 262, 264–
66, 269, 270, 273, 274, 277
Moloch, 14, 43, 44, 149, 158